THE TRUTH
ABOUT
SUNDAY MINOR

H.R. Young-Lira

THE TRUTH ABOUT SUNDAY MINOR

H.R. Young-Lira

gatekeeper press
Columbus, Ohio

THE TRUTH ABOUT SUNDAY MINOR

Published by Gatekeeper Press
3971 Hoover Rd. Suite 77
Columbus, OH 43123-2839
www.GatekeeperPress.com

ISBN: 9781619848467
eISBN: 9781619848450

Printed in the United States of America

Dedicated to my mother.
The words from my childhood still ring in my ears,
'Tell the truth. I may not like what I hear, but I'll respect you
more if you do.'

"The truth will set you free. But not until it is finished with you."
–David Foster Wallace, *Infinite Jest*

Contents

Acknowledgements 1

Introduction 3

The Dream 5

The Talk 9

Saved 15

The Life of Minors 35

Crybaby & the Cinnamon Roll Man 49

Miss Doddy, the Dutchess & the Orphans 57

Rose Village 63

She Can Fly 71

Different Kinds of Blind 85

Dr. Faus & the Three-Pronged Approach 103

The First Lady 107

The Mark on the Bed 119

The Horse Thief 133

The Padded Room 139

Contents

Thorazine 145

The Destroyers 149

No Contest for Fire 169

Finally a Friend 177

A Taste of Freedom 179

Prize Fighter 193

Breaking Out 199

Fair Price for Reprieve 209

Life According to Webster 215

Four More 229

Mothballs 237

Cakewalk 249

Minor Truths 257

Square One 269

Epilogue 275

Acknowledgements

....

FIRST AND FOREMOST, thank you, thank you, *thank you* to the real Sunday Minor. Without you, your story would not exist and this novel could never be written.

Next, my dear husband, I am eternally grateful to you for the space and time to follow my heart, for listening to me read virtually every word of this book aloud–more than once, and for telling me you're proud of what I do.

I am also brimming with gratitude for my group of beta readers who freely contributed a serious amount of time and thorough feedback: Joseph Johnson, Anita Hacker, Jessica Hoffman, Dena Traweek, Alex Cherry, Justyna Akyondem, Kathie Clark, Sindy Young and Katie Iupe. I chose each of you for a specific reason, and I am fortunate you accepted my invitation. Your commentary and critiques were invaluable.

Karl Monger, I'm glad I found you. Your editing propelled this project forward in ways it couldn't have been otherwise. Jakob Clark, once again your creative genius guided me to my best first impression. Lindsey Clark, I called on you in the eleventh hour and you totally answered. Sincerely, thank you for that. And Consuelo Hacker, thanks for the advice. You rock the book stacks.

Last, a huge thanks goes to the team at Gatekeeper Press for the extra handholding, conference calling, and revising until the final product was perfect. You took us over the finish line.

THE TRUTH ABOUT SUNDAY MINOR

Introduction

FOLLOWING THE EVENTS depicted in this book, decades of difficult work assembling her version of "normal" couldn't prevent the real-life Sunday Minor from continuing to grapple with her past. Ordinary life scenarios would evoke flashbacks that triggered anxiety, insomnia, dark and self-deprecating humor, and manic depression. In her mid-forties, she began writing a memoir of sorts titled, *No Family Reunion*, and she jotted memories down as they came to her until she passed the journals on to me.

I wanted to help. We spent the next year talking regularly, sometimes three or four times a week, as I collected strands of detail and twisted them into the threads of truth I would weave into a fictionalized tapestry of Sunday's early life.

I decided that, together, if we could transform her journals into something we could share, then perhaps *you* could read her story and share it with others, too, and then maybe *together* we could all make light work of lifting the weight of the world Sunday has always felt she carried on her shoulders alone.

She related to me a number of times throughout our discourse the importance that you, our readers, know that *she* knows this book represents *her* truth. She realizes these chapters are a compilation of *her* experiences the way *she* remembers them. And they are a single perspective among many who bore witness to the events.

Although the characters in this novel are an amalgam of her recollection and how I imagined them to have been, the events of the novel you hold in your hand are crafted around written accounts and oral discussions of the time between Sunday's earliest memories until she was seventeen. To that extent, this story is true.

THE TRUTH ABOUT SUNDAY MINOR

The Dream

SUNDAY MINOR BENDS, clutching her middle with one hand, bracing herself on her knee with the other, staring blankly at the forest floor. She is heaving. The chattering grackles above fall silent. She whips her head to the right. She stares through the junipers into the pitch black, listening hard. The smell of rain and whispers of an argument are carried on the breeze. She spies two silhouettes through the trees...a woman–the First Lady–and...and her older sister.

The woman pleads, *That's not the way it works.*

The girl is resolute. *Then we can't talk to you.*

Sunday still has time.

She bolts, weaving in and out of the underbrush, oblivious to the rocks tearing at her soles and the low wiry branches clawing at her bare shins and arms.

Lighting splits open the sky, stopping her in her tracks, and the rain pours down. A glimmer of light draws her eye downward. Without thinking, she reaches for the tattered bible lying on the ground before her, the gold embossed lettering wet and shimmering. *How did this get here?*

Under the bible is a dictionary with "Webster" printed in silver. She picks it up, too. *Strange they should be left out in the woods.*

Crack! Sunday snaps her head up, her eyes lock on the quickly widening gap in the earth beneath her, a growling hiss splits the air as of molten lava surges below.

She drops the books and bolts forward again, aware of what she must do. She glances over her shoulder repeatedly, eyes wide.

Disoriented by the electric strobes of lightning, she scans the surrounding woods. The rain is beginning to collect into streams that flow among the gnarled juniper roots. An illusory Cherokee princess, tall and regal, materializes from the darkness pointing the way. Sunday spies the large cardboard box glowing in the distance like a soft beacon pulling her in. The figure dissolves in the mist. Sunday takes flight.

Thunder booms overhead. Fat raindrops snap against her face. She slides across the last few feet of mud separating her from her shelter, and in.

She sits up inside the box, lit by a candle that doesn't exist. Her brother, appearing next to her, reaches out to touch her arm, startling her. His words want to comfort, *It's okay, Sunday. It's okay now.*

The din of the storm bears down overhead, and she vaults her eyes toward the paper roof. Her heart races as the box dissipates above her. She reaches out to her brother as his form wavers before her and vanishes. A hiss from her mother reaches her through the rain: *He wanted me to have an abortion anyway.* The candlelight snuffs out.

The black rain beats down on her head, turning to hail. She flinches under the blows coming down harder and harder until they become her father's fists. His voice booms in time with the thunder, *If you don't like the way I run things, get the fuck out!*

The phantom fists rain down blows. Nowhere to be seen, only the whisper of her brother's voice comforts her in the dark, *It's okay now. It's okay.* She shields her head and squeezes her eyes tight as she curls into a ball. She tries to fly away.

She's desperate to escape the endless blows. *It's okay now, Sunday.*

Her soul is tangled within her contorted limbs. She can't fly away. *It's okay.*

The fists pound faster on the back of her head and down around her shoulders.

THE DREAM

It's…
not…
workiiing!
She screams.

The Talk

S UNDAY'S EYES SNAPPED open, her heart still pounding. In the dark, she sucked at the air, but she couldn't fill her lungs under the 200-pound weight on her chest.

With a soft click, the bedside lamp came aglow, illuminating the room. Her foster father, Mr. Kindly, loosened his grip across her shoulders, and whispered, "It's okay, Sunday. It's okay now."

The girl nodded, and he lifted his mass off of her upper body as she inhaled deeply. She reached for her glasses and slid them up on her nose before zeroing in on his mouth until his face came into focus. He turned on the edge of the bed and dropped his face into his hands.

Her heart slowed as she shifted her gaze down to the foot of the bed, where her foster mother, Mrs. Kindly, cupped her face, puffy and red from crying. Sunday rolled her head toward her twelve-year-old foster brother, Ira, who was peaking in around the doorframe, tearful eyes wide.

Mr. Kindly said soothingly, "It was just a dream."

In the dining room dimly lit by a single bulb from the kitchen, the worn out woman slid into the chair next to her husband and across the table from the sixteen-year-old girl. Sunday followed the second hand gliding past the hour on the polished copper starburst clock above Mrs. Kindly's head. It was 3 a.m.

Only a couple of months had passed since Sunday arrived, but her foster mother already appeared older, haggard. The girl nervously traced the small circular scabs on the palms of her hands as Mr. Kindly leaned on a balled fist, staring into his cup of coffee.

The couple studied each other until Mrs. Kindly's chin quivered. "Sunday, honey. We've been trying for weeks…and, well…you're hurting yourself."

9

Sunday knew what she meant. She saw the day coming. She was sure her foster father was at his wits' end. She'd learned his wife had struggled to recover from a miscarriage the previous year, and how hard they worked to make this fostering situation happen. She could tell her nighttime episodes were starting to have an affect on Ira's normal life, too. The night terrors, those were something Sunday never could have anticipated, and obviously the Kindlys couldn't have either. This was something they weren't equipped to handle.

They told her that during the first incident they awoke to the smell of cigarettes and burning flesh coming from her room. Sunday had been in a trance-like state, puffing the smoke before snuffing the butts out in her palms. She became violent when they touched her, swinging her arms and screaming for them to leave her alone until she shook herself awake.

She'd been told some nights she spent shuffling in circles at the foot of her bed, murmuring what sounded like words and their definitions. They went on to explain that on other nights they found her curled up under the heavy cotton sheets, hugging herself tightly, sobbing uncontrollably. On others she flailed and thrashed, banging her head against the solid oak headboard, crying out in pain.

Still, if not for the golf ball-size knots on the back of her head and the sores on her palms Sunday never would have believed what they told her. The evidence was baffling. The few hours she wasn't fixated on how her brother and sisters were still trapped in her mother's house, she tried to make sense of why these things were happening to her in the night. Nothing of the sort occurred during the month-long stay with her friend, Sarah St. Christopher, right after she left her family. The only reason Sarah's parents let her go was because the courts declared Sunday a ward of the state. She couldn't remember the dreams. Those nights were a blank space to her. If *she* couldn't understand why she couldn't "act right," there was no way anyone else could either.

So, yes, she knew the end was coming. Of course, she would still be punished for not being normal.

Mrs. Kindly continued. "We've spoken with your case worker, Ms. Folly, every day and have worked very hard to follow her advice. We've done our best to protect you from yourself…we agreed you would leave your cigarettes and lighter in the kitchen overnight… we gave you the lamp so you're not frightened when you wake up…"

Mrs. Kindly studied the surface of the cherrywood dining table as if the right words were written there. "We've tried to provide a stable and loving home…"

She searched her foster daughter's eyes, but what could Sunday add when decision already clouded the air? The dark voice in Sunday's head sounded off. *Bet she never thought in a million years she'd be having a conversation like this, eight weeks in.* Sunday could tell Mrs. Kindly didn't know what to say either. *No happy ending here.*

Her foster mother went on. "The doctors said waking you when you're sleep walking is too dangerous…you understand? We only want what's best for you."

She sighed and glanced at her husband as he put a finger to his lips and shook his head. She slid a thin pamphlet across the table to Sunday. "Well, honey, we don't know what else to do…they've recommended you spend some time at Rose Village…to help you… process this."

What exactly do they think I need to process?

Sunday never heard of Rose Village before, and she had no idea what lay ahead for her. Nevertheless, she trusted the Kindlys, and when they said they wanted only the best for her, they were telling the truth. Sunday reached for the pamphlet and stared at the cover before pulling it down into her lap. Her mind churned through the last few weeks, searching again for a solution, something that would allow her to promise to be normal, some explanation she could give to ease the pain revealed in her foster parents' eyes. There was nothing.

Instead, she nodded slowly and mouthed, "Okay."

The three of them rose to go back to bed. Sunday pulled her comforter up under her chin and stared at the ceiling above her until the room began to gray with the nearing of dawn.

She awoke to the sound of Mrs. Kindly gently rapping on her bedroom door. "Sunday, honey, come down and have some breakfast before you have to gather up your things."

The truth of what had happened overnight came rushing back, and her heart sank. She rose. Despite the uncharted journey that lay ahead, her foster mother's familiar direction offered some semblance of comfort. Eat breakfast, gather your things–these were clear-cut instructions, and Sunday was especially expert at following instructions.

After breakfast, she scanned her bedroom. Although she was grateful for all the things Mr. and Mrs. Kindly had provided her, she felt sad she couldn't be what they wanted in return. Living in a normal house with a normal family wasn't anywhere on the learning curve of her previous life. She was sorry for having so awkwardly responded to Mrs. Kindly's showered affection. She couldn't accept this life, not when her brother and sisters were still stuck under the Minor roof, enduring the mad reign of their mother and probably scarcely surviving.

At school, Sunday kept her distance as best she could. She'd promised her brother she would. There were moments the two of them felt brave enough to steal a glance, flash a smile or share a few words with one another, but she couldn't be sure how they were all legitimately doing because she couldn't risk being responsible for what would happen if her mother found out they'd spoken.

She scanned the room again for what she thought the Kindlys might expect her to take. None of these things were hers–not really–but she couldn't go back downstairs empty handed. She couldn't bear to disappoint them again. She wouldn't be able to stand Mrs. Kindly's furrowed brow. She couldn't take causing

Mr. Kindly to drop his head and stuff his hands into his pockets once more. So she compromised, settling on the book bag they'd gotten her the day she arrived. *I could use this.*

She unzipped the dark blue canvas satchel and carried it to the closet, then dropped into the plush green shag carpet on her hands and knees and slid open the door. She reached into the far back corner and pulled out her neat stack of things from home. She laid the items in a row in front of her. There were the clothes she was wearing the day she left: the pair of denim-print cotton pants she'd made herself, a flower-print short sleeve button-up blouse her mother had sewn years ago, and her worn white canvas tennis shoes. The other clothes were what she'd grabbed when the sheriff led her home for the last time: another pair of home-sewn slacks and a thin black turtleneck.

The only other thing she'd carried with her was that tattered bible. She ran her fingers across the cover–the surface rippled like a naval orange–wondering why she still hung on to it.

Her fingertips paused over the gold embossed lettering, and she sank into a memory. She was eight years old again. And she was going to be saved.

Saved

"**J**UST AS I am, without one plea…" This was the hymn that signaled the end of the preacher's sermon and the beginning of the altar call at church every Sabbath. "God accepts me just the way I am." That's what the song said. Sunday thought the words were true, and if she were saved her life would change and she wouldn't make mistakes anymore–or if she did, no one would detect them. *I would be cloaked in the blood of Christ. I would be invisible to everyone. Jesus Christ is gonna save me. He's gonna protect me. No matter what I do or what I say, he's gonna protect me.*

The feeling always started with the bass line right in the pit of her stomach. That bass moved the tenor voices among the congregation. The sound would flow up and into her heart, the tones surging in her chest. The notes swelled higher and higher into her throat in time with her breathing. She could have sworn her spirit was what spilled out from her mouth in a sound that swam through the rest of the voices until it was lost. The way she sounded on her own didn't matter; they were together, blending into one voice. The hymn swirled around her. *I am a part of that beautiful sound.*

Though she never quite understood the flood of emotions that refrain had been triggering the past few weeks, it sent tears coursing down her cheeks. Each time, she would fight the urge to walk down to the front of the church and meet with the others, who seemed to feel the spirit the way she did. She didn't dare to step away from her family, afraid of what her momma and daddy would say, what they would do. That was, until the last time the choral played before she was saved.

To Sunday, a sermon was a crazy dance, the preacher yelling of hellfire and damnation, and on that day Brother Smith delivered a particularly frightening one.

"My *frieeends-uh*."

Brother Smith's palms opened to the sky, then he balled his hands into fists and he shook them toward the heavens, hissing every "s", spitting every "t"…"Hell exists-ah. This place was maaade for the Devil and 'is angels-ah. It was maaade, therefore, as a place of punishment."

He dropped his hands to his sides and shook his head, and said, "Not a place simply to go. No." His voice boomed, "Hell is desiiigned for punishment. The Bible says it is a place that is calllled hellfire."

Sunday glanced across the pew at her family while Brother Smith scanned the faces of his flock. "Now, if you're very smart today, have half intelligence, you oughta be doin' some thinkin' about where you're goin.'"

He opened his throat and called out, "Hell is a place! A place that existed before you were ever born-ah."

An "amen" hurled from the back of the room, seeming to rekindle the fire in Brother Smith. His words rose and fell. "Hell is there-ah! It's gonna be there-ah! There is no salvation in Hell-ah!" His arms waved and the words shot out in rapid fire. "There-is-no-savior-in-Hell-there-is-no-blood-of-Christ-in-Hell-there's-no-altar-in-Hell-there's-no-forgiveness-in-Hell-ah!" His feet stomped out every point. "Whatever goes to Hell, staysss in-ah Hell-ah! It's permanent. Settled. Over with. The underworld is waiting."

Sunday clung to every image, mouth agape. Bother Smith's eyes widened, and so did hers. He painted a picture of the grim fate awaiting his flock. "Hell has much patience. Hell knowwws that every soul lost without God will enter into its mouth." He simulated Hell's arms reaching for the group and drawing them in. "It will take its clutches and wrap them around that soul and pull that soul down into the midst of Hell itself-ah."

Between the wide wooden rafters set against the bright white vaulted ceiling above, Sunday played the scene of Hell's scaly hands and blood-red talons dragging her down into its gnashing teeth. She snapped her jaw shut and gulped.

Brother Smith cried out, "That's whyyy Jesus Christ came two thousand years ago."

He spun a full circle. "He didn't diiie to make you rich."

He stopped to face the congregation, leaning far forward with narrow eyes. Sunday was sure they were locked on her.

"He didn't diiie because of who you are. He didn't die to create this hellhole you know about."

Sunday nodded. *I do know about it.*

Brother Smith stood up straight, shooting his finger into the air, calling out to the rest of them, "He diiied to keep youuu outta Hellll-ah!"

His shoulders slumped. "There's only one name that can keep you outta Hell. There's just one naaame that can keep you outta Hell-ah. That name is the naaame of Jesus Christ."

Another "amen" was flung into the air somewhere behind Sunday.

He shook his head and asked, "Where will you be? Where-will-you-*beee*-where-will-you-*be*?"

In Hell.

He pointed an accusing finger at them all. "You're allll going to Hell-ah!"

The congregation was stunned into silence.

I am already there.

Brother Smith leaned in again and whispered the secret. "It doesn't have to be this way…There is a way out."

Sunday's hymn was cued, and as the first notes were played, the tension in the room dissolved with a unison sigh.

Brother Smith swayed to the rhythm of the hymn as he shared his truth. "If you do *not* want to go to Hell and burn-ah, if you wanna go to Heaven instead-ah, if you wanna sit beside the throne of our King and our Savior for*ever*more…Accept Jesus Christ into your heart, and peace will be yours."

With that, fresh tears sprung from Sunday's eyes, giving her away. The salty flavor of relief blended with the bitterness of understanding. *I'm an embarrassment, crying in church like a little baby.*

She'd already been whipped several times over her tears. Each time they arrived home, her momma screamed about how embarrassed she and her daddy were, having a child cry for no apparent reason in the House of the Lord. Between uncontrolled lashes of the belt, which came faster than Sunday could defend or even respond to, her momma screamed out between blows, "You [*whack*] know [*whack*] what [*whack*] you [*whack*] did! [*whack*] Again, Sunday [*whack*], goddamnit again!"

Out of breath, she would loom over the girl with pointed finger and accusing eyes. "You know [*heave*] the whole goddamn church [*heave*] is lookin' at you."

She would turn her back on her daughter and throw up her arms like she'd given up, whining, "Why? [*heave*] Why are you doing this to me? [*heave*] Why can't you just act right?"

Sunday's momma told them repeatedly that they were respected Christians. They arrived single file every week, the seven of them, one after the other. Her momma worked hard to present her good Christian family, two parent saints and their five little angels, squeaky clean, hair combed, patent leather shoes shining, marching in like God's soldiers. "Yes, ma'am...No, sir." These were the only acceptable responses whenever any of the children were directly addressed. If a compliment was paid, "thank you" was permitted. Crying, fidgeting, falling asleep–the children paid a price for those things. *I'm eight years old. Old enough to know better than to cry for no reason.*

She stared down at the teardrops as they landed on the toe of her patent leather shoe. She didn't want to get in trouble. She didn't mean to cause a scene. No matter, there she was again, tears flowing, heart aching, adrenaline pumping. The only thing she knew for sure was somehow Jesus had accepted His punishment in order to protect her from hers. Today, the message exploded in her mind. *Jesus. Jesus must be calling me down to the front of the church. He already took the blame for me, and promised to take the punishment, too. He promised.*

She wiped her cheeks with the backs of her hands, and she decided. She stepped sideways, and then hesitated. *They're not gonna let me out.*

She pushed Friday and Wednesday backward anyway and eked past them. She edged in front of her momma, who was swaying baby Tuesday on her hip in time with the hymn. The steady movement was enough to prevent anyone from noticing June's dagger eyes, their two angry slits honed in on Sunday. Her lips were pursed into a tight white ring. June's hissed thought reached Sunday: *Wha-d'you-think-you're-doin'?*

Sunday saw her daddy catch the silent exchange. Chester pressed his hand against her momma's arm, warning her to let Sunday by. She passed her daddy, too, on the end, and out into the aisle.

Instantly the chapel seemed to lighten. *I am free.*

The child drifted into the sea of sinners and floated down the aisle in a daze, only vaguely aware of her family's eyes burrowing into the back of her head.

Once she found a space at the front of the stage, she was led through the sinner's prayer, confirming loudly she was absolutely sure she wanted to walk with the Lord for all eternity. Her journey across the pew and down the aisle was already proof enough His promise was true. How could she have passed otherwise? She'd arrived safely there at the front of the church, after all.

He will shield me from them for the rest of my life.

Sunday was scheduled for baptism the following Sabbath.

The Minors made their way to the car after service, and Sunday's newfound peace gave way to fear. *I caused a scene. I drew attention to myself. I didn't ask permission. It'll wait 'til we get home.*

19

She climbed into the backseat of her daddy's '57 Chevy and began to pray silently. *Deliver me from evil.*

The children immediately changed into everyday clothes, like always, as soon as they arrived home. Sunday waited on the edge of her bed, her assigned seat for as long as she could remmeber, still only half-certain she'd actually been saved. The other half of her was certain of the whipping to come.

"Sunday, getcher ass in here," her momma yelled from the other room.

Sunday's heart sank. *They're gonna make an example outta me.*

She held her breath as she walked down the hall and into the kitchen. Her momma was making potato hash for lunch. "Peel the potatoes."

That's it? No screamin'? No cussin'? No lecture? No belt? Secretly, Sunday was overjoyed, although she struggled not to let the truth creep into her face.

Sunday's daddy grabbed a jacket on his way out to the drag races after lunch, and her momma spent the rest of the afternoon on the phone. June ran her finger down the smooth white pages of her little black faux leather address book. One by one, she dialed ever number on the list to extend an invitation to the church next weekend.

"Sunday's going to be baptized! She's saved!"

The beatings resumed the next day for everyone but Sunday. She thought the Lord had built a shelter around her, protecting her from their madness, and not a whole day passed before Monday, Wednesday, and Friday perceived the considerations made for her, too. Of course, there were still a few days until Sunday was actually baptized. She understood that things might not be perfect until after.

Behind traveling down that church aisle without recourse, the second bit of proof of Sunday's new protection came later that day in the form of an incident with the laundry. She was getting ready for school, and only after she'd pulled them up over her tiny waist did she discover that the elastic had come out of her panties again. Aware that only a few seconds remained before her momma's ticking time bomb went off, she raced aimlessly around the house for some solution, until the tiny sparkle on her bedroom floor stopped her in her tracks. *A safety pin!*

She pulled up her skirt, cinched and folded her panties over, pinned them as best she could, smoothed out her skirt, and raced to the car, with no one the wiser.

Off to school they went. Not once that entire day did the girl have to wriggle, shimmy, or dig to get those underpants back into place. In fact, she completely forgot about them.

The children had already cleared and cleaned the dinner table and dishes, and moved on to ironing their six pieces of laundry each when Sunday's momma yelled at her from the other room. "Sunday! Getcher ass in here!"

In an instant the girl stood at attention in front of her mother, where she sat on the floor sorting darks from lights. She held Sunday's tiny cotton pink panties above her head. "What is this? What. Is this?"

Sunday recoiled in front of the evidence. "A safety pin in my panties."

"You're walkin' around with safety pins in your panties? Why?"

"Because the elastic tore, and they wouldn't stay up," Sunday said, flinching at a phantom backhand.

"What if you'd gotten into an accident and ended up in the hospital? Huh? They woulda said we don't take care of you!" She threw the underwear into a pile, and huffed, "Your daddy and I work hard to take good care'a y'all! Y'all just tear shit up faster'n we can replace it!" She waved the girl away. "Get outta my sight."

No backhand, but her words stung the same. *I shouldn't have pinned them. That was bad. I must be in trouble because I'm not baptized yet. I only got a few more days. Still, I'm not gettin' whippins, and that sure is somethin'.*

21

The following evening, Sunday couldn't hold back any longer. There was only one fair thing to do. She sat her brother and sisters down in the girls' room after dinner and witnessed to them. She stood over them like Brother Smith and spun an eight-year-old's theories of divine intervention. "Getting saved is the secret weapon," she professed. "You're cloaked in the blood of Christ, after all." She pointed out the proof. She hadn't gotten in trouble for leaving their pew. She didn't get whipped for putting the safety pin in her panties. They'd witnessed their momma passing her over themselves. She hadn't been whipped in three days counting that one.

Her sermon worked. Her sisters and brother wanted the Lord's protection, too. She convinced them each to go forward in the church the next chance they got.

The following night, she was given yet more proof. That night the waft of fried chicken, one of her favorites, saturated the air at the Minor house. Sunday's ravenous tummy grumbled in anticipation. She devoured her drumstick and immediately asked for seconds. Around the table rang a chorus of "me-toos" from the others. June's angry eyes flashed in Sunday's direction. "What, I can't fucking feed you enough?" She jerked up out of her chair and grabbed the children's plates, throwing them in the sink one by one, and screamed, "You goddamn kids eat too goddamn much!"

The children froze. Sunday silently reasoned, *Once I get baptized, after that He's really gonna save me. Then the protection will start for real. Besides, Momma's right. There's a thousand Chinese babies out there that don't get nothin' to eat at all. Fried chicken is only one serving. The nasty things like the giant pot of greens, the mountain of liver and onions. We can have seconds of that. Spanish rice is a good one, and there's plenty of that, too. Potato hash comes in the great big cast iron skillet. Beans! Those are made in a pot bigger'n my head! I'll remember.*

June stomped out of the kitchen, and the children crept to their rooms. Sunday was positive Jesus was responsible for making June forget to actually punish them.

The last major incident that proved she now walked under the cloak of the Lord was witnessed not by one, but by all her siblings.

The end of the six-weeks was upon them, and the children each slid their report card in front of their momma as she sat at the table before falling back into line—as always, in order of birth. June examined the number grades first, granting judgment and sentence, one card at a time, reviewed conduct grades afterward. She always doled out punishment for poor conduct as a group.

Wednesday got a 93 in science, lower than last six-weeks.

"Damnit, Wednesday," June glowered at her oldest, "why'd you let this happen? You showed me you can make higher grades, and now you've gone and fucked it all up. You're grounded."

Wednesday wrung her hands as she glanced at the belt grimly laid out on the table. Sunday felt the shame radiating off of her sister, the smartest one of the bunch.

The boy was next. "Goddamnit, Friday..."

Sunday didn't catch the rest. She was already visualizing her own report card. *My grades are good this time. No low ones. I did talk in class once. I was just telling Heidi how she was doing her 9-times tables all wrong. That's why I got that 'U' on there. It's gonna be okay. I'm saved now. I'll be safe-*

"Sunday! I'm talking to you!"

Sunday snapped her head up.

"What's wrong with you? You're grounded!"

Sunday wasn't sure why.

Last, June poured over Monday's grades. The woman closed her eyes and sighed deeply, visibly struggling to stay seated.

See, Monday was plagued by two tics-one in which she'd blink hard, squeezing her eyes so tight there's no way it didn't hurt her. The blinking happened often, and became worse when she was under pressure. The other thing she would do when she was anxious was snap her hand down hard, like the boys do, bringing her arm up before flinging it back down to make a loud *snap*! when her finger hit her hand. She couldn't help herself, and the tics sent their momma into an absolute fury. "Stop!" June would spit, "People are gonna find out you're retarded!" The screaming only impelled the girl's tics, and June would rage on, "I said quit! People are gonna say you're stupider than you already are!"

So Sunday wasn't surprised by the anger creeping into her momma's face with every one of Monday's involuntary gestures. Monday never did get good grades. She'd always claimed she didn't care about school anyway, that she just wanted it to be over. Her tics told another truth, though. When she said she wanted it to be over, she wasn't exactly talking about school.

"Obviously you're grounded."

Monday's brows shot up as she locked eyes with Sunday. *That's all?*

Sunday nodded back, still feigning solemnity in front of their momma.

Grounded. The concept was a secret joke among the children. *Grounded? She never lets us go anywhere anyway. Daddy's the one who lets us go for walks when she's not home. Grounded from what? Goin' in the back yard?*

June skimmed the opposite side of the children's report cards for anything that wasn't an "S" for satisfactory. This time they had all gotten at least one "U" again. June stood and scooped up the belt. She loomed over them as she prepared for rounds, carefully wrapping the soft leather around her hand.

Sunday eyed the heavy square buckle hanging loose on the other end. The prong clinked against its brass counterpart with every wrap. The girl's skin twinged where the buckle-sized marks permanently lived.

This ritual, the wrapping of the belt, was something her momma did ever since she broke her hand swinging at Wednesday too hard one time. Since the break, when Chester wasn't around, June would do the ritual of the wrapping and leave the buckle dangling.

She laid into each of them, screaming, "This! [*whack*] Every [*whack*] time! [*whack*] Why do we have to do this? [*whack*] Every [*whack*] time!" [*whack*]

The buckle punctuated each line. "Why can't you just act right?" [*whack*]

June swung again, and Wednesday cried out as the metal caught her hip, and she doubled over in pain.

"How difficult can it be to keep your mouth [*whack*] shut?" [*whack*]

Friday was next. He reflexively ducked away from their momma. The belt wrapped around his head, and the buckle licked his temple. He gasped and covered the side of his face. He kept the scream firmly lodged in his throat, but he couldn't stop the tears from pouring out.

"You sons of bitches! They think we can't raise decent kids!"

June lunged toward Sunday, breathing hard. "And *you*."

The girl inhaled the lingering scent of tomatoes and ground beef from dinner on her momma's hot breath and didn't breathe out until the belt dropped to the woman's side. Nostrils still flaring, she locked onto Sunday's eyes. "I've *got* to do laundry now."

Sunday didn't dare breathe a word. The children stood in place stifling their moans as the belt unraveled from June's hand and dropped to the floor. She walked out. They glanced at one another. Sunday could tell they were baffled, but she wasn't. *Jesus distracted her.*

Tuesday peeked around the doorjamb, breaking the spell, and the rest of them scurried after their momma to keep up with her shifting mood. Riding her waves was the only way to survive. The universe stood still as they all fell into a trance, working like a fine-tuned assembly line at the ironing board: Wednesday at the head of the board, carefully folding a freshly ironed crisp white kitchen towel, calling out orders; Friday leaning into the iron to ensure the sharpest crease on a pair of his own khaki pants; Sunday plucking and whipping the next white cotton tee before laying it out for her brother as soon as the pants were pulled from the board; and Monday on the end, arms stretched as wide as possible, fingers barely clasped in front, making sure none of the precisely twenty-four items dropped to the floor.

June appeared in the room as the last fold was doubled over, and like someone flicked a light switch back on, she yanked the cord from the iron, doubled it down, and turned to Monday, screaming about penmanship, swinging with every word. "What [*phwap*] is [*phwap*] wrong [*phwap*] with [*phwap*] you?" [*phwap*]

Monday curled over to take the licks on her back, glaring at Sunday from under her arm as she sobbed. The corners of Sunday's frown stretched down deep. *Monday knows Momma skipped me.*

Sunday couldn't be sure how much time passed before her momma tired out, but when she did, they immediately filed out and headed back to their rooms.

As her sisters checked themselves over so they could decide what to wear the next few days to cover up, anguish gnawed at Sunday's insides. She hated that they hadn't yet had a chance to be saved like her, but she was also secretly relieved. She compromised with a promise to herself: *I'm gonna try harder to be good next six-weeks. It's the right thing to do when you're walkin' with the Lord.*

The thought never once crossed Sunday's mind there might be another reason, a real reason, she had been overlooked.

The night before her baptism, Sunday's momma scrubbed her from head to toe, like she was a potato just pulled out of the dirt. June set Sunday's hair in the black brush curlers with pastel pink pins. She rolled them so tight Sunday could feel the bristles sticking into her scalp. June jammed the pins straight down into Sunday's tender head and scraped them forward to be sure they wouldn't budge in the night. She smirked and sing-songed to Sunday, "Remember, beauty comes at a price."

Socks, panties, and slip were all bleached twice, and Sunday's powder blue satin dress was starched extra crisp. Her swelling hope kept her from slumber most of the night.

As the Minors filed into the church the next morning, Sunday's daddy held her back so she could sit in the aisle seat this time instead of him. At the end of the sermon, while every head was still bowed in prayer, Sunday felt a tap on her shoulder. She sought her daddy's approval, and with a single nod, he granted permission to follow the deacon to one of the bible study rooms behind the baptismal. Her momma followed the two of them through a great wooden door on the right side of the podium.

Sunday took in the room around her. The sun fell through the tall, narrow stain-glass window on the back wall, pure and bright. There were no other lights on. *A sign from God. Everything is good. I'm following His will.*

Her eye followed the strip of sunlight that crossed the deep maroon carpet and fell over a cluster of beige metal folding chairs. Ladies' dresses and stockings were draped over them, several pastel pillbox hats dotted the seats, and assorted pumps and flats were stowed beneath. The women there were already stepping into their white cotton baptismal gowns.

I'm the only kid.

Sunday pushed her anxiety back down into her stomach. *We're all girls in here. I don't have to worry about getting undressed in front of strangers.*

Her momma chose a far corner, standing between her and everyone else. June pulled a folding chair close and sat down. She pulled Sunday's dress over her head, and spun her around while the girl contemplated her new life.

I'll need to start talkin' more like Brother Smith. I need to start usin' words like "ye" and "thou." Will I get laughed at since none of the other kids use those words?

She never put two and two together–that perhaps her mother thought there was bound to be someone in the church who would question any bruises or belt marks. The idea that June might have actually been performing a final check for visible signs never occurred to her.

When the inspection was complete June stopped spinning the girl, and pulled the gown down over her head, straightened the hem, and licked a thumb before rubbing away a final nonexistent smudge on her cheek. Sunday squeezed her eyes shut to stop from being dizzy.

"Here, child, follow me." The deacon led Sunday out to the front of the baptismal, which was hidden from the congregation by a wall, without her momma this time.

No one spoke. The old wooden steps creaked even under the weight of her bony forty-five pounds, and at the top she focused on where the water met the stairs inside the deep basin, hoping to distract herself from how deep the pool might actually be. *Brother Smith said you have to have reverence. We're just lowly sinners. We're not good enough 'til we're washed of our sins.*

The fear crept back in, though. She was petrified by the idea of deep water. She hadn't learn how to swim yet. *Lord, please save me if I start to drown...*

Before she could finish her prayer, the pastor called her name. As she tried to muster some grace to glide down the first step, she was sure her sharply drawn breath gave away how hard the icy water was pressing against her body.

He didn't seem to pay any mind, though, as his hand slipped under her thin arm. He floated her over to a step stool they'd placed there in the bottom for her, but he never let go, holding her steady.

He raised his right hand into the air, and his voice thunderered out over the congregation. "Do you believe in the Lord God almighty?"

Peering up into his face, she nodded.

He fixed his eyes on her and asked with the same power, "Do you believe that Jesus was the Son of the Lord God almighty?"

She nodded again.

"Do you believe that Jesus, the Son of the Lord God almighty, died for your sins, so that you shall be allowed to enter into heaven?"

I do believe it.

As she nodded, she caught a glimpse of herself, and instantly felt the heat rise on her neck and ears. *The water made my white gown see-through. Brother Smith can see my underwear!*

She was mortified. She reached to cover herself, but the pastor caught her hands, and folded them gently across her chest. He raised his right hand above his head and pronounced to the masses, "I baptize you in the name of the Father...the Son...and the Holy Ghost."

His right hand came down to cradle the back of Sunday's head in a way her momma and daddy never did. He gently pinched her nose closed with his left hand, and lowered her into the water. He smoothly lifted Sunday back up...but her feet! Her feet slipped out from under her, and her back hit the water. *Fwshh!*

I'm falling! Lord, take care of m-

Brother Smith instantly swept her up and out of the water, as if she were a feather floating on the surface of a lake. "Walk with the Lord for all eternity."

No one laughed at her blunder. She was not an embarrassment. *God already started. I'm not in trouble. I am washed of my sins.*

As Sunday dressed, the congregation filed out to the instrumentals of the final verse of her favorite hymn.

Sunday stumbled along behind as June pulled her by one arm directly to the car, where her daddy, Chester, had already loaded the rest of the children in. Her head was in the clouds. She smiled to herself. *I must be glowin' 'cause I'm a child of God.*

She thought the whole family would stand in awe of the change she felt deep inside. *I will always be good now. I'm gonna have to tell them again how they can be protected from being bad, too.*

The Minor family headed for home to change clothes and prepare their covered dishes. There were a few things June needed from the store for the celebration, and Chester said it'd be all right for her to drive herself to get them.

Sunday was nothing short of ecstatic about the party to come, and she'd already taken off her shoes, socks, and dress when her father called her into his bedroom. Reveling in the freedom promised by a new life, Sunday bounded down the hall into the room.

Though the blinds on the window with the A/C unit across the room were shut tight, light shone bright from the long narrow window above the bed, filling the room. That window was set high enough that no one could peek inside. She noted their gold sheets and blanket were still rumpled; they never left the house without perfectly made up beds. *Today's different, though. We had to get to church early. Momma and Daddy didn't have time to make their bed. He probably needs my help makin' the covers back up before everybody gets here.*

Modesty was never a virtue of Chester Minor, so Sunday was not surprised or intimidated when her father stepped out of the bathroom completely nude. He reached over her head and closed the door behind her.

He instructed, "Go on and get in the bed."

Sunday thought the request was odd, but she didn't detect any foul mood so her guard was down, her mind still on the party. She obediently climbed into the bed.

He gently pushed her backwards, forcing her to recline on the pillows. He slid her slip up to her chest, and pulled her panties down over her feet. Her face warmed with embarrassment, and she immediately tried to cover her exposed body. Her daddy, just like Brother Smith had done when she reached to cover herself, reached back. Except instead of crossing her arms over her chest protectively, he placed them at her sides.

Sunday knew better than to question. She lay there stiff, eyes wide, waiting.

The man spread her tiny eight-year-old legs wide and positioned himself between them.

She shot a glance downward to get an idea of what was happening. She'd seen his penis before, but this time it was different, bigger than when he came out to watch TV after a shower when her momma wasn't home. It was sticking out now...and darker, like a new bruise.

He leaned over her, supporting all his weight on his left hand next to her head. With his right hand, he pressed his penis into her. He pushed forward with his hips. Like lightning, the shock of pain from her crotch bolted deep into her stomach, up through her chest, into her throat and out of her eyes as bright white stars.

He pulled back to examine Sunday's face. She didn't make a sound. The tears forged trails down from the corners of her eyes. Strange she could feel them pooling in her ears.

He licked the fingers on his right hand and wiped the spit on his penis. Then he shoved in again. He thrust hard over and over. Sunday held her breath, afraid to scream, convinced he would rip her apart like the wishbone from a Thanksgiving turkey.

She couldn't take the pain. She needed to get away. She inhaled as slowly and deeply as she could. As she exhaled, she pulled her soul out of her legs, and as breath was drawn again, she drew her arms into her heart, and on the third inhale, she pulled herself, all of her soul, into a ball right there in her heart and her lungs, and with an equally deep exhale, she flew out of her mouth, away from her body, and up into the corner of the room.

Floating above, she glimpsed a shock of her own blonde hair on the pillow below the back of her father's head. She peered down at her own tiny hands gripping the golden sheets. He heaved each breath from his belly. The odor of stale coffee and eggs rushed from his mouth and pervaded her space.

Each time he withdrew, she thought he was through. But he thrust forward again and again, spearing her hollowed body to the bed. From the high corner of the room, she turned what was happening over and over in her mind. *I'm not bad. I wasn't being bad. I'm not being punished.* No whipping she'd ever gotten in her whole life hurt as much as this. She turned her gaze to the window as a breeze rustled the leaves of some far-off tree. She thought to herself, *This must be what it feels like to be stabbed to death, murdered. Actually murdered.*

The reflection of the sun off the Chevy windshield flashed against the ceiling. *Momma's home.*

In one fluid motion, her father pulled out, and Sunday was sucked back into her torn body. He dismounted and slid into the bathroom before she heard her mother even open the car door.

Sunday shot straight up in the bed and crossed her arms over herself.

Over his shoulder, Chester called out, "Get changed, kid… and listen. Won't be necessary for you to be discussin' this with anyone, about what happened here, understand me?"

His voice came to her like a faint echo. She wiped the tears from the sides of her temples as her eyes fastened on the corner where the wall met the ceiling. That bed…those walls…her world spun around her. Thoughts fired out of control, shooting across the dark sky of her mind. *What happened? What does this mean? Why does it hurt so much? How does this fit into my new life, walking with God? Maybe He doesn't know I'm only eight. Is this something God was supposed to protect me from? Maybe he accidentally gave me a purpose for grownups. Is this a part of his plan for me?*

. . .

Sunday stared blankly at the last bit of home laid out before her in the room the Kindlys called hers. A lifetime seemed to have gone by since that afternoon.

So deep was her recollection, she was completely unaware of Mrs. Kindly padding up behind her until she tapped her on the shoulder and whispered, "It's time."

Startled, Sunday jerked her finger from the gold text on the cover of her bible, scooped up her things, and stuffed them into the bag.

They both stood and turned. Sunday followed her foster mother to the door. Mrs. Kindly whipped around and embraced her tightly. Sunday stiffened in the woman's arms. Mrs. Kindly leaned in, pressing her cheek to Sunday's, and whispered, "I'm sorry."

The Life of Minors

M R. KINDLY PULLED onto the main road leading out to the interstate while his wife pressed each thick radio button until she settled on a station playing a song Sunday didn't recognize. Mrs. Kindley glanced back at the foster girl and flashed a weak smile before turning around to sway in time with the music–a feeble attempt to throw a lukewarm blanket over the cold hard truth, if you asked Sunday.

The girl focused inward, combing through the harrowing details for clues that might point to the root of her problem.

Countless incidents wove themselves around her every attempt to escape–teachers noticing this strange injury or that, the stranger who came to visit that one time, even family members witnessing the harsh reality of living under the Minor roof–all with no result. The children were left to fend for themselves. At first, when the punishment became too much, Sunday discovered she could simply "fly away." Of course, that came with its own set of dangers forcing her to stay put as often as she could. There was the time she'd run to God for shelter, but her daddy was certainly quick to dispel any notion of divine intervention. When a pact with her brother and sister to find a way to endure the pain wasn't enough anymore, she ran... twice. The first time, she ran *away.*

Well, the second time...

She was twelve when she realized none of what she'd endured was about her own imperfections. With her self-assurance came the realization that endurance wasn't about only surviving; enduring meant appearing to strive for perfection while surviving long enough–four more years, if she's counting–to get out.

The second time I ran…I ran toward *something, didn't I?*

She still clung to the belief that the truth would ultimately set her free.

Not until I'm normal, I guess. Who are we, anyway? I'm Sunday Minor. We were the Minors…

. . .

The life of the Minors had begun in Stensonfield, an army base turned makeshift subdivision in San Antonio, Texas. Sunday's first memories of the place were that there were six of them. And before they left that little army barracks flat, there were seven.

There was a daddy and a momma, of course. They were called Chester and June. The children put their heads together once they learned to count and figured out that eight short months after their parents married, along came the first girl, Wednesday. A year later there was her brother, Friday. Only six months had gone by when June delivered "The Dead Baby Boy," and almost a year to the day, Sunday was born. Monday came after fourteen more months passed, and two long years and some months later came Tuesday, the last. "Irish Twins" is what some people called the first four on account of them all being born so close together. The children thought the nickname was funny. Chester did not.

Chester Minor was a hard and angry man, only outwardly pleased by orderliness and hotrods. He used to be a military man, honorably discharged from the U.S. Army, not because he was a hero, but because he fell inside a tank during a training exercise and hurt his back. There were times when Sunday thought her life might have been different had he continued soldiering on past his six-year stint. Most of the time she thought probably not. Nevertheless, he carried his pride home, commanding the same diligence from his family as a drill sergeant would of his soldiers. Everything in its place or there was hell to pay, and he was equally as hard on himself.

As far as Sunday knew he never puffed a single cigarette, and the only evidence suggesting he ever drank anything other than water was the single photo of him and June taken one year at the annual Sears & Roebuck Christmas party. He was holding a glass of something brown served over ice.

Inside the fridge was Chester's pitcher. The children called the container "Daddy's Water." If he came home and the tall plastic pitcher wasn't full and ice cold, he'd say, "I work damn hard all day every day, and y'all can't even keep a goddamn pitcher of cold water in here for me."

The children never drank from it. Not only because they were not allowed to drink "Daddy's Water," but also because there was mildew lining the edges of the lid. June never made them clean the thing, and Sunday was glad of that.

She assumed he never realized because sometimes he even drank straight from the spout. She imagined the spit dribbling back into the pitcher when he did and decided that's where the mildew came from–his spit. "Nasty!" the children whispered, and snickered quietly among themselves. He wasn't so perfect like he thought.

Once, Sunday caught June secretly snickering, too.

Chester only ever seemed truly happy in his garage, under the hood of his latest project, or at the drag strip adding to his collection of trophies, which numbered in the dozens. More than occasionally he could be found standing tall, hands on his hips, staring with proud, glassy eyes and a faint smile at the perfectly aligned collection on the wall. He spent every spare dollar and minute he found on his hobby.

Chester repeatedly reminded Sunday and the others that he possessed the IQ of a genius. He was also a bigot, often imparting the story of Nazi Germany with a puffed chest and a wide grin. He shared that Gramma and Grampa Minor, who were of German descent, adopted him as a baby, and his responsibility was to his "German roots." He freely used such terms as "niggers," "japs," "jews," and "spics" when he was talking about anyone that wasn't white like him. He wasn't shy about espousing his belief they were ruining this country either. Although he did grant that the occasional "meskin" might surprise you by "damn near passin' for one of us."

Still, a direct connection between German roots and upholding Nazi values was hard for Sunday to imagine. Take Uncle Vernon, for instance. He was always kind. He was the one who gave Sunday the old and tattered bible she still carried around. Uncle Vernon was born German. He was the actual son of Grampa Minor, not adopted like Chester, but his momma was not Gramma Minor. Gramma Minor never much liked their uncle because of that fact, and Uncle Vernon never really liked Chester. Sunday thought maybe that was why he was always particularly nice to Friday.

There was one time in particular Sunday could recall him sticking up for Friday, right there in front of all of them. Uncle Vernon would usually stop by without calling ahead, but that time he called first. Friday got excited because Uncle Vernon liked him best. The visit also gave the boy an excuse to bake a pineapple upside down cake from scratch.

...

June was behind the Singer and up to her ears in flowery cotton fabric and thread, sewing short sets for the coming summer. She'd tasked Sunday with things like pulling out the measuring tape, pinning the patterns, and handing her thread.

Friday ran into the room, excited. "Momma, Uncle Vernon's comin' over. Can I bake a cake?"

June didn't bother looking up from the sewing machine. "What kind?"

"Pineapple upside down cake. It's his favorite!"

"I dunno if we have the ingredients."

"Well, if we do, can I make one, Momma?"

She waved him away. "I don't give a shit. Can't you see I'm busy?"

Sunday knew she was only pretending not to care. She was probably going to be the one to eat half that cake anyway.

Friday bounded back into the kitchen, where he rummaged through the cabinets and the fridge, gathering up everything he needed. She remembered wishing she wasn't stuck helping her momma so she could help Friday bake his cake.

Before Uncle Vernon even arrived, waves of sweet, warm pineapple and sugary vanilla cake had begun wafting through the house, drawing his sisters one by one from their various posts and duties into the living room to sit quietly so as not to be banished as pests once the grownups settled into conversation. No one wanted to miss out on that cake. Sunday's mouth watered. Their momma crept out to sit down, too, when Uncle Vernon and Chester sat down. She didn't want to miss cake either.

The men talked of muscle cars and racing while June feigned interest with an occasional "Is that so?" and "Well, wouldn't ya know." Sunday expected she couldn't care less.

Friday brought the first slices out to the grown-ups. "I made your favorite for you, Uncle Vernon! Pineapple upside down cake!"

Uncle Vernon started to say thank you, but Chester cut him off. "Yeah. The damn queer, he can't do a goddamn thing like a man, but he sure as hell can bake a cake. He's gonna make somebody a damn good wife someday."

Chester smirked, but Uncle Vernon wasn't amused. The giant grin on Friday's face fell to the floor and clutched his middle like he got punched.

He tried to make up for Chester's words. "Well, goddamn, boy! That's a damn fine cake. You said you baked this cake for me?"

39

He didn't wait for Friday to answer. "Well, then, your daddy ain't allowed to eat one goddamn bite. It's my goddamn cake."

A nervous chuckle escaped Chester's throat. "Yeah. He cooks real good, but I dunno about that son-of-a-bitch."

Friday headed to the kitchen and soon returned with four more slices for each of his sisters.

Uncle Vernon shot back, "Let 'im alone, Chester. He's a good boy. He's just tryin' to find his way."

Friday set the plates on the coffee table and walked to his room without a word. None of Friday's sisters said anything since their daddy was liable to turn on them, too. Monday stood up and went in to give him her slice. Sunday snuck out to the back patio to eat hers.

. . .

Though his logic was never sound, Chester always maintained there was reason for the things he did and the way he did them, whether he said so out loud or not. He told his children while he beat them–sometimes nearly to death– he punished them because there was some lesson that needed learning. And when he finally admitted to raping *all* his children, he reasoned it was so he wouldn't cheat on his wife.

June Minor made sure to tell the children in any number of ways that she never led the life she deserved, although Sunday could plainly see she tried very hard to make it so.

Even when the calendar showed they were well into the 1960s, Sunday thought June could have stepped right into Mrs. Cleaver's shoes if she wanted to. With her perfect hourglass figure impeccably wrapped in carefully hand-sewn dresses and her ever-coiffed hair, at the very least she certainly looked the part.

Once over bologna sandwiches, June told Sunday that because Chester took great pride in order, after naming her first daughter

Wednesday–the day she was born–she named each new child a subsequent day of the week. Chester chimed in at that point. "Yeah, but Thursday and Saturday woulda been stupid names so you oughta be glad we didn't name none'a y'all that."

They were consequently named in order of birth: Wednesday, Friday, Sunday, Monday, and Tuesday.

June had also ingrained in Sunday the notion that appearances must be kept up precisely in public, and more than once she'd gravely warned on the way out the door "Children are to be seen, not heard."

Every afternoon when the children were small, her momma carefully balance preparing dinner, her hair, her makeup, and her dress before her daddy came home; and once a year, for the Sears & Roebuck Christmas party, Chester allowed her to go all out and dress to the nines.

She bought a special dress for a couple of those occasions, and made dresses for the others, but she *always* paid attention to style. Each year she would drop the latest Christmas vinyl onto the turntable of Chester's hand-selected, top-of-the-line, all-in-one console before calling the girls out of their room and gliding in to get ready.

While Tuesday rolled around in one of the two twin beds, June carefully pulled up her delicate stockings and shimmied into her satiny floor-length ball gown. She spent the better part of an hour perfecting her dark waves before moving on to her makeup, all with the use of a single hand mirror.

The girls would peek in, in time for her to neatly clip the clear teardrop stones onto each ear and fasten the glamorous companion necklace, arranging the stones so they lay just so upon her collar. Afterward, she would pull the tiny bottle of Chanel No. 5 from a secret pouch brought out into the light of day only on special occasions and dab each of her wrists and behind her ears before hiding the petite glass bottle away again. Finally, she would slip on her heels, the ones that shimmered in the light, and glide out of the girls' room-turned-boudoir and into the living room with all the grace of a Hollywood star. Sunday's momma said she felt like Dorothy Dandridge.

She would ignore the astonished gasps of her children, who were stunned by her beauty. Instead, she would parade in front of her husband while he sat on the couch, and ask in her most nonchalant manner, "Chester, dear, do I look *okay*, hmm?" and start to smile as she took care to do a full spin for him. He gave the exact same response each year: "Yeah, you look fine. Are you ready to go?"

Her smile would fade and she would try to hide her disappointment. "Yeah, let me get my purse."

Each year, Sunday thought to herself when her momma's smile faded, *Daddy, she's beautiful. Why didn't you say so? Do you see how beautiful she is?* She never found the courage to say the words out loud.

The rest of the year, amidst the monotony of daily cooking, cleaning, sewing, and laundry, June changed out her classical and big band records, read up on the latest fad diets, and thumbed through Avon catalogs. She would often go on about Egyptian cotton sheets and how Egypt was all the rage.

If any of her children dared to interrupt her, cross her, or remind her in any way that perhaps the life she was leading wasn't the one she acted out each day, she would snap. She spit venom and rained blows down on her target. Her rage was the kind that could not be quelled. Not ever. She seemed to be a slave to her fury, nearly collapsing when her madness finally released its grip, but the fire never truly went out; the cinders only died down into smoldering embers barely beneath the surface, still burning, always gathering fuel until the next eruption. Even when she finally attempted to break free and end it all, Sunday was convinced only one question held her fast to this life: "But then…what would the neighbors think?"

Sunday never thought she was as smart or as pretty as her

older sister. Wednesday was the very first child and the apple of Chester's eye, if there could be such a thing. She was a blue-eyed beauty with white hair that was straight as a board. Growing up, she was never fat, but she was never so thin as Sunday. She was quickest to understand the rules, she was cunning, and from the start she had a tongue like a whip. So when she was old enough, five or six, she easily slipped into the role of caretaker in a household where more and more through the years there was none. Though she gobbled up every book she could find as soon as she learned to read, there was never a printed guide to playing second momma–only the model provided by the tempestuous and pounding dramatics of June Minor. Wednesday grew to rule by barking orders, frequent tongue-lashings, and sometimes dishing out some of the brute force they'd been shown.

She and Sunday were oil and water. Everything she did was nearly perfect. "Why can't you be more like Wednesday?" was a common refrain in the Minor house, and the pedestal isolated her older sister from the others. Sunday grew to accept that she would never be able to meet such a standard. Wednesday set the bar high, and her accomplishments became a benchmark, a rule of thumb, among them. She easily doled out criticism, detailing every shortcoming of the others. Sunday felt like it just wasn't right.

At the same time, there was an undeniable inner strength about her sister, a fierce will to survive and a calculating mind. The oldest girl analyzed every possible outcome of every one of her moves. Sunday preferred to believe the reason Wednesday told on them so often, and sometimes fibbed, was because she was absolutely cornered and telling was the only way she could think to save her own hide.

Whereas Wednesday was Chester's pride and joy, Friday Minor was June's, at least until Tuesday came along. The shock of waves on his head was as black as Wednesday's was white. His face was round and his middle was soft when he was young.

Later he grew tall and his shoulders grew wide, helping to hide the fat little boy he remained inside. He strongly resembled his momma, and he desperately sought her approval. He clung to the things she bothered to teach him–how to sew and bake and set the girls' hair. Their similarities ended there.

He was stoic from the start. His gender set him apart from the others, and so he was made to stay in his own room and deal with his own set of rules and responsibilities. This isolated him from the others, too.

He was smart like Wednesday, but unlike her, he was considerate. And in accordance with his mother's wishes, he was a child of action, not words. Though his troubled thoughts betrayed him at times, acting out where his mind came to no solution, most often his own motherly instinct shined through.

Sunday could never match her brother's innate sense of caring and protection. He was Sunday's heart. He was her friend, her foil, and even when she said nothing at all, her confidant. He stood by her when there was no one else, expecting nothing in return, and for her part, she would go to the ends of the earth to do the same for him if need be.

He hadn't learned his empathy from anyone. He didn't need a lesson in compassion. The true, deep care he felt for the wellbeing of others came naturally. He shared everything he owned that he was allowed to, he loved animals and nature, and he tried to account for the good in everyone and everything. He tried hard to be joyful, too, and when he grieved, he didn't try to change things. He understood "that's just the way it is."

He was also an artist deep down. Sunday could tell by the way he neatly kept a cigar box of scarce supplies–a few charcoals, a single smudge stick, and his sketchpad–and how he carefully pulled out individual tools only when he needed them. She would sometimes sneak in and flip through his sketchbook, which revealed perfect country hillsides, deer in shadowed forests, and far off mountains as if drawn from the valleys below.

He also valued order and cleanliness, like his father. There was never a speck of dust on his belongings, nothing out of place, and every stitch of clothing was starched stiff and creased and hanging neatly in his closet. All proof of the work he did to please Chester. He pined for his father's approval, at least in the early years, but eventually, he too came to understand he would never have the connection, and *that's* just the way *that* was.

Monday Minor took on the tint of brass in Chester's hair and the brawn of June's family roots. She was as stubborn as an ox–about as graceful, too. Even as ferocious as Sunday could be, she couldn't hold a candle to her younger sister.

Their parents called Monday stupid plenty of times in front of Sunday, though she didn't believe them. Plain as day, early on her sister had simply given up any hope of ever coming as close to perfect as Wednesday. Neither of the girls could be as forgiving as their kind older brother. The only thing left to do had been for the pair to work diligently enough to avoid punishment when they could. Because of these things, Sunday found a sense of equality to Monday she couldn't with the others.

In the meantime, Monday lived for her mission to stand for the underdog, righting wrongs and carrying out whatever was fair, always defending her convictions with her fists. Not that Sunday didn't care about the underdog, she simply didn't think about saving the little guy as much as Monday. Sunday saw her younger sister as owning a kind of place among heroes for her deeds, though her approach sometimes isolated her. Sunday always fell back on her brother's coin, understanding fully "that's just the way she is."

Tuesday Minor was the baby, several years younger than the rest, and a chubby replica of June with thick, dark hair, peaches and cream skin, and the same dramatic black lashes circling her big, round, bluest of blue eyes. She became the apple of *every* eye. June exploited the attraction at every opportunity. From her virtually fixed place on June's left hip, Tuesday inhaled the attention and breathed it back out again in coos, smiles, and baby belly-laughter in a way none of the others ever remembered doing.

A vision of innocence among grownups, the little cherub became a source of intense resentment among the rest of the children, as affection they'd never received continued to be showered upon her. At first only the tenderness shown by her parents and strangers isolated her from her siblings.

Later, Tuesday herself seemed to sense that she was somehow more special than the rest. In time she used her charm against the others. Behind her back, they nicknamed her "the spy" for the way she always carefully inventoried every detail of their mischievous goings-on, and holding them over their heads, threatening to spill the beans whenever she wanted to be a part of some plan the others hatched without her. Even when she got her way, if she saw fit to do so, she tattled anyway, and when rounds of punishment were being doled she was spared, every time, no matter if she was a co-conspirator or not.

Sometimes they taunted her. "Momma and Daddy talkin' about you, and well, sorry to say, you're adopted." She'd give a suspicious, "Nuh-uhhh," before they pointed out how she didn't have any of the same features as her sisters. Nevermind she was a carbon copy of her mother and brother. "Yeah. They aren't happy with you right now, and I think they're gonna give you back," they'd say.

Sunday could unequivocally say she'd never been a little tattletale like her youngest sister. Eventually, she and the others managed Tuesday by simply not including her in anything they did because she couldn't tattle on what she didn't know anything about.

Over time, the baby of the family grew more and more reserved until she said little about anything at all. She merely stared at life through her big round eyes.

These days, Sunday didn't feel much of anything for her. Tuesday was just there.

In the end, not counting Sunday's aunts and uncles and all the grandparents and great-grandparents, the life of the Minors amounted to four "bad kids" doing what they could to bend without breaking under the tyranny of two unsatisfied parents with an insatiable appetite for perfection…and a baby who never even had to try.

...

Sunday cracked the car window and raised her head to breathe in the fall air, still no closer to an answer than when Mrs. Kindly gave her one last shot to make her case that morning.

The truth about Sunday Minor was she was never trying to be a hero. She was trying to survive. Between the two of them, Chester and June, the best odds for that were to blend into the background or, if the spotlight happened to shine in Sunday's direction, to work diligently to meet an unattainable standard of perfection. Otherwise, prepare to suffer the consequences–consequences that only seemed to magnify as the children grew.

Sunday thought for so long that the inside of the Minor house *was* normal, but even after the truth came out, what then? Shelter from a friend that couldn't let her stay; placement with a foster family stumped eight weeks in; and now there in the Kindlys' car, uncertainty rode like an extra passenger beside Sunday toward the next destination: Rose Village.

Mrs. Kindly clunked down the row of radio buttons once more until the sounds of Cat Stephens' *Wild World* filled the car. She sat back and relaxed, bobbing her head again slightly to the music. Sunday curbed the impulse to point out the irony of her foster mother's selection.

Crybaby & the Cinnamon Roll Man

....

SUNDAY LURCHED FORWARD as Mr. Kindly pressed on the brakes and shifted the car into park. She shook off her foggy reminiscence, and looked out the front windshield at the doughnut shop. The Kindlys turned toward her in unison, all smiles.

Mr. Kindly asked, "You wanna come in and pick something out, sweetheart?"

Sunday nodded and opened her door.

As she set foot in the bakery, the sweet scents of sugar and spice filled her nose, and her mouth began to water. The thick, buttery aroma reminded her of The Cinnamon Roll Man. *Things weren't all bad back home. At least not in the beginning.*

• • •

Saturday mornings back at Stensonfield, that's when The Cinnamon Roll Man used to come.

He strolled the barracks with his big cardboard tray filled with those giant brown oil-stained paper bags, "50¢" scribbled in black marker on the outside of each one. He went door to door selling half a dozen giant fried cinnamon rolls at a time. If the children performed well enough the night before, and if their momma was in a fairly good mood, they could safely assume breakfast would be special.

The Cinnamon Roll Man was a tall tower of a man, taller than their momma, and real, real skinny. He was older than old, his wrinkles set deep into his leathery neck and face. The biggest, bushiest white eyebrows hung over his eyes and a ring of white hair outlined his flat, bald pate, held up on either side by giant, rubbery ears.

Before he even knocked on the door, the kids could smell him coming. "Momma, Momma! The Cinnamon Roll Man's here!"

They'd squeal and bunch up behind her, nudging her forward to open the door.

He'd bend way over, lock eyes with Sunday, and ask in a deep, gravelly voice, "How y'all young'uns doing this morning?"

Grownups didn't often speak directly to the children.

Sunday instantly shied away, hiding all but her eyes in her momma's skirt, and barely above a whisper they all chimed in unison, "Fiiine."

He stood tall again, holding out a bag from his tray, and nodded to June. "Ma'am. How, may I ask, are you?"

She would say with a sweet smile, "Oh, very fine, I thank you."

She would take the bag and hand it down to whichever child was closest, and pull fifty cents from her coin purse and drop the change into his great big hand. "Good day to you, sir."

He'd tip an imaginary hat and head out toward the next door.

Sunday and the others were careful to conceal their excitement as best they could as June closed the door and turned to take the bag back. If they were too loud or too jumpy, June was liable to turn on them, tell them they're "just awful" when she's "tryin' to do somethin' nice" for them, and "this is the thanks" she gets. She'd hide those magical rolls away for herself.

Otherwise, she would reach in and pull the top one, the one that was always layered with the thickest icing, out for herself before handing the bag to Wednesday and saying, "Okay, now go on outside. Each of you can have *one*…and you better stay where I can see you."

Sunday remembered thinking once, *If Jesus ever visits us, not only in our hearts but in real life, he would bring these with him… and if heaven is real, I just know we're each gonna have our very own Cinnamon Roll Man.*

Those rolls *were* heaven. Their spirals were so thick and warm. One cinnamon roll was as big as Sunday's two hands–

no–as big as her face. The children all ate them the same way. Only after Wednesday passed out the last one and pulled her own from the bag did they all sit down in a row, in order of birth, and begin.

The roll was one long hot spiral, crispy on the outside and fluffy as a biscuit on the inside. Each of them sat perfectly still and slowly unfurled their roll, revealing the massive, crunchy bits of butter and cinnamon and brown sugar clumped together and hiding between the layers. Sunday licked her fingers after every bite, and rolled out the spiral a little more.

Sunday was careful not to waste one sugary morsel. If June found even a trace on any of their clothing, they were whipped. If anyone accidently dropped some, the instant the crumb hit the fabric, they'd peek around at the others to determine whether anyone caught the mishap. Someone else always did–usually Wednesday–and whoever witnessed the crime would chime, "Well, that's what you get because you wasted some."

In the event Sunday's shirt was the one smeared with cinnamon, the punishment didn't matter. She'd already the eaten the delectable roll, and a full, happy belly was plenty to get her through the beating to follow.

. . .

In the bakery, Mr. Kindly pointed at his wife and told the baker, "She'll have an éclair. I'll take two chocolate glazed and...a bear claw."

Mrs. Kindly crossed her arms over her chest and sighed, feigning disappointment, like she'd given him an inch and he'd taken a mile.

Sunday knew he was pretending not to see his wife when he winked at her. "What'll it be, young lady?"

No matter how good it might be, nothing would ever match that magic from the past. Still, she put on half a smile and said, "I'll take a cinnamon roll, thank you."

Mr. Kindly pulled the car out onto the interstate again, and the couple chattered on about the superb taste of their handmade goodies and what secret ingredients they must combine to make them that way. Sunday unrolled her treat a bit at a time, doing her best to ignore the sense that she was being dropped off in some remote shelter like an unruly, unwanted pet.

She thought about the pet *her* family had taken in so long ago.

Daddy never wanted her, but even Crybaby had a good enough home with us.

...

The last winter the Minors spent in Stensonfield was also the third day of the first snow Sunday ever saw. Grandaddy Paw already came by the house once that flurry-filled week, and he always came around after church for dinner. So she and the rest of the children were taken by surprise when he burst through the door that day.

He wore his thick brown garage jumpsuit with the zipper all the way up and tucked under his chin. While he stomped off the snow in the doorway, Gramma slid in behind him, weighted down by the brown paper grocery bag in her arms.

The children clustered around his legs, squealing and giggling at the snow fluttering down around him, melting the instant the crystal flakes hit their warm skin.

As Granddaddy Paw shook off the last of the cold, the children noticed his chest wriggling around. Every eye widened. They'd heard of the abominable snowman. The same silent question bounced from one child's face to the next: *Could it be?*

Wednesday took the lead. "Grandaddy Paw, why's your coat movin'?"

The kids waited for an answer.

Gramma broke the silence. "How y'all doin?" She winked at Granddaddy Paw and waddled toward the kitchen, balancing the bag in one arm and waving for June to follow behind with the other. "Honey, you need groceries or anything?"

In the meantime, Chester stepped out of the restroom still drying his hands, nodding to each of them. "Cora...Paul..."

He folded the hand towel and set it down on the dining table before reaching for a handshake. Friday scurried behind him and picked up the towel immediately returning the cloth to the bathroom rack where it belonged.

Grandaddy Paw tugged at his zipper and started in, "Chester, that boy needs to start learnin' some responsibility. Every boy oughta have one."

The children waited patiently as their daddy mulled the idea over, nodding slow.

At the same time, the furry little thing popped up out of the top of that suit and the children screamed with glee, "It *is* an abominable snowmaaan!"

This set Grandaddy Paw to laughing while he finished unzipping his overcoat. As he doubled over, the caramel-colored chow puppy tumbled out onto the floor.

The girls dove down to touch the curious little thing. Only Friday remained at a distance, concentrating on the two men as they went on.

Grandaddy Paw dropped his head down to the boy. "Go on'n take a look at your dog, boy!"

"That's *mine*?" Friday wasn't convinced.

Chester sighed. "Well, Paul, exactly how much does it cost to feed a dog?"

"Ohhh, not much at *all*, son. Couple bags of food and"–he turned to Friday–"if you watch 'im real good–"

Friday interrupted, "It's a girl."

"Take good care of 'im–"

"It's a girl."

53

"There shouldn't be any vet bills at all. Now go on and play with 'im."

"But Grandaddy Paw! It's a *girl*."

Grandaddy Paw feigned suspicion. "Well, just *how* do you know the difference?"

Friday popped down on the floor and pulled the puppy close. He turned her over. "Look! Her pee-pee is under her tail instead of on the tummy." He glanced back up at his grandfather and said once more, "She's *mine*?"

Grandaddy Paw glanced back at Chester, who nodded approval, before confirming, "Yessir, she's all yours."

Chester murmured into the air, "Now what of a name for 'er? Hmm?"

The group began throwing out all kinds of names. Meanwhile, the puppy dawdled her way over to the kitchen step where June had set two small bowls of food and water. The pup started whimpering when she couldn't clear the step, and before long her mewl turned into a howl. Everyone but Chester chuckled.

He said very seriously, "We don't need no crybaby 'round here." Hand on hip, pointing his other finger at the puppy, he said sternly, "You can't be a crybaby."

Grandaddy Paw almost shouted, "Now *there's* a good name!"

Chester stood with his arms crossed.

"Now, Chester, she won't be doin' that her whole life. Crybaby. That's a fine name for the pup."

. . .

Sunday smiled, thinking about that day. The only time Crybaby ever made a sound was when she was a puppy and couldn't hurdle that step. Friday took care every time to put one tiny paw up on the step after the other. He never lifted her up into the kitchen; he only gave her a boost.

She also remembered those steamy nights late in the spring before they moved, when she would sneak out into the living room and slide under the pullout sofa bed where her momma and daddy slept with only the screen door pulled to so they might catch a random breeze. Crybaby would pad out to join her and curl up and sleep until her parents stopped breathing so deep. Then as quietly as she'd stowed out she would creep back to her room before anyone was the wiser.

There was still never any question whether Crybaby was Friday's dog. The dog, the bike, those things were for boys, not girls, and he did a good job making sure his girl was fed and watered.

What she didn't remember yet was that on some nights, ones she hadn't snuck out into the living room, Chester was the one who did the slinking, entering their rooms under the cover of the dark.

Mr. Kindly slowed and turned his blinker on to exit the interstate. He veered left under the highway and came to a stop sign.

They cruised under the thick branches of a grove of lazy oaks, their remaining leaves barely turning over and drifting back to sleep with the cool fall breeze. The grove opened up to a row of houses and a small community park, where Sunday couldn't help but stare at a handful of young children whirling on a merry-go-round. She smiled to herself. *Maybe they're orphans.*

Miss Doddy, the Dutchess & the Orphans

THEY'D GOTTEN CRYBABY soon after Sunday turned five, but even before the extra body, and even with Wednesday gone to kindergarten part of the day, that barracks flat had already seemed to shrink to a size too small to hold all those kids. So the time not allocated to sitting on the edges of their beds was spent in the yard. That is, if the gravel pit lining the front of the building plus the patch of grass surrounded only on three sides by a white picket fence could be counted as one.

There they played games in the gravel like checkers, using the makeshift board Friday configured by clearing a square of the gravel straight to the dirt and colored pebbles; or a game of house, complete with mud pies and grass salads. After they grew tired of the same old games, they each found a shady spot, and fell asleep until the light crept over them or they were called in, whichever came first. Of course, you can't make a mud meatloaf without getting a little mud on your hands. So when the children went inside, the leather belt was always waiting.

June screamed between lashes, "God [*thwhack*] damnit! [*thwhack*] You're filthy! [*thwhack*] What the hell did y'all do? [*thwhack*] I'm not gonna do laundry [*thwhack*] all day long [*thwhack*] when y'all [*thwhack*] are just goin' outside [*thwhack*] and wallowin' in the goddamn mud!" [*thwhack*]

That yard was Sunday's only view of the outside while living there. Until the Minors started attending church after they moved to the house on Rock Knoll, the only other people Sunday ever met besides the Cinnamon Roll Man or the occasional family members were Ms. Doddy, The Dutchess, and the orphans.

Across the Minors' patch of grass stood two two-story barracks buildings, also converted into apartments. They were much nicer than where the Minors lived, with fat, round white columns out front and intricate white railing lining the second floor balconies. Miss Doddy lived there.

Her door was the one upstairs on the left. She said once that her grown son lived in a place called Overseas. He was a soldier in the Army like her daddy used to be, and Miss Doddy's German Shepherd called The Duchess stayed behind to protect her while her soldier was gone.

Miss Doddy was older than Sunday's momma, but she was beautiful like an old Cherokee princess. Her features were similar to Sunday's Gramma, but with longer hair, white instead of dark gray, pulled back in a long ponytail. Her smooth skin was brown and her almond-shaped eyes always seemed to smile even when her mouth didn't. She wore the same thing every day—navy and cream plaid pedal pushers with a different colored tank top and the same brown sandals. Sunday's daddy said she was "a damn hippy."

For a while, Miss Doddy occasionally came knocking, asking June up to coffee. One of those very afternoons, The Duchess saved Tuesday from certain death. Well, the kids thought so anyway. Sunday's momma sure didn't see it that way.

Sunday and the others took their places along the top of the fence while Tuesday peeked through the picket slats near the ground to follow June and Miss Doddy up the stairs. The children set out for a game of balance beam.

They didn't realize Tuesday had inched her way to the front of the house and halfway across the field after June until the four of them had already traversed the fence line down and back at least twice.

Monday doubled over and let out a belly laugh, almost falling off the fence. "Would you look at that!"

Friday and Sunday gasped in horror. Sunday hushed her sister, and stared at the baby. "Oh no! She's outta the yard! What're we gonna do? We can't leave the yard to get her!"

Wednesday wagged her head. "Serves 'er right. You wait 'til Momma sees her. She'll get it then."

The four of them stared as Tuesday dawdled up each stair, swaying dangerously backward before plopping down on the step in front of her.

Just about the time Tuesday edged herself around onto her haunches ten or so steps up, The Duchess appeared below, and froze, her nose zeroed in on the baby, one front foot raised and the opposite back leg stretched straight back, tail straight down. Sunday and Monday burst into laughter. "She's come to save the day!"

Tuesday bobbled around and grinned at them from across the field. The Duchess bolted around the front of the stairs and up to Tuesday, who was almost at the top, wobbling and giggling. She scooped the baby up by her snapsuit collar and carried her back down to the ground floor. About that time, June stepped out onto the landing.

She raised a hand to her brow to block the sun, and placed the other on her hip where Tuesday usually sat, and yelled, "What the hell are y'all doing over there?"

Monday pointed at the dog with the baby in her mouth, and yelled back across the field, "Look, Momma! The Duchess thinks Tuesday's 'er puppy! She saved 'er!"

The children broke out in laughter again.

June gasped, "Oh my god!" and trampled down the flight of stairs faster than she'd ever moved according to Sunday, screaming, "The dog is attacking my baby! Somebody! Help!"

The Duchess gently laid the girl on the ground and stepped back, awaiting the next command.

Miss Doddy trotted down after June. "No, no, no! She's fiiine! Look at 'er. Good as gold!"

June brought her prized possession up to eye level, turning her over and around, examining for damage. She was always hovering over the baby, and she certainly never left her alone with Chester. Only recently she dared to venture from the house without the girl attached to her hip, and this is what had come of it. She didn't say anything to Miss Doddy; she didn't even glance in her direction. Instead, she shot an icy glare toward the fence line and marched back to the house. Miss Doddy stood there slack-jawed, eyes burrowing into their momma's back.

All smiles dropped to the ground. The children were at the door when their momma got there. Sunday knew that look. They silently followed her into the house.

Inside, June sweetly cajoled as she set Tuesday gently on the couch. "Myyy precious baaaby." Then she stood straight up with her back to the rest of them. Through gritted teeth she commanded, "Get the belt."

Miss Doddy never knocked on the Minors' door again.

Now and again the children trekked around the supporting beam of the little picket fence to peer up into her window, never seeing more than a flutter of her shears. During one such trek around the fence the children did, however, discover something new–*real* orphans.

Not George the Orphan Cat With White Eyes. He was the fat, gray tabby they sometimes found curled up in the baby cart deemed months before as "ruined, just shit" and banished from the house after accidentally being left outside overnight. No, George didn't count.

Monday was the first to behold the children playing together out in the field by the foundation slab piled high with rubble next to Miss Doddy's building.

"Y'all! Get up here! Look at 'em!" she cried, nearly falling off the fence.

Wednesday, Friday, and Sunday scrambled to the top of the fence, and teetered across to where she balanced.

Wednesday wondered aloud, "Who are they?"

Friday slid up next to her. "There's no parents!"

Sunday wobbled over. "Yeah… Nobody's watchin' 'em."

Monday seemed most amused. "A pack'a stray kids, huh?"

Wednesday shook her head. "No, they're orphans, like George. So sad."

Thereafter, a study of the orphans became their afternoon activity. They filed across the fence to watch them play games like freeze tag and red rover. Their number varied from day to day, but there were always five to ten of them.

The Minor kids dubbed freeze tag "swingin' statues" because that's what the kids became when they were tagged and they froze. They observed how dirty they were with their blue jeans and messy T-shirts, speculated on where they came from, and opined on how unfortunate they must be having no one to care for them.

Closer to dusk, the orphans disappeared one by one, until there wasn't anyone left. The Minor kids filed back down the fence as the last of the orphans was gone, jumping off one at a time to mimic a game of "swingin' statues" themselves until time to go in.

No desire to actually play with the other children stirred in them. The idea never occurred to them as even a possibility, so firmly were June's rules set into place. A warning always rang in Sunday's ears: *You better stay where I can see you.* They simply believed the children were alone with no parents, no place to go, and no one to love them.

...

Riding with the Kindlys on the way to nowhere, Sunday thought how silly it had been to think those kids were orphans. She was the *real* orphan now. And she was the one who'd made it so.

The tires spit gravel against the undercarriage of the car. A particularly large stray pebble cracked loud against her door, snapping Sunday back to reality.

As Mr. Kindly rolled through a set of limestone walls supporting a great wrought iron gate, Sunday read the beautifully weathered iron plaque on the left:

Rose Village
Psychiatric Hospital

Rose Village

THE GROUNDS APPEARED as inviting as the cover of the pamphlet the Kindlys slid across the table to Sunday so early that same morning. The brochure boasted being her hometown's first and largest freestanding private psychiatric hospital, and alluded to its expert care and three-pronged treatment approach. There weren't, she noticed, any pictures of what she would find inside.

At the institution's great wooden doors, Mr. and Mrs. Kindly hugged Sunday goodbye, after which she was promptly ushered into something of a marble-floored holding tank.

She found a seat in the back corner of the room. There were thirty or so other people of all ages hovering and wandering aimlessly about the space. Wide-eyed and alert, she searched the various faces for some sign she was in the right place. Although she'd called her momma crazy, and she surmised her daddy was sick, until now, she'd never seen just what "insane" really looked like.

Judging by the strength of his jaw line and olive complexion, Sunday saw an older man near the window closest to her had been quite handsome in a former life. Now he was gaunt and graying. He never so much as blinked as he stared despondently through the glass.

She planned her flight path as an obese middle-aged woman lumbered in her direction before slowly pulling her shirt over her head and unfastening her bra. The woman's pendulous breasts swung side to side from her beefy shoulders. Sunday leaned forward, on her mark should the woman get too close, but two orderlies rushed the woman in the nick of time. One covered her with a blanket while the other picked up her clothes. They ushered her through a door to the left of the nurses' station.

Nearby, an elderly woman rocked a baby only she could see. Her forehead wrinkled over a worried brow. Bags underlined her eyes and spilled into deep creases curving down her face and around her frown.

Sunday had never witnessed sorrow like that before, not even the single time June spoke within earshot at any length about her own lost child, The Dead Baby Boy. *Come to think of it, she'd seemed so...empty...about the whole thing...*

In the kitchen at Stensonfield, a few months before Tuesday was born, she listened in to the few details about the dead one. Sunday couldn't have been more than three years old. Her mother's description was so odd, and she never forgot the blue pictures she'd drawn. Strange she remembered the conversation so clearly.

· · ·

Gramma had come by for coffee, and brought coloring books and a few eight-packs of Crayons for the kids. June sent Sunday and the others to their places in the kitchen with the gifts to keep them occupied for a while.

Gramma settled in at the dining table while Sunday's momma set the water on to boil. June carried over two full cups balanced on two saucers with two spoons and set them on the white and gold-flecked Formica table top. They spoke in hushed voices.

"Dixie, honey...."–that's what Gramma called Sunday's momma–"it just wadn't meant to be."

June talked about the dead baby the same way someone else might talk about toenail clippings or a load of laundry. "He had dark hair like his brother. Slanted eyes. They were blue, like the girls'. He had little bitty hands. No fingerprints. No footprints. That's how we knew something wasn't right."

Huh? He got no fingers and no toes? Just little blobs.

Sunday couldn't shake the images, so she drew them inside the outline of a little bear in her book for a close-up view, careful to keep in the lines so no one would think she was coloring wrong. She colored the blobs at the ends of the arms and legs blue.

Her momma didn't cry. Instead, she stared above Gramma's head, talking on in the same dull drone. "His skin…was so thin… so clear you could see right through. You could see his blue veins."

Sunday paid careful attention to her picture so she wouldn't be caught listening in. *You could see blue veins?*

Sunday saw her Gramma reach across the table and touch her momma's hand. "Well, it wadn't in the stars, Dixie…You have enough already. With Wednesday…and Friday….and now you've got Sunday and Monday." She shook her head and said again, "Just wadn't meant to be."

June pulled her hand away. "I know Momma, but that's…that baby's still *one.*"

"I know, honey," she said with a raised eyebrow and a slight nod down to June's middle. "Well, and now you've got this one on the way."

June finally broke her stare and whined, "I'm getting older, Momma. I'm twenty-two now, and I'm getting older. Good god, I'm having another one. I've got all these kids."

"Yes, dear, but you're only havin' one more," Gramma comforted.

Sunday darted her eyes back down to the book, sensing the conversation coming to an end. She scribbled the rest of the bear in blue before anyone found out about what she'd drawn. *Color the blobs. No fingers, no toes…and skin you can see right through.*

· · ·

Sunday blinked back at the childless mother across the holding tank. The woman met her gaze; her frown deepened and her chin quivered. Sunday averted her gaze, surprisingly feeling like an intruder.

In the other direction, a girl not much older than herself sat perched on one knee in a metal armchair with thick orange canvas cushions, staring at a blank TV screen, pushing buttons on a remote control resting on the arm of the chair. Sunday's gaze lingered on the girl's nails, bitten down to the quick, reminding her of the incident with the chewed up doll fingers back at the flat.

...

A few weeks before Christmas, Gramma and Grandaddy Paw gave Wednesday a baby doll with a set of clothes and a pushcart. Sunday remembered Chester's jaw muscles flexing at the sight of the lone doll on the bed. He *loathed* things that weren't perfectly symmetrical, and two beds with four pillows could never be complete with a single doll. He muttered once, "For Christ's sakes, what was that woman thinking buying one damn doll?" One of the girls having something the others didn't wasn't fair. He used to say, *What's good for one is good for all.*

Every night he would seethe at the sight of the single doll during inspections, but this one wasn't the girls' fault, and so, firmly planted in the safe zone. Still, she wasn't surprised to find three identically wrapped gifts the same size as the box Wednesday's doll came in under the tree that year. She thought even that probably irked him, placing only three under there instead of four.

Christmas morning came and went, and before noon, as was customary in the Minor household, the children picked up all traces of the holiday and put their gifts away, most of them along the back wall of the closet floor, not to be touched again except with special permission. Their new dolls were to be placed on their beds.

When the family feast at Gramma June's was over and the Minors settled in at the house again, the children went about their daily routine: dishes, baths, and inspections. Only then did Sunday finally see the sweet relief visibly wash over Chester's face and down through his body. She even thought she saw him waver from the dizzying satisfaction of finally making the girls' beds perfect. One doll on each pillow, precisely as it should be. And that is exactly where those dolls stayed ninety-nine point nine percent of the very brief time they kept them.

One afternoon a month or so into the new year, the weather too nasty for them to go outside, the children were commanded to the edges of their beds. Sunday shared a bed with Wednesday for the first half of their lives, and Monday was assigned beds with Tuesday, naturally, so they could lay in order of birth. Monday was in charge of making sure the baby stayed safe on the bed, and developed a system of pillow dams and barriers to keep her contained, but Tuesday hadn't learned to sit still on the bed to wait for instruction the way the others did. Instead she spent her time rumpling the bedspread, stuffing corners of pillows and sheets into her mouth, and taking turns swinging the dolls and slapping at them when they fell.

The girls paid no attention to Monday's doll until she turned to check on the baby. She cupped her mouth and gasped. "She bit the fingers off."

Sunday and Wednesday hopped off their bed and onto Monday and Tuesday's. The three of them leaned in close enough that their foreheads touched, examining the hands of Monday's doll.

Tuesday stared blankly back at the three girls.

Monday pursed her lips and glared down at the holes where the fingers were supposed to be. "She's evil."

Sunday and Wednesday giggled in agreement.

Monday poked Sunday in the side. "Trade me."

"No."

"*C'monnn, trade me,*" she whined.

"No way! She's gonna bite mine off, too."

Monday shot back, dead serious, "No, she's not. She's full."

Sunday understood Monday was afraid she was gonna get a whippin', but she was *not* gonna be the one to get whipped instead. She shook her head to make sure the point was sinking in.

Wednesday taunted, matter-of-factly, "Well, she can't get mine because my babydoll's on the other bed."

Monday pulled back a balled up fist. "I'm gonna hit 'er."

Wednesday grabbed Monday's hand and pressed it to her belly. "You can't. Momma's gonna get mad."

Monday plopped down on the bed and crossed her arms. "Hmph."

"Look!" said Sunday, pointing at the baby gnawing on the fingers of her own doll. They kept their seats and observed.

Reality set in quickly, though. The dolls were ruined. Sunday and Monday tried tucking the dolls in under the sheets. "There, now they won't notice."

Wednesday chided, "That's not gonna work. Daddy doesn't like for the sheets to not be straight."

They pulled the dolls out and tried to arrange them close together so that each little hand was hidden behind the other. The three stood in the doorway to survey their handiwork.

Sunday shook her head. "No, I can still see 'em."

The trio stared down at the foot of the bed where Tuesday lay curled up and asleep. Monday quipped, "I guess she's full *now*."

June called the children in to prepare for dinner. Wednesday grabbed Tuesday, who remained asleep, and everyone filed out, forgetting all about what'd happened for the time being.

The moment Chester stepped through the door they glanced nervously at one another from their posts in the kitchen. Sunday held her breath as he treaded across the living room to the bathroom. She almost fainted when he paused by their bedroom door, and sighed when he closed the bathroom door behind him.

Safe.

Sunday kept one eye on him when he stepped back out and cocked his head, peering into the girls' room for a long time–too long. He walked to the bed and leaned over the dolls. He ripped each fingerless doll from the pillows by the head and shook them as he yelled, "What in the hell happened to these dolls?"

June darted in to assess the matter. She shot an accusing glare at the girls, who'd already lined up behind her in order of birth.

Monday called out, "Tuesday bit the fingers off."

June zeroed her icy stare in on Monday. Monday shifted her eyes to the floor as she automatically revved up and snapped her fingers.

Chester threw one doll back on the bed and boomed, "Well, Jesus, Monday, why the hell didn't ya stop 'er?"

She stared harder at the floor and snapped her finger twice more. "Momma woulda got mad."

June rolled her eyes at Chester as if to say, *That is ridiculous.*

Chester chunked the other doll onto the bed. "They're all shit now. They're just shit. Goddamnit!" he barked, fuming at the group. "We pay good money for toys for these goddamn kids, and all they can do is fuck them up."

She stepped out of line, scooped up one of the dolls, and rocking back and forth, tried her best to treat it like she thought a loving mother would. "We can keep 'em, Daddy. Look, they're just crippled."

"No. No, no, no, *no*! We're not keepin' no torn up dolls in this house," he told the kids before turning to his wife. "Jesus Christ, June. Why the hell can't you keep an eye on these kids? You got one damn job and that's takin' care'a this house while I'm out workin' all goddamn day to pay for those damn dolls. And this is what happens!"

He shook his head and stomped past her out of the room, calling out behind him, "You better fuckin' do somethin' about this."

June turned to Friday, standing outside the door. "Goddamnit, Friday, go get the belt."

· · ·

Sunday turned away from the girl with the chewed up nails sitting in the orange chair as the sound of her name emerged from the window the nurses' station and bounced across the marble tiles. The nurse was leaning out over the counter jutting from the windowsill. She raised her head, as if to say, *Yes, you,* motioning Sunday over with a wave and a nod.

As Sunday made her way toward the window she ducked with a start when a gangly man, no taller than Sunday's five feet six inches, peeked out from the shadows of a thick square column, giggling into his hands. She picked up her pace as an orderly stepped out from the same door they'd taken the half-dressed obese woman through. He was six foot plus and, Sunday thought, at least half as wide. Sunday wasn't so sure she *was* in the right place.

"Sunday Minor, yes?"

"Yes, ma'am."

"Welcome to Rose Village."

She Can Fly

....

WITHOUT TAKING HER eyes off the newspaper in front of her, the nurse put her hand to her heart and introduced herself. "I'm Colleen." She stretched an open palm to the giant orderly. "And this is Oliver. You can call him Olly."

The orderly nodded.

"You'll need to follow him in for a couple of checkups…and a quick test. First is your physical. Next a few questions about yourself. Last, you'll join a few others for a short written exam so we can place you in the correct class level for continuing education. When you're done there, Olly will show you to your new room."

"Yes, ma'am."

Olly lumbered down the corridor; Sunday followed close behind. The pale yellow walls reflected the fluorescent light in a way that Sunday didn't feel quite so small as she had in the holding tank, which she was relieved to leave behind. She almost wasn't aware there were no windows. Instead, there were doors on either side every few feet, each marked by a single faux wooden plaque bearing a white number.

Olly stopped short and counted the doors from the end of the hall. He turned to his right and pointed at the door in front of them. He twisted the knob and flipped the switch on the wall, illuminating the exam room inside. "Here ya go."

He stepped aside, showed Sunday in, and gestured for her to have a seat in a silver metal chair next to an exam table. "The doctor will be right in."

Sunday nodded and sat down as the orderly pulled the door to. She noticed a cobweb swaying under the stale, frigid air stream blowing from the dusty vent above. The girl with the chewed up nails still on her mind, she glanced down at her own left hand and ran the fingers of her right over a barely visible scar on her ring finger. The first time she could remember ever being in an exam room like this, the doctor had frozen off a wart there. She lifted her gaze to the red metal cabinet over the sink in front of her, not really focusing. So much had happened that the timelines were fuzzy, but the details were still so clear. She must've been four. She hadn't learned to "fly away" quite yet. *That's too bad. Woulda been useful if I had.*

...

The bump on her finger was like a tiny mountain range. She discovered the blemish coming up weeks before her momma. On the occasion she accidentally knocked her finger against something the growth would start to bleed. Other than that, she didn't mind her new addition at all. Having her own little set of mountains to look at any time she wanted made her smile.

Out of the blue, June told Sunday they were going to the doctor. It scared her that her momma didn't tell her why. She assumed the situation must be terrible, though, because her momma pulled the pale blue dress with lace all over out of the closet. *The doctor's not church. Why's this a special occasion? Something must really be wrong with me. I'm dying!*

As Sunday struggled to force the peanut forming in her throat down to her stomach, June pulled the white lace-fringed socks over her ankles and buckled her patent leather shoes.

In the exam room, the doctor took her hand and examined closely. He pushed on the wart. "Does that hurt?"

"No."

He turned to June. "We can take that off."

"M'kay. When should we schedule an appointment?"

"I mean we can handle the removal right now."

Sunday gasped, wide eyes cast toward her momma. *He's gonna cut my arm off.*

June sounded pleased. "Okay, let's go ahead and do it."

Sunday's mouth snapped shut and she gulped.

Only when the doctor arranged the jar of cotton swabs, a bottle of rubbing alcohol, a pair of tweezers, and only a single band-aid, did the room stop spinning around her. *One band-aid.* She would, in fact, be keeping her arm.

The doctor rolled a machine over next to the exam table. Connected to the side was a coiled cord like the one on a telephone, except instead of a receiver there was a pin-looking thing attached.

"Now this, young lady, is called a laser!" He dropped the goggles down from the top of his head 'til they rested on his nose, and flipped a switch. A high-pitched buzzing tickled Sunday's teeth.

The doctor winked at her. "This isn't gonna hurt one little bit."

Tears sprouted from her eyes, and she buried her face into her mother's shoulder. The doctor leaned in and pressed the pin to her skin. "You're gonna be fine, honey. You're not gonna feel a thing."

June gripped the girl tightly. Not to comfort her, though. Sunday was in trouble. *I'm crying and nothing happened yet.*

Sure enough, the pin didn't hurt at all. The sickeningly sweet aroma wafting up through the space between her mother's sweater and her face, filling her nose, was what sent the girl over the edge. The air smelled like rotten barbecue. Sunday gagged. *Momma's gonna be so mad. I'm gonna throw up on 'er and ruin everything.*

Her momma did nothing to console her. She gagged again and cried harder. The doctor leaned back and pulled his goggles back up. He reached backward and flipped the machine switch off. "Honey, am I hurting you? Can you feel this?"

The girl shook her head.

"Why are you crying, sweetheart?"

The lie just popped out of her mouth. "I'm gettin' Momma's shirt wet."

June rolled her eyes and sighed.

The doctor saw her exasperation and consoled the girl. "You're okay, sweetie. We're almost done."

He switched the machine on again, and dropped the goggles back down. Sunday swallowed each gag hard as another minute passed before he finally turned the machine off for the last time. He leaned back with a grin and spread his arms wide. "All done!"

The doctor picked up the band-aid and pulled the wrapper apart. "Now," he said, pressing the bandage to her hand, "we're all set."

Sunday's daddy asked when the pair reached the car, "Is the situation taken care of?"

June heaved her door closed and grunted, "Yeah."

"Did she behave?"

June threw her hands like she'd given up on the girl. "No. She cried the whole damn time."

Chester craned his neck in Sunday's direction, as she pressed herself against the seat as far away from them as she could get. "Did they hurt you?"

"No, sir."

"Well, what the fuck were you cryin' for then?"

"I was scared."

He rolled his eyes, and now he took a turn throwing his hands up. "Oh, god."

He slipped the key into the ignition and raised his voice. "You aren't even hurt."

He revved the engine and yelled, "Oh, my god, Sunday, what the hell is wrong with you?"

June cocked her head to the side. "You know, Chester, they *live* to embarrass us…"

Back at the house, Chester and June sat Sunday at the dining table.

Her momma grabbed her hand out of her lap. "Doctor said we gotta take this band-aid off now. We gotta get some air to it." She ripped the bandage off, and Sunday winced at the sting around the wound, although where her tiny mountain range used to be was completely numb.

Chester loomed over them, gasping at the sight. June wrinkled her nose at the offense. A black hole with white strings hanging from the center now replaced her tiny mountains. It was so ugly.

Chester boomed from above, "And that's supposed to make 'er look better?" He shook his head. "Jeeesus Christ, June."

June couldn't take her eyes off the disgusting wound. "He said they burned the thing off or something..."

"Well, is her hand gonna look like *that* the whole rest of 'er life? I don't see what the fuck's the difference if she's gonna stay ugly anyway."

"I don't know, Chester. I don't know."

A few weeks later the scab fell off and all that was left was that faint white scar.

· · ·

Sunday unconsciously ran her fingers over the indention on her hand again. *Why couldn't she have just explained what was happening? Why couldn't she have hugged me and told me everything was gonna be all right? Why couldn't she ever love us?*

If she'd discovered she could fly away beforehand, she probably wouldn't have cried. Her daddy was right, though. *It was truly nothing to cry a-* The exam room door opened and the doctor popped his head in. "You still need a few minutes?"

Sunday was confused.

"Your gown? You'll need to change into that gown." Sunday followed his finger to the white gown with blue polka dots wrapped in plastic sitting on the counter. She nodded, and the doctor closed the door.

Sunday sighed as she crossed the room and unwrapped what amounted to a slip of tissue paper. She set the gown back on the counter while she pressed each toe to the back of the opposite heel, slipping out of her canvas tennis shoes.

To keep herself from slipping out of her own body, she replayed the moment she'd shared with someone that she could fly away. She never told anybody before–or after–that conversation with Friday in the back yard on Niagra Drive. Their talk was more of a monologue, with her rambling on while Friday, for the most part, just listened. The first time it happened she was five.

. . .

She and her brother were sitting on the back patio, hot, bored and pushing rocks around on the ground. Nothing else came to mind, so Sunday tested the waters. "Sometimes, when I'm waitin' for things to happen to me, I can fly." She studied Friday's face for signs that he believed her. He rolled his eyes.

"No, really! Sometimes I can fly when things're actually happenin', but mostly only when I'm scared and just waitin'." She went on to explain how flying worked. "All I have to do is think real hard for a minute about my body. I breathe in real deep and hold my breath for a long, long time–long as I can. Next, I blow out real hard, and pull aaalll the feelin' outta one'a my legs. Afterward I breathe in real deep again, and hold my breath for a long time again. And when I blow out real hard, I pull aaalll the feelin' outta my other leg. Once I'm done with my legs, I do it for one arm, and I do it again for the other one. That's when I can see I'm in a tiny little ball right in the middle of my heart. And then, when I blow out real hard the last time, I fly...straight outta my mouth. Everything is blank around me, and from there, all of a sudden, all around me, I can see I'm right there in the air. I'm in the air, floating above everything."

Sunday detected he still didn't believe her. "I'm not pretending. I'm not usin' my 'magination. I am flyin'...If I'm still too close to myself, and they can still reach me, I blow out again, and again, and I go higher and higher, 'cause if I go high enough they can't reach me. If they can still reach you, you can get sucked right back in. You have to stay far enough away. So I always go up. They can't fly. They can run, and they can chase you. They can get in the car and follow behind you. But they can't go up. When I fly, they can't reach me."

She grasped that he was still listening because he hadn't gotten up and walked away like he did when he was done with the subject at hand. She carried on while Friday stared at the dirt. "My favorite time to fly is on a swing. When I know I done somethin' wrong, and it's only a matter'a time before they find out, I think, 'I'm gonna get on this swing, and I'm gonna fly.' Next thing I know, I'm swingin', and I fly like a bird. There's no ceiling to stop me, so I can go as high as I want, and nobody can reach me...Except if I'm swingin' and I didn't do somethin' wrong, and I'm not scared, I try to make myself fly anyway. I swing higher and higher and point my toes real hard to try'n touch the sky. I never can fly away when I'm swingin' for fun. Either way, I sure have fun swingin'."

She peered over at her brother again, searching for some sign he might want her to shut up. He'd picked a blade of grass and fiddled with it while he stared out across the yard. Good enough for her. She kept talking.

"Remember when we first moved? I was playin' with Paul, and I hurt my arm real bad? That's the first time I did it. At least I think so. That's the first time I remember."

Paul and his momma and daddy lived next to the Minors at their new house. They were called "The Velas."

Sunday chattered on. "We were playin' pirate ship. We brought out a stool from their house, and were rockin' back 'n' forth like pirates on the high seas. A big wave crashed into the boat and turned us over, and I fell on my elbow and hurt it bad. I was cryin', and Paul's momma came runnin'. I was tryin' not to cry, and I was tellin' 'er 'It's gonna be okay,' and 'I'm okay,' and 'It's not that bad,' and stuff. She didn't even listen. She went over to get Momma anyway. I was so scared Momma was gonna be mad. Maybe 'cause Mrs. Vela was innneruptin' 'er day. Or I thought she might have to take me to the hospital, which I was right. I knew that'd make the steam come outta her ears while she was whippin' me for sure. Or worse, I thought she might scream at me and whip me right in front of Paul and his momma and everybody, which I was wrong. I was still scared she might. Either way, she was gonna be so mad, so when Paul's momma was walkin' over to the house to get 'er, I plopped down on the ground and flew straight up in the sky to wait…As soon as I saw Momma crossin' from our front yard to theirs, I thought, here comes Momma, and snap, I was right back there on the ground where I oughta be. I guess I just somehow figured out I needed to get back…See, nobody can tell I'm gone 'cause my real body stays right there. O'course, I can't do anything else with my real body if I'm flyin', and that could be dangerous."

Friday nodded. Sunday knew *he* knew things could get dangerous if you couldn't at least run from June.

"After that first time I flew away, I tried again when I was gettin' whipped. I went like a ragdoll, and Momma dropped me straight on the floor."

Friday nodded again.

Their momma'd already begun to change by the time they moved; she got meaner, and more and more often, at that. He'd been there when Sunday had gone limp right before June dropped her. He told her when she woke up he'd been scared she was dead.

The children learned quickly they could cry and beg when their momma was in a rage, and swinging whatever weapon she'd picked up before lunging at one of them, but they were not allowed to scream. In fact, they *should* start crying and begging right away, so she knew the punishment hurt. If not, she'd beat them harder and longer until they did. Sometimes, though, if she hit the same spot more than once or twice, the third and the fourth and the fifth time simply hurt too much. Sometimes the screaming couldn't be helped. Most often the scream accidently slipped out when they were trying to stay still.

June would do this thing. She'd drop the belt and clamp one hand over their mouths and use her first finger and thumb to squeeze their noses shut tight, and with the other hand, she would press the nape of their necks forward, hard, and lift. The child would be dangling only a few inches above the ground, high enough to silence them within a minute. If there was no air going in or out, then there was no scream.

The first time June grabbed her, Sunday imagined her head was a pumpkin and she was a jack-o-lantern with a body built on. A few minutes would pass as she dangled from her momma's grip. She clawed desperately at her fingers clasped tightly over her face, and she felt her eyeballs bulge out of their sockets as she pictured the tiny holes at the bottom of each of the creases between her momma's fingers where she imagined there were tiny streams of air flowing through them–she couldn't feel them, but she had to believe the air was getting in–until she grew weaker…and weaker…and finally blacked out.

The dead weight must have shocked June out of those rages because without warning her momma would simply let go. The child would drop to the floor. Afterward, while the others held fast to their silence, their momma would start to cry, and always, she'd say with a sigh as she walked out, "I don't know what you people want from me." Monday always called out behind her, "We just want you to love us, Momma."

Sunday believed Friday nodded because he'd both witnessed and been subjected to the same ritual.

"Yeah. That's what happened to me the first time she dropped me. I coulda hit my head or somethin'. They could do anything to me, and I wouldn't be able to do a thing about it. Now I know I can't fly when it's time to take what I got comin' to me."

Sunday rambled on. "Anyway, when Momma bent down, to squeeze my arm after we were playin' pirates and I fell off the chair and Paul's momma went to go get ours and she came out to get me, I jumped outta my skin, 'cause my elbow hurt so bad…She squeezed again, and made me wanna throw up. I must'a turned green 'cause Momma didn't squeeze anymore. Instead, she looked down at me with her lips real tight and her eyes squinted at me real mean, and said, 'You're gonna have to wait 'til your daddy gets home. Now go on home.' I got up and went straight to the house. I sat on the couch and waited for him…I watched Momma put meatloaf in the oven. Then I saw her brushin' her hair. You know how she's always brushin' her hair and puttin' on lipstick when she knows Daddy's almost home?"

Friday nodded once more, signaling to Sunday she held his attention for only a little while longer. He tossed a rock to her. She stood and tossed it back.

She spoke faster between tosses. "I heard Daddy's car comin' down the street. So did Momma. I didn't mean to, but the second she walked out the front door to tell him what happened, I went blank…That time, I didn't fly away. I tried real hard, but I couldn't. Everything was just black."

Sunday stared off into space, trying to remember anything other than blackness in the moment. Only her parents' voices swam through the darkness. "I heard them come in, and Momma tellin' Daddy what happened. 'Can you believe the hell she's puttin' us through? I think she's gonna have to see a doctor. Lord knows what she's gonna cost us this time.' 'Well, June, did you call a doctor?' 'No, I was waitin' for you to get home.' 'Why? Jesus, well, let's go.' That was all. I couldn't hear anything else after that."

She focused on the stone in her hand to be sure before tossing it back. "Nope. Everything was just black. I think maybe I needed more practice at flyin'…Anyway, I must'a really went away that time because I don't know how I got there, but I woke up right there on a stretcher in a hallway in the hospital. Momma was next to my head, leanin' on the wall with her arms crossed. I could tell she didn't wanna be there. Well, I didn't either…The doctor's big face was right next to mine, and the nurse's littler face was right next to his, both of 'em starin' at me. He said, 'Does that hurt?' I don't even know what he was doin'. I couldn't feel a thing. I said, 'No.' 'Does that hurt?' 'No.' After that the nurse turned her little bitty face and whispered somethin' into his great big ear. I didn't listen to the whole thing, only the end: '…her toes.'"

She was glad Friday's eyes widened with renewed interest.

"I saw him touch my arm. I didn't feel his hand, but I saw him squeeze, and they both looked down at my toes. I was afraid I'd do somethin' I wasn't supposed to, so I didn't look down, but I wanted to real bad. I wanted to see what they were sayin' about by toes. They stopped askin' me if my arm hurt, and every time they moved, they stared at my toes."

Sunday paused to catch her breath from running on so.

"Later, they wheeled me into a dark room, the one for X-rays. People would stop by and try'n straighten out my arm. The doctor and the nurse came back in and the nurse tried moving my arm one more time while the doctor stared at my toes. The nurse said, 'She's extremely protective'–talkin' about me–'but she's not cryin'–because I wasn't…and the lady said, 'Is she in shock?' The doctor said, 'No, I don't think so'…They gave me a shot after, which hurt real bad, and I didn't want to be there anymore. I tried to fly up to the ceilin' to see. Instead, I went blank again."

Friday caught the rock and walked over to Sunday. He told her, "Hey, that's real crazy, but I'm gonna go on in and get a drink and do my drawings."

He started for the door, so she whined, "I'm almost done. Can't I just tell you the rest?"

He turned back around. "Okay then."

They sat down and she spit out the words fast as she could. "I came to, and I was standin' on the floor next to the stretcher on the table with wheels. The nurse was pullin' my shirt over my head, tellin' me, 'You're gonna stay a couple nights with us, honey. We're gonna go ahead and get you into a gown'...I looked around at where I thought I was gonna stay. There was a red box on the wall with tools in it, I think. At least the box was the same color as the one Daddy has in the garage. The doctor was gone, and only me 'n' her were in there. I didn't know what was happenin'. All I knew was my arm was hurt and I was takin' care of it. She pulled down my shorts, and I helped her as much as I could with my good arm. Afterward, I pulled up my panties where they slipped down a little. She said, 'Oh, no, honey, those have to come off too.' That's when I started crying–when she told me to take my panties off. I dunno why I was cryin'. I just was."

Friday nodded, slowly this time.

She babbled on. "The nurse made a sad face, which I thought was real nice of 'er. She said, 'I'll be right back.' I knew she was goin' to get Momma 'cause that's what they always do so I tried to sniff up my tears so I wouldn't be cryin' when she got back. The door opened and Momma came in. The nurse was behind her. Momma bent close to my face, mad again, and said to me real quiet, 'You need to do what you're told, and quit actin' like a baby.' I thought she was gonna whip me right then and there if I didn't, so I stopped. I just let 'em take everything off. They put a paper nightgown on me and tied the strings in the back, but I didn't feel one bit better about the whole thing. Even though they tol' me to lay back down on the table with the wheels in the hospital, and nobody could see the back'a me, I felt like everybody could see me naked...They rolled me out of the room on the stretcher on the table with the wheels into another room in the hospital. I was cold. And I waited forever. I was real tired by that time, so I went to sleep."

Friday stood again, obviously ready to go, and Sunday jumped up. "I'm almost done, I promise!"

Friday crossed his arms over his chest and sighed.

"I stayed in the hospital for three days. The doctor said my arm wasn't broken, that I had done somethin' real special–I dis-lo-cated it."

Friday nodded. He'd also been there when their momma and daddy talked about what it meant to dislocate your arm.

"I popped mine out the wrong way. I accidentally shoved my top arm bone down in between two other bones on the bottom. Anyway, the doctor and nurses came in a couple times a day to pinch my fingernails and tell me to wiggle my fingers. I heard 'em talk about putting pins in. I don't remember how they fixed my bones, but they must have done something because they put my whole arm in a real neat crane to hang above my head...Momma stayed with me. She didn't talk to me much, but she watched TV and made me order nasty stuff off the menu." Sunday imitated her mother's whine. "'Get the asparagus. You'll *like* that.' Yuk!"

Friday chuckled.

"She knew I wouldn't like veg'tibles, and when the food came, she'd go, 'Oh, you don't *like* that? You want *me* to eat your veggies *for* you?'...Daddy came to visit once. That was the first time he ever bought me a present without Momma like at Christmas or somethin'. He bought me that little troll doll with white hair all the way to the top of the plastic tube it came in. Pushin' the belly button made the nose light up."

Friday turned back toward the door, and Sunday skipped behind. "Gramma came once, too. She brought me a Donald Duck coloring book and a new pack'a eight colors. Since my arm was just hangin' in the crane, not doin' a thing, I thought up a perfect way to use it. I made a scoop with my fingers and put the Crayons up there like a little Crayon tray. I could reach them with my other hand easy."

He paused at the door to let her finish. She shrugged and offered a final thought. "Anyway, so now you know, I can fly."

...

What Sunday was aware of for the first time as she eased herself atop the thin paper covering the exam table was that maybe, technically, she could say that her ability to "fly away" signaled her first attempt to get away.

She shivered, noticing a chill in the stale air.

Yes, flying away was only a temporary solution, but she had discovered a way to escape. Being able to pull herself up into her chest and blow herself away from what was happening below, she honestly thought she could fly. Although she did quickly learn her gift was not something that could be invoked for fun on a swing set under the afternoon sun–she couldn't *make* herself "fly." Dissociation and defense mechanisms were not well-mapped concepts, even for the experts of the time, and certainly these were not part of a child's vocabulary. Her knowledge was limited to understanding that she could fly away when all else was out of her control, like an instinct. And in times of crisis, it was a way to survive.

Different Kinds of Blind

SUNDAY, STILL THINKING about that moment in the exam room after dislocating her elbow, shivered again when the air kicked on and the breeze blew down the front of her paper dress. *I cried when the nurse told me to undress. Why?*

The doctor rapped lightly on the door and peeked in again. "Ready for me?"

The doctor slipped into the room, staring down at his clipboard as he closed the door behind him. He was tall and thin, with salt and pepper hair. He wore thick black-framed glasses and a Hawaiian button-up shirt and khaki pants. His shoes were black orthotics, kind of like women's nursing shoes. *Moon shoes.*

"Hmm," he said over the clipboard in his hands, "Sunday Minor?"

She nodded again, and the doctor set the clipboard on the counter. He pulled a pair of latex gloves over his bony fingers and said flatly, "Is there anything you need to tell me before we begin the exam?"

"No."

"Do you know why you're here?" He glanced down at her shaking foot and scribbled on her chart. She curled up her fingers to hide her own chewed up nails. He scribbled again.

"Because I'm having nightmares."

"How tall are you?" He felt her neck and behind her ears.

"Five-five."

"How much do you weigh?" He draped a stethoscope around his neck.

"Seventy-five."

He stopped what he was doing and flipped back to the front page of her chart to scrutinize something. "How old are you again? Sixteen. And you really think you only weigh seventy-five pounds?" He motioned for her to get on the scale as he rose from his seat.

Sunday stepped onto the scale. "I weighed seventy-five last time they checked in P.E. I've weighed seventy-five for a long time."

The doctor shifted the block counterweight to 100 lbs, and it clanked heavily to the right. He shifted the block back to zero and moved the smaller counter weight far over, where it eventually rocked ever so slightly. "Eighty-two."

He raised his eyebrows and scribbled on her chart again. "Still underweight for your height."

Sunday shrugged off the fact she guessed wrong about her own weight. The last couple of months, away from her mother, she must have put on a few pounds. *It's not a contest.*

He ran through some more questions and went on to conduct a general health check, noting the knots on the back of her head, the scars in the palms of her hands, and the slightly misshapen left side of her torso. Last, he pulled a tongue depressor from a drawer. "Open wide for me and stick out your tongue."

The doctor pressed down, and she gagged. He pulled the wooden stick from her mouth. He snapped off a glove so he could scribble on Sunday's chart. He muttered while he scratched something out, "Has had nooo dental work."

Sunday bristled. "Yes, I have."

She described how a dentist pulled her whole second row of teeth when she was seven and said her baby teeth never dissolved because of something her momma ate while she was pregnant. Wednesday called her "shark mouth" until they were removed. Sunday kept that detail to herself.

"Really? Okay."

Really? This guy is calling me a liar? He doesn't know me.

Her confrontational posture was met with silence. Was that a sense of having been slighted that was creeping up into Sunday's chest? She couldn't be sure.

The doctor pointed to the eye chart, and without waiting for instructions, Sunday cupped the left lens of her glasses and called out the letters on the chart across the room. The doctor signaled her to switch hands, and she covered her right eye to repeat the exercise.

"That's about all I need." The doctor, still focused on his chart, nodded toward Sunday's clothes. "Go ahead and get dressed. Olly'll take you down to the Psychiatric Director's office for a few questions."

The doctor walked out, and Sunday pulled her glasses down her nose and peered over them at the blurred chart. She smiled, slid off the exam table, and began to dress.

She'd been wearing glasses since she was six. It was so neat how crisp things could become by wearing a couple pieces of glass in front of her eyes.

. . .

In those days, Sunday thought when she looked at things she saw them differently than everyone else. Like her bruises…

They're there, and I can see 'em, but nobody else can. I can see the outline of the belt buckle, and I can see the puffy red bumps all around it, and I can even see the tiny little scabs and dots and baby bruises inside the buckle mark. They are red and blue and purple at first. If Momma and Daddy don't use the belt, there's no dots, just kind of a circle.

Sometimes they have black in them. After a while they turn green and yellow and brown. And then they go away. Sometimes I wonder why nobody else can see them. At least no one I know because nobody ever said anything about them. Well, I can. I know they're there.

I can see the marks on my sisters and my brother, too. I'm not sure if they can. At least I don't think they can see them, not as good as me anyway.

She used to call her ability secret eye powers, and only she possessed them.

I can stare at the sun and not go blind, like everyone says. The sun moves. Well, not the sun by itself, but the black rings spinning around it in a perfect circle. It looks a lot like my bruises do with all those rings. I can't tell anybody about it or else they'll go blind when they try to do it themselves. Besides, if they can't see the bruises, they prolly can't see the rings either. But I can.

And so the news came as a big surprise when her first grade teacher told her she couldn't see. Sure, Sunday needed to pull things close in order to read them, and when she was doing her writing exercises, she couldn't always identify the letters of her vocabulary words the blackboard well enough to copy, but *blind?*

She would concentrate hard at times. Other times, as she stared at the faint white chalk lines on the big green board, her thoughts would wander. *Why do they call it a black board anyway? The board is green, not black.*

During one of those daydreams Ms. Tucker bent down next to Sunday. She eyed the blackboard from the girl's line of sight, before studying Sunday's paper again. Then she walked away.

After the test was over and the class was taking turns reading *Tip and Mitten* aloud, the teacher pointed to Sunday and wagged a finger for her to approach. Ms. Tucker leaned forward and whispered to her, "Honey, is your momma aware you can't see that well?"

Sunday was shocked. "I can see fine. I'm not blind. I can see there's writing, and I can see my paper. I can see."

Ms. Tucker pushed herself out from the desk, and stood up. She motioned Sunday to come around. She leaned in and said, "Okay, well, we're gonna go ahead and test your eyes in a minute."

Sunday shrugged. "Okay."

The teacher walked to the door, and leaned out to whisper to Ms. Gregory in the next class over. Ms. Gregory murmured something, and stepped into Ms. Tucker's room. The teacher told the class she'd be right back. She wiggled her finger again at Sunday, and the girl followed her down the hall.

In the nurse's office, Ms. Tucker said to her, "Morning, Glory! We need to borrow your E chart, ma'am."

Sunday glanced at the top line of the chart hanging on the back wall. *They're not Es, they're a bunch of bars goin' every which way.*

The nurse handed Sunday a big plastic spoon, and told her to cover up one eye, "Now, tell me which way the E is facing as I point at them. You can show me with your hand like this." She made the number three with her fingers and pointed them sideways and toward the floor.

Sunday did as she was instructed.

"Okay, now, let's switch." The nurse moved Sunday's hand with the spoon to cover the other eye. "There. Again."

Sunday repeated the exercise.

"Honey, you didn't get any of those right except for the top row."

What?

The nurse picked up a notepad and wrote something down. She grabbed a stapler, and stapled the note to Sunday's shirt.

Anxiety squeezed her ribcage. *Daddy's gonna be mad about those staple holes.*

At recess she snuck a peek at the note. The sheet was close enough, but hard to read upside down, and Sunday didn't recognize all the words. She saw her name. She realized the note was about her. And she could see those sentences were long. Fear clamped her throat. *Oh, no! They're tellin' on me for not being able to see!*

The rest of the day, she tried to stuff the thoughts deep down, but they bubbled up anyway. *They're sayin' I wasn't paying attention or somethin'. They're gonna tell me I'm not tryin'…*

She trudged back to class, trying to ignore the rustle of the paper against her shirt.

Sunday crept into the kitchen when she arrived home. Chester glanced over from where he stood in front of the fridge pouring a glass of water from his pitcher. He elbowed the fridge closed and slammed the glass down on the counter.

He ripped the note from her shirt. "Jesus. They can't send a fucking note in a folder? They gotta put a mess'a goddamn *holes* in your shirt to make a point? We paid good money for that shirt."

He read the words Sunday couldn't, as June toted a basket of laundry through.

Chester said, "Sunday's fucking blind. We gotta take her to the damn doctor and send a goddamn note back with 'er saying she went."

June rolled her eyes and kept heading toward the garage. "Well, there's an eye doctor in town, if you wanna drive us up there."

Chester set the note on the counter and walked away as June kicked the garage door closed behind her. Sunday was relieved she wasn't going to be whipped for the holes in her shirt.

Chester drove Sunday and June to the doctor's office the next afternoon. He stayed in the car while they went inside.

Sunday thought the optometry chair was something straight out of the Twilight Zone. She leaned her face into the giant machine in front of her.

The doctor instructed, "Now tell me what you see."

She squinted through the eyeholes at a chart on the wall in front of her. She imagined there were needles in the machine ready to shoot out of the eyeholes if she didn't get the answers right. There were letters on the chart this time, not just Es.

As soon as the doctor made the first adjustment to the lenses, Sunday flinched and blurted out, "*I-can-see-now.*"

"Okay, sweetie, tell me what the letters are."

"D. E. F..."

He clicked the lenses over, blurring the chart, and clicked them again so they became clear.

Sunday flinched. *Oh, no. I got that wrong.*

"Okay, now try'n read 'em again for me."

"O...B...E..."

"Good. Okay, now let's do somethin' a little different."

What now?

The doctor flipped a knob up, "Okay, is this better?" and back, "Or is this better?" Up, "Is this better?" and back, "Or this?"

Sunday could tell the glass changed, but the letters weren't affected enough to tell which was better. *I don't know!*

The second hand on the clock she couldn't see snapped against her eardrum. *Thwak. Thwak. Thwak.* She stared hard. *Thwak! Thwak! Thwak!* She felt beads of sweat forming over her brow.

"Now! That's good! I can see!"

He leaned back and pulled the giant machine away from Sunday's tiny face.

She sighed. *I got it right.*

He focused behind Sunday on June. "Okay...she's gonna need glasses."

He stood and helped Sunday hop down from the chair.

As they filed out to the storefront, he told her momma, "We also detected that she's burned her retinas. She's gonna need sunglasses, too."

Two kinds of glasses?

June cooed with feigned concern. "Well, thank *goodness* we caught the problem early."

Sunday hovered close to June under the front counter while she spoke with the doctor and his attendant. "Okay. Mmhmm. Okay."

Sunday inspected the other people around the store. Some were sitting with attendants at shiny, cream-colored plastic tables slipping frames on and off of their faces. Others were perusing the glasses lining the walls.

June grabbed Sunday's hand and led her to a wall of smaller frames. "These are for children."

She pulled down a pair. "What about these, Sunday, hmm?"

Ugh! They look like a black cat with horns!

"Hmm? What do you think, dear? Now you'll be just like *me*."

They even held the same rhinestones on the tips of the horns. "You know, I wear glasses, too, sometimes."

June slipped the frames into Sunday's left hand and grabbed her right, pulling her toward the sunglasses. She reached up high to bring down an identical pair of frames, except they were powder blue.

Even worse!

"Oh, now these. These will match your eyes. Oh, everyone is gonna *envy* you. They're gonna wanna get a pair just like yours."

She handed the second pair of frames to Sunday.

Nobody's gonna envy me. Nobody that's six years old wears glasses. And none of 'em wear sunglasses either. Prolly not in the whole world. That's for grownups…and Hollywood stars.

Sunday stared down at the two pair of horn-rimmed glasses. June jerked the blue ones away from her. Her momma's patience was clearly wearing thin, so she reached for the first ones on the lowest shelf. They were cat eyes, too, creamy white with a shimmer and the same rhinestones on the horns. *I don't care anymore.*

June cocked her head to the side and blew out. She grabbed Sunday's hand and dragged her to the checkout counter. There, June opened her hands and Sunday dropped the glasses into them.

Two pairs of ugly glasses.

June turned and laid the frames on the counter and wrote a check. She talked with the woman a little more while Sunday remained fixed squarely on the door.

June dragged her back out to the car, where Chester was waiting. "Okay, we've gotta make a trip back down here in two weeks to pick 'em up."

Chester shifted into reverse. "Did you pay for 'em already?"

"I had to. They weren't gonna make 'em 'til I paid for 'em."

"Well, maybe this'll get 'er ass in gear so she can start makin' better grades."

This! *This is the reason I'm not makin' good grades. They're gonna be prouda me next time. I'll show 'em.*

She always assumed her imperfection was her own fault, so she was thrilled there might be some other explanation. Completely oblivious to the fact that she was only six years old, hardly learning to write her name and three-letter words, Sunday tried to contain her excitement about her future report cards while Chester moaned on. "Jesus Christ, this girl is gonna put us right into the poor house with two goddamn pair'a glasses. We're destined to goddamn poverty 'cause Sunday can't fuckin' see..." His bellowing from the front seat the whole rest of the way home hardly registered.

Two weeks later, Chester took them back to the optical clinic. Mother and daughter were greeted at the door and ushered in to one of the tables Sunday saw other people sitting at the last time she was there. The attendant went to the back. June stared straight ahead with her hands in her lap, so Sunday did the same. The attendant came back to present Sunday with her ugly glasses. She leaned over to position the black pair on Sunday's face.

"Now, these are your daily wear glasses. We're gonna try these on, m'kay?"

They slipped down on Sunday's nose, almost falling off her face. The lady pulled them off and set them in front of her. She reached under the table and pulled out a tray of sand.

While she pressed the frames into the sand she explained, "Now the sand is very warm, making the glasses soft to help me make them fit you. Makes the plastic pliable."

Sunday thought that was real neat. The attendant pulled the frames out of the sandbox, and ran each earpiece through the heated granules a few more times. "Now..." She pushed and pulled the earpieces a bit, and slid the glasses back onto Sunday's nose. "Is that better?"

Momma and Daddy don't ask us what's better. You get what they give you. Everybody knows that.

"Yes." *If they give something to you, it's better.* "They're not fallin' off now. That's better."

"No, I mean, are they rubbin' your ears, honey?"

We don't complain. That's the rules. "No, it's fine."

"Are you sure that's not too tight?"

Sunday pumped a leg under the table. "Yeah, this is fine. It's perfect." She added a big nod and widened her eyes so the attendant would believe her.

The lady worked over the cream pair of sunglasses next. "Now these are for when you're out in the sun, sweetheart."

They went through the whole bit again. June shoved the glasses into Sunday's hands at the end of the visit, and the girl ran behind, barely keeping up with her momma's swift, long stride back out to the car.

Sunday kept herself quite entertained, pulling her new glasses down on her nose and peeking over them to compare. She would also peek around the edges as people passed by her to note what they looked like with them, then without.

I never knew I really couldn't see. I didn't know there were different kinds'a blind.

She scored well on every writing test after that. All the colors around her were prettier, too. Blue was bluer and purple was more purple. And when a bruise turned yellow and brown there were three or four other yellows and browns Sunday could clearly make out in the rings. She could see the edges of everything from far away. Even all the way across the playground, she could count exactly which monkey bar other kids were on at recess.

The sun wasn't too much different, but the shade from the sunglasses sure made staring at it easier. She could see *all* the black rings now swirling around the center.

I never knew there was so many!

There were only a couple of things she didn't like at all about her glasses.

For one thing, she tripped over every little thing for the first few days–a divot in the sidewalk, a step she thought was closer, thick grass that covered up a dip in the yard. June would chastise, "Good Lord, Sunday, can't you see where you're goin' after all the money we spent on those?"

Her momma told Chester one evening when she was within earshot that she thought maybe Sunday's feet were turning back in again. They talked about when she'd only begun to walk and how she'd worn braces on them for a while.

Another thing she hated about the glasses was that by the end of the first week of wearing them, she developed blisters behind her ears. The earpieces rubbed against her skin there, and the spots stung. She didn't want to get whipped for the blisters, so she didn't tell anyone. June discovered the sores when she was setting Sunday's hair for church the evening before. She stopped scrubbing Sunday's head in the kitchen sink and yelled into her face, "What in the hell happened to your ears?"

"I dunno." Sunday winced, waiting for a backhand.

"Goddamnit, Sunday, you've been diggin' and playin' with your glasses, haven't you?"

Sunday's neck was aching from holding steady over the sink. She could barely eke out a "No." Her momma was liable to pop her hard over the head with the brush if Sunday didn't hold still. She'd been popped plenty of times before for less important reasons so she squeezed her eyes shut just in case.

June scrubbed furiously, and Sunday opened her eyes again. Her momma incessantly blinked back the rage. Through gritted teeth she promised, "Well, we're going back 'cause they obviously did somethin' wrong."

The next day Chester huffed and puffed, swinging things around and slamming them down again. Taking them back to the optometry clinic meant missing a trip to the drag strip after church.

The woman at the doctor's office peered around Sunday's ears. "We thought you said they fit?"

The girl shrugged. "They did." *What do they want from me?* "Maybe my head grew?"

The woman put the frames back in the sand before setting them on the girl's face.

"How does that feel?"

"It's fine."

The woman stared down her nose at Sunday. "You're sure?"

What could she say that would make the attendant happy, but that also wouldn't get her into trouble? "They're hurting my sores."

The woman behind the table smiled and sat back. "Okay, honey. We're gonna loosen them up a bit 'til they heal. You can come back and see us then, and we'll finish up."

Ugh. Another visit?

"Now, let's go ahead and pull out those sunglasses, too."

"No. It's okay. They're fine."

She raised her chin for fair warning. "We need you to put those on for us."

She meant business, so Sunday pulled them out and put them on.

"Honey, these are almost the same as your day glasses." She pulled them from Sunday's face. "Let's see what we can do."

The moment Sunday thought they were home free, the attendant sprung another surprise on them. "Okay, now let's get you some chains so you can wear 'em both around your neck."

Sunday's jaw dropped. *Granny chains?* Gramma Minor wore those.

"Honey, this'll make changing them out easier when you go outside. It'll be great."

Sunday hated them. She already felt like the only one in the whole school with glasses… two pair…and now granny chains.

Every one of Sunday's teachers checked daily that she carried both pair around her neck, and that she changed them out at recess. *Stupid chains hangin' while I'm tryin' to do the monkey bars, always gettin' in the way.*

At least when they slipped down after that, they wouldn't fall all the way to the ground and get scratched or broken. At least there was that.

Sunday did get the belt when they returned home, though, because she was to blame for her glasses being too tight in the first place. She kept her mouth shut, and this is what happened.

How tight are glasses supposed to be? She'd never worn glasses before. If Sunday had complained, her momma would have called her a crybaby and whipped her anyway. There was no winning with June.

Sunday blamed the only other thing she hated about her new glasses on Wednesday. Her big sister started calling her "four eyes" the day she came home wearing them. Sunday couldn't stand it.

Their great-grandmother, Momma June, picked them up for church once, and Wednesday yelled at Sunday from the front porch, "Go on, *four eyes*. Get out to the car. You're gonna make us late."

That was the last straw. As soon as Sunday climbed into the car, she pulled the glasses off. She stared out the window and thought about being a "four eyes," absentmindedly flipping them back and forth by one earpiece in her hand. All of a sudden, the earpiece broke off and the glasses fell into her lap. Sunday gasped.

She fit the pieces back together and carefully slid them over her nose, gently tucking the earpiece behind her ear. *Maybe if I stay real still...* The car hit a bump and both parts dropped back down into her lap. She whipped her head around to her brother. "Friday. Look." She uncurled her hands, revealing the pieces. "I broke 'em."

His mouth dropped open and he whispered, "Oh, God."

Sunday tucked the glasses into the triangle in her lap and covered them with her hands all the way through church and for the whole ride home. She ran straight to her room to sit on the floor between the beds, hidden from anyone who might pass by. Friday snuck into his closet where June kept the gift-wrap and ribbon, and pulled down a tiny bottle of glue and a roll of Scotch tape.

They tried to glue them, but when the glue dried the earpiece wouldn't close.

"I can't leave 'em on my neck with one arm open. They'll notice."

Friday scooped them from the floor and bent them apart. They tried tape instead. Friday held up the glasses and scrutinized the giant wad of tape in the light, then folded and unfolded the frames a couple times. "I think this'll work."

He slid them onto Sunday's nose. "There."

He pulled a strand of her hair forward and over the corner of the glasses where the tape was. The deed was done. They parted, never speaking of the matter again.

Sunday didn't care she looked even stupider than before. At least she wasn't getting in trouble. That's all she cared about. The solution worked for months, until one day at breakfast Chester walked past Sunday and then turned on his heels. He stooped down next to her and examined the glasses. He took a deep breath and stood straight up again. He put his hands on his hips and shook his head, eyes to the floor, before he yelled at June across the table, "How long've her glasses been like this?"

June jumped and leaned in toward Sunday. "Whaaa?"

She regrouped when her bit of acting concerned didn't work, and said confidently, "Two months."

Two months? Waaay longer…

"My god, June, she's walkin' around with tape on her glasses like we can't afford to take care of 'er."

"Well, Chester, you're never around, and I've got to take her back to the eye doctor to get 'em fixed."

He ripped his jacket from the back of a chair, and stomped out of the house. June disappeared and reappeared in an instant holding the belt. She punctuated every lick. "By [*whack*] god [*whack*] we [*whack*] paid [*whack*] good [*whack*] money [*whack*] for those [*whack*] glasses [*whack*] and you're [*whack*] gonna [*whack*] wear 'em!" [*whack*]

The three went back to the clinic when Chester returned. None of them said a word all the way there.

As the attendant cut the tape, she quizzed June. "So now, how long have these been broken?"

"Oh, just yesterday," June said.

The attendant rolled her eyes at the lie. "Well, this is pretty easy to fix. We'll take the hinge off and replace the screw."

There were no questions for Sunday this time, and for that she was glad.

June pressed a hand firmly into Sunday's back, ushering her to the counter, where she pulled the checkbook from her purse. "And how much should I make the check out for again?"

"Oh, no. There's no charge."

"Hmm?"

"Well, when you bought the glasses you bought the insurance. No charge for a year. If anything else happens bring her back in, and we'll handle the repairs. You've still got six months on the insurance."

June masked her surprise with a smile and slipped her checkbook back in her purse. "Oh. Yes, of course. Well, nothin' else is gonna happen."

You're dang right. I'm not gettin' one more whippin' on account'a these glasses.

In the car, Chester asked, "And how much did *that* cost?"

"It was free."

"Now, why on earth would they do something for free?"

Her momma lied again. "Well…that's their policy. Fix them for a year for free."

She just doesn't wanna get in trouble. Anyways, I sure do love to look at things back 'n' forth through my glasses.

...

As Sunday pulled her second shoe back on, the old glasses slipped down her nose. She pushed them back up, and chuckled to herself about her childhood secret powers. Who else could see the world through her eyes? Who else could fly?

Olly knocked hard and loud one time. "Ms. Minor, are you decent?"

"Yes."

He opened the door and leaned in. "C'mon with me."

As they turned the corner at the far end of the hall, he said to her, "I'm taking you to Dr. Faus. He'll ask you a few questions, explain a few things, and then I'll take you to your room."

The cool blue-gray walls were trimmed in dark walnut. On the left were floor-to-ceiling bookshelves of the same deep brown wood, and filled with volumes of medical encyclopedias and stacks of psychiatric periodicals. A bank of windows ran the length of the wall to Sunday's right overlooking a courtyard. Sunday followed the tops of the lofty old oaks, as their almost bare branches bent in the fall breeze. Below them were several concrete benches, one under each oak tree.

There was a woman with dishwater-blonde hair down to her waist wearing a floor-length white nightgown and no shoes, examining a patch of grass as if she possessed vision superpowers, too. An old man hunched over one of the concrete benches, scribbling fervently on a notepad. Another woman, older than him, sat under a different tree gazing up into its branches, smiling the same way Sunday did when she was just a girl on a swing, learning to fly. Sunday sighed, focusing on the next great wooden door ahead.

Dr. Faus & the Three-Pronged Approach

··

T HE DOOR CLICKED shut behind Sunday as she stepped toward the desk. Dr. Faus looked up from his periodical over a pair of thin wire spectacles. "Ah," he said, waving Sunday over, "one Ms. Sunday Minor, I presume."

"Yessir."

"How are you today?"

"Fine."

He pulled her chart from a stack on his desk as Sunday slid into the leather chair in front of him. "Do you know why you're here?"

Jesus, is everyone gonna ask me the same damn questions? She wasn't interested in repeating herself after being called a liar once today already. "No."

"Well, I understand you're having bad dreams…and that you might be hurting yourself. So we're gonna see what we can do about getting you feeling back to normal."

Sunday smirked. *Back to normal. Tell me more about this "normal" I'll be getting "back to."*

He pursed his lips and said dryly, "What we offer here is a multiple method combination of therapy. We take a three-pronged approach, as I'm sure you read in our brochure. Part of a patient's time is spent in individual therapy. Part is spent in a group therapy environment. And there is a third *pharmaceutical* component."

"Pharmaceutical?"

"Yes, a regimen of Thorazine."

Sunday curled her shoulders in and crossed her legs. The only drug she'd ever taken was Aspirin.

"Have you heard of it?"

"No." Anxiety pushed over the heat in her throat. She swallowed hard.

"Have you ever taken any prescription medications?"

"No. I'm allergic to penicillin."

He shot her a quick glance before focusing on the chart in front of him again. "Have you ever used anything for… entertainment?"

She glowered at the top of his balding head. "No."

"Nothing at all?"

She said more firmly, "No."

Only his eyes darted up over his specs.

He doesn't believe me either!

The pair sat in silence.

Sunday's knee began to bounce. "What about school?"

"School…yes…if it appears you will need an extended stay, you will attend classes here on the facility campus. Your test will determine in which level you will be placed."

Extended stay? She decided not to probe. Instead, she clung to the promise of attending class. School was normal. She could be normal in school. Besides, when she told her daddy she couldn't live with them anymore, she promised him she would finish school.

"We do have a fairly strict routine here. We find the practice helps our guests adjust more quickly to a new environment– helps them tackle their problems head on."

Sunday skimmed the words printed on Rose Village letterhead he set in front of her:

TIME   ACTIVITY

TIME	ACTIVITY
6:00 a.m.	Morning Medication
6:30 a.m.	Adolescent Wing Breakfast
7:00 a.m.	Leisure / Study
8:00 a.m.	Morning Class Sessions
10:00 a.m.	Mid-Morning Medication
10:30 a.m.	Leisure / Study
11:30 a.m.	Adolescent Wing Lunch
12:00 p.m.	Individual Therapy Sessions
2:00 p.m.	Mid-Afternoon Medication
2:30 p.m.	Group Therapy Session
3:30 p.m.	Afternoon Class Sessions
5:30 p.m.	Leisure / Study
6:00 p.m.	Evening Medication
6:30 p.m.	Adolescent Supper
7:00 p.m.	Leisure (Television / Physical Activity)
10:00 p.m.	Final Medication / Lights Out

Please note there may be some variance of schedule depending on individual needs and specially scheduled group or class activities.

"As you can read there, your schedule will also include ample leisure time in which you can participate in a variety of group activities such as bowling–we have a bowling alley right here on the campus–and arts and crafts. I understand there is no additional parental funding to be contributed, so you'll have to forego the field trips. I'm sure you'll be able to find an interesting read among our shelves to fill those hours."

She didn't respond, so the doctor pointed at the paperwork before him. "Well, says here you don't appear you have any medical issues. I think we're done for now."

How does he know I don't have any medical issues? I barely walked down the hall.

He called out, "Oliver."

The door creaked open. "Yessir."

"Can you accompany Sunday down to the aptitude test room, please?"

"Yessir."

Sunday followed Olly out.

The First Lady

....

SUNDAY QUICKLY SCANNED the large, cold testing hall, taking in the four by ten configuration of desks: *Forty seats.* Only three other test takers dotted chairs in the first and second rows. She headed for the chair closest to the door.

The facilitator called from behind her desk, "Ah. Last, but not least. Sunday Minor?"

Sunday nodded, and the woman picked up a thick packet of papers. The click of her heels echoed through the still airspace as she walked over to lay them in front of Sunday. She spoke as if the room were full. "You will have one hour to complete your test. Keep your eyes on your own work. Please begin."

Sunday glanced at the clock above the facilitator's desk: 2:05 p.m. She skimmed for context clues, raced through the basic word problems, and punctuated her final short answer on Newton's Laws. She checked the time again–2:27 p.m.–and laid her pencil down and turned the test over. She glanced at a girl chewing at her bottom lip so furiously the skin had torn and begun to bleed. Sunday cringed and averted her eyes to the window across the room.

How are these people gonna help me? The closest anyone ever came to helping was that woman who–

"Are you finished?"

Sunday snapped her head toward the front. The others glanced up nervously from their papers, first at the clock, next at Sunday.

"Yes, ma'am."

The facilitator rolled her eyes and clacked toward her. "We'll see."

She picked up the completed test and clacked back to her desk. As she flipped through the pages she eased herself back into the chair. She murmured under her breath, "Oh my," and laid the stack on the desk. "You may go."

Go where?

Sunday stepped back into the hall.

Olly jogged down toward her. "You finished?"

"Yes."

That woman who came. Why didn't she do anything? She understood we needed help.

. . .

By the time they lived on Niagra Drive, the Minor children had been looking after themselves when their parents were out for quite some time. Sunday was already nine, and they all carried the weight of their parents' rules and the ever-increasing gravity of the consequences when they broke them–especially in their momma and daddy's brand new house. They didn't need anybody to babysit them. They certainly knew what *not* to do whether Chester and June were home or not:

Among other things, you do not lose a single point in any subject at report card time; you do not ask for seconds when there are none–a new house don't mean luxury vacation; you do not leave a dirty dish in the shiny new aluminum sink to stink up the place; you do not leave a drop of moisture when drying them or you're liable to cause the new white paint in the cabinets to bubble up; you do not skip a single slat when you're dusting the bright white Venetian blinds; you do not leave a speck of dust on any of Daddy's trophies; you do not forget it's six pieces of ironing each, unless you want Momma to help, which means you have to stretch the cloth tight while she irons between your fingers...which sometimes means burnt fingers; you do not forget to mop immediately after you sweep; you do not make a mess of the house Momma and Daddy worked so hard to get us. You do not complain. You do not question. You do not go outside when Momma and Daddy aren't home, not even inside the attached garage. And you do not, under any circumstance, let strangers in the house.

The children came running when Wednesday called, "You kids come in here...*now.*"

They all stopped short at the sight of the stranger.

Sunday thought, *Here we are, Momma and Daddy gone off to the movies, and I don't know who let her in or who said she could sit down, but there she is, sittin' on the nice couch in the good living room. If Momma and Daddy find out, we won't be outta long sleeve turtlenecks and tights for weeks. Wednesday must'a let her in.*

They crept further into the room and slipped onto the couch, which they'd rarely been allowed to touch outside of chores and special occasions.

The stranger seemed younger than their momma and just as pretty. She dressed like the First Lady, the one on the news with blood on her dress the day her daddy came home early because the President was shot.

Why is the First Lady in our house? Did Daddy shoot the president? He shot the president! She found out my daddy shot the president.

The woman wore white, two-inch heels. She wore pantyhose, a straight yellow skirt, and a white blouse with buttons down the front. Her short, black, helmet-like hair curled under the same way The First Lady's did. *She's got a perfect ring'a bangs all the way around to the back.*

She donned a set of pearls like her momma wore on special occasions, too.

Sunday noted how her purse didn't match her high-class outfit. The worn wrap-purse had a snap-close and a thin strap. Every few minutes the stranger pulled it closer up under her leg.

There was no blood on her dress. Sunday comprehended that she wasn't the *real* First Lady; she was too young. Sunday liked the idea anyway, and technically she *was* the first lady that ever came inside the house that wasn't her Gramma Minor, her

Gramma, her Momma June, or any of her aunts. The woman was fidgety, clicking her pen in a constant, steady rhythm. She carried a clipboard with a folder under the clip.

"Is this everyone?" She slipped the folder out from under the clip and flipped it open. "Is everyone here?" she asked again, studying each child's face.

Wednesday fired back, "How many of us do you think there are?"

"We have reports on two."

"Which two?"

"Is this everybody?"

Wednesday didn't miss a beat. "Do you want me to take roll call?"

Talking back to their parents meant punishment, but when their parents weren't around, the children didn't hesitate to exercise their own voices, and this visitor was a stranger. Wednesday could sass if she wanted to. Sunday had no doubt word games were sport for her. *She acts more and more like Momma when she's not around.*

With a titter of nervous laughter the stranger tried to keep things calm. "Ohhh, no, no, no. That won't be necessary."

"So who are the reports on?"

"Well, dear, we can't tell you that."

"How are we supposed to give you what you want if you can't even tell us who you wanna know about?"

"Well, let's start with some general questions, why don't we?"

Sunday leaned back, trying to swallow a laugh as Friday rolled his eyes. Trick question. Their momma would ask the same thing. "Lemme ask you a *general question.* Have y'all been in the living room today?"

Starting off with a "general question" is a sure sign they're trying to trick you. Oldest trick in the book. That's when you know you have secret information they want. And if you're not careful, you're liable to slip up.

"Y'all are all pretty slim, aren't you?"

Sunday shifted her head slightly toward Friday to hide from Wednesday and the woman. She puffed out her cheeks to fatten them and stared cross-eyed down at her nose as surely a real fatty would. He took a turn at choking back a laugh. He patted his belly. Friday definitely wasn't slim.

Wednesday shot back again, "Well, if *your* dad weighed a hundred 'n' twenty-five pounds when he got married at twenty-two, and *your* mother had a nineteen-inch waist when she got married at sixteen, *their* children would be small, too, *huh*?"

The woman stretched a little taller in her seat and smoothed her shirt through the middle at the indirect comment on her weight. "Okay, well, do y'all have regular meals? Do you have enough to eat?"

"Any of us look dead?" Wednesday said.

Well, Sunday thought, *even I know that's a stupid question. Of course we do. Don'tcha think we all remember who's turn it is to get up every morning at 6 o'clock to make eggs or oatmeal for everyone else? Don'tcha think I make sandwiches every night for the next day at lunchtime? We're the ones that can tell you exactly how much we eat, too, because it's us that have to wash the dishes. We dry them. We put them away. We wipe the counters gleamin' clean, and we sweep and mop that floor good enough to serve tomorrow night's supper on.*

The woman's eyes fluttered closed and she sighed.

Clearly she wasn't asking the right questions. She didn't inquire about their favorite foods and whether they asked for seconds. She didn't find out how come while most kids were going to be riding bikes or going swimming, the Minor children would be cleaning house, doing chores, and sitting on the edge of their beds the whole weekend. She didn't ask if they ever went on family vacations. She didn't ponder aloud what kinds of things their parents did to make sure the children knew they loved them. Wednesday wouldn't have any witty comebacks to those questions.

Instead, she said, "All right, all we need here…is to determine…whether you all…are being taken care of."

"Well, what do you want from us?"

"We've got reports that a couple of you might not be in the best…circumstances."

"*Two* of us are not in the best circumstances? Do you see there are *five* of us sitting here?"

Yeah. Two of us? Two of us are worse than the rest of us? No, we all get everything exactly the same; it's only fair. Well, except for Tuesday…So somebody cares about only two of us?

"Well, we only have reports on two."

Reports? Reports were never good. No matter how hard any of them tried, Chester and June were never satisfied with reports of any kind.

Wednesday repeated, "Which two?"

"I can't tell you that…Look, how about if I have a conversation with you separately?"

"No. We're all right here. What's said in front of one of us can be said in front of all of us."

Sunday's cogs began to turn. There was more going on here than she'd first thought. *If we have to talk to this lady, what are we suppose'ta say? What are we not suppose'ta say?* She could tell this wasn't another one of Wednesday's little word games. She genuinely didn't want anyone saying anything.

The stranger chose her words carefully. "We understand… that y'all are being…punished harshly…Are y'all getting disciplined?"

Still not the right question.

"Well, everybody gets in trouble, don't they? Nobody's perfect. Everybody gets a whippin' when they're bad."

The woman gently pried. "No, this is extreme."

She was getting closer. Wednesday nodded slowly, chewing her lip, before timidly asking, "What are you gonna do if we talk to you?"

112

Her tone unnerved Sunday. *What is she thinkin' about for so long? Why is she so quiet now? Talk to her about what?*

"Well, we're doing an investigation to find out if y'all are okay..."

Wednesday tiptoed around the truth. "We're not."

The stranger's eyes brightened. "Well, that's what we're gonna look at." She nodded. "This is the second stage of the investigation."

Wednesday jerked her head back at the new information. "What was the *first* stage?"

"The receipt of the report."

"Who filed the report?"

"I can't tell you that."

Wednesday's voice rose an octave. "Well, then we can't talk to you."

The woman pled, "If you don't talk to me, we can't help you."

She thinks we're just gonna open up and talk to her...a stranger? Wait, what is Wednesday hiding? Are we all hiding something?

Wednesday steadied herself. "If we talk to you, what's gonna happen?"

The woman nodded again. "I'll take the information, and we'll complete the investigation in order to determine whether y'all need to be relocated."

Relocated?

Wednesday remained suspended in silence for a micro-eternity. Then she looked the woman dead in the eye. "If we tell you everything, you have to take us now."

Sunday's mind reeled. *What's happening? What does Wednesday mean by everything? What are we hiding? Where is she taking us?*

The woman lowered her eyes and shook her head. "We can't do that. We have to finish the investigation first."

"Then we can't talk to you."

"Then I can't finish the report."

The back-and-forth–whether they would talk to the woman, what would happen if they did, who filed the report, which two of them were involved–went on for several minutes more before Wednesday finally shut the negotiation down. "No. You don't understand. If we do talk now and you don't take us, somebody's gonna end up dead or *worse*."

Dead? Worse than dead?

The woman's shoulders slumped. "That's not how it works."

Wednesday closed her eyes and rolled her head back. "Then we can't talk to you."

"Do you mind if I speak with them individually?"

Wednesday didn't budge. "You can't talk to them."

A silent standoff ensued. Minutes passed, with no one saying a word.

The stranger finally conceded. She closed her folder, slipped it back under the clip on her board, and stood. She sighed. The children shared nothing that any other kid wouldn't. She clicked her pen one last time and dropped it into her purse. "Well, I guess that's everything."

Wednesday stepped toward her like she was going to say something, but thought better and stepped back to join the other Minor kids in line, in order of birth, of course.

The First Lady glanced around the room at Sunday and the others once more. "Do any of *you* have anything to say?"

They all turned to Wednesday, and Wednesday turned to her. "Nobody here wants to talk to you."

The woman's white two-inch heels barely crossed the threshold when Wednesday slammed the door shut behind her. She whipped around and glared at the others, hands on her hips like June. They agreed without a word: *Nobody is to breathe a word of this to Momma and Daddy.*

Wednesday answered the next question before they asked. "Well, if Momma and Daddy do find out she came here, they'll also find out we didn't say anything."

Friday asked, "Say anything about what?"

Wednesday, already headed toward the kitchen, called out behind her, "About any of it."

Friday trotted up behind her and raised his voice. "So…"

Wednesday spun around, and they were nose to nose.

Friday issued his challenge slowly and clearly. "If Momma and Daddy…find out that she was here…then they'll find out we didn't say anything…about *what*?"

Wednesday gritted her teeth and spit, "It doesn't…matter."

Sunday held her breath, waiting for the exchange to turn into a full-blown fight.

Friday retreated to a lighter tone. "What if Momma and Daddy *do* find out?"

Wednesday relaxed. "What I'm saying is, if Momma and Daddy find out she was here, they're also gonna find out we didn't saaay anything."

Friday pushed again. "Say anything…about *what*?"

Wednesday shook her head and sighed. "I don't know."

Friday summed up the recount for the last time. "So. If Momma and Daddy find out that somebody was here asking questions…they'll find out we didn't say anything, too… because we have no idea what any of the questions were about."

They all flinched at the fire in Wednesday's eyes. "Yes."

Sunday didn't fully understand what any of that meant.

Monday rushed to Friday's side. "C'mon, let's go." She tugged at the crook of his elbow. "You wanna go play?"

He turned toward his younger sister, eyes still locked on Wednesday. "Okay."

"It'll be fun," she said, dragging him toward the girls' room.

The First Lady never did come back.

...

Olly ushered Sunday to the end of the hall and through a set of doors underneath a wooden plaque that read "Adolescent Ward" as a girl brushed past her in a hurry going the opposite direction. Sunday was too wrapped up to pay much attention. *If only the stranger had asked the hard questions...*

There was no way she could have guessed that in the Minor house, "being bad" meant the quarter didn't bounce off the bed sheets pulled tight into military corners during inspection, or that the plush maroon and gold faux Persian rugs weren't precisely positioned on the floor, or that the itchy wool throw pillows on the good couch weren't arranged gold, brown, gold. Everything must be perfect all the time. Otherwise, their momma screamed, red-faced, while they were whipped incessantly. How could she understand "being bad" meant something so insignificant as sneaking a cookie out of the pack? Or that "being bad" meant if no one confessed, they all got rounds? And no one in the world could have ever assumed that for Sunday's daddy, "being bad" meant eating an Oreo cookie incorrectly. He said they were *sandwich* cookies, meaning they were meant to be eaten like a *sandwich*. The woman would never find out about how the first time they ever got Oreos–they each got three. And that when the children then screwed off the tops at the same time and began eating the stuffing first, their daddy got angry, and went down the line, ripping the other two cookies away from their innocent grasps, knocked each of them hard upside the head, and yelled, "Y'all stupid sons'a'bitches can't even eat a goddamn cookie right."

And there was no way that such simple questions could ever uncover the fact that in the Minor house, "getting a whippin'" meant stripes and bruises, black and blue belt buckle imprints, and turtlenecks and tights, even in the dead of summer. Sunday never had any inkling that being beaten nearly to death for an accidental pen mark on the furniture was excessive, or that an all-day beating between cups of coffee from their momma qualified as abuse.

She didn't like what happened to her, but that was instinct, she guessed. And already with the flying away, and trying to be saved…she'd even run away once by that time…she'd done her best to find an escape.

That lady should have done something.

This life was all she knew. It was Sunday's normal. A few years would pass yet before she came to realize on her own that what went on there truly wasn't right.

The hallway they traversed this time was white. Doors lined both sides. There were black lines in a diamond pattern on each window of every door. Sunday glanced into some of the rooms as they passed. Four beds lined the walls in each one. Some people were sitting on their beds playing cards. Others were sleeping. Others were talking. Some rooms were empty.

Olly turned and opened the third to last door on the right. Three perfectly made-up beds obviously weren't being occupied; only the fourth was being used.

"You're lucky. You got one roommate. Her name's Bo. She don't talk much. She's in private therapy right now. You might'a seen her on the way to Dr. Faus's office. She'll be back in about an hour."

The Mark on the Bed

A LONE IN THE third room she could call her own since she left home, Sunday sat down at the foot of the made-up bed farthest from the door. She smoothed the thin mustard-colored comforter neatly over the edge.

Almost the same tone of gold as the one Momma and Daddy bought new for their room at the house on Niagra.

...

Sunday only caught them speaking about the move once.

Chester raised his voice at June after several minutes of badgering. "What we have is perfectly fine. We have beds for everybody, and we still have the black couch."

Chester always made sure they owned nothing but the best in his home, so June played the card. "Well. We might as well keep livin' in this shack if we're not gonna have decent furniture."

Chester threw up his hands. "Jesus, June. Fine. You can have one room."

In her six-year-old mind, she didn't understand he meant her momma could redecorate one room. She imagined all their furniture–their beds, their dining table, themselves–all sardined into one room. *All our beds are gonna fit in one room?*

They already shared barely enough space on the floor to color and spent most of their waking hours in the yard. Now her momma wanted to get more furniture for the one room her daddy was gonna give them? *It won't work.*

Sunday's parents never actually said they were moving. They got the kids up early, and even before breakfast, loaded them into the car and dropped them at Gramma June and Grampa Herbie's house for the day. They didn't come back to get them until after dark.

Pulling into the driveway at the Niagra house for the first time, she took in her new surroundings. The house was big and stood alone, not connected to any other house, with a driveway of its own leading straight into an attached one-car garage. A large picture window separated the garage and the front door. The children peeked in while Chester fumbled with the lock. Sunday could see across the living room into the kitchen and out through the edge of another picture window overlooking the back yard, which she couldn't quite make out on account of the sun long set by that time. The kids filed in behind their parents, in order of birth, to find every stick of furniture had been set in place already, including the new bedroom set Chester purchased for June.

The pair glowed as they revealed the new master suite with the small bathroom inside. The fancy ebony laminate set consisted of four pieces: the double-bed, which was placed squarely under the narrow window set high on the wall, a mirrored dresser with nine drawers, another taller chest of drawers, and one bedside table positioned on his side of the bed. The laminated pressed board bedroom set was her momma's idea of high quality. To accentuate the polished black surfaces, they shelled out enough for a gold satin bedspread with matching sheets and installed gold loop carpeting in that room. June said the whole room was "so Egyptian," and "Egypt is *all* the rage."

There was no central heating or air conditioning, so Chester and June brought in a handyman to add window A/C unit in the lower, wider window on the far side of the bed.

After the grand tour, her parents showed them to their new rooms.

Within a few days the Minor children settled into their new house. Aside from the increase in size, which for them meant more space to clean, there were only a couple of changes in the routine, one having to do with lawn work, the other being directions for the new window unit.

Every afternoon during the week, the first person to come home was supposed to go into Chester and June's room, turn on the air conditioner, and close the door so the room would be cold by the time they went to bed. Wednesday was usually the first to arrive, so the task usually fell to her.

By the time the others got there, the room was always colder than anywhere else in the house. They weren't supposed to go in there, but at least eight months out of the year outside temperatures were high enough a make a kid sweat on a four-block walk home from school. On sweltering afternoons, whenever the kids got home their routine included sneaking in to steal a few minutes in front of the cold air to dry the sweat from their faces and backs. They all did it. And none of them told on one another.

Three years into their time on Niagra, on a particularly hot fall afternoon just after she'd turned nine, Sunday arrived just after Wednesday turned the A/C on.

Chester and June wouldn't be home for several more hours, so she decided to do her homework in there. She settled into the thick gold carpet and leaned against the long mirrored dresser with her book, some paper, and a pencil.

She'd already finished ten or so math problems when Friday came in for a turn in front of the A/C. For fun, Sunday jumped up and slid in front of him.

She smiled mischievously over her shoulder so he'd get the idea she was playing around. Friday smiled back and shoved her shoulder hard. She stumbled to one side. She laughed and pushed him back, starting a shoving war until they were tumbling all over the bed trying to pin each other down.

Friday finally pinned his sister, and offered up a truce. "Okay, we gotta hurry and finish our homework before he gets home." Friday never called Chester "Daddy."

Sunday complied, but they were hot again after roughhousing, so they agreed sitting on the bed, high enough to feel the cold air blowing on them, would be best.

Sunday picked up her things from the floor and spread them out across the right side of the bed in front of the air conditioner. Friday grabbed his stuff and laid everything out across from Sunday.

Friday announced, "I'm still hot. Trade places with me."

"No."

"C'monnn." He reached over and pushed Sunday to the side.

She almost fell off, but he grabbed her arm and pulled her up. She pulled back hard and leapt forward, trying to pin Friday again. No luck. He rolled his sister over, and tumbled off the end of the bed and onto the floor, laughing. They wrestled some more. Friday won again.

As Friday began to gloat, Wednesday burst into the room. "Y'all better have things cleaned up in here before Momma and Daddy come home. It's already four-thirty."

The two didn't move right away.

"I mean it! Straighten up that bedspread. And pick up your books and papers! Get outta here!"

After some half-hearted grumbling the two did as they were told. Friday stacked all his work, and while he carried his books and paper to his room to dump on his own bed, Sunday stacked her own homework to take to her room. They returned to straighten up. As they each grabbed a side of the gold comforter they saw it.

No longer than an inchworm, at the foot of the bed on the right side–Sunday's side–was a thin blue line of ink, plain as day. The mark on the bed blared back at them like a neon sign. Their jaws dropped.

The words tumbled out of his mouth. "I'm-sorry-I-forgot-about-my-pen-I-just-put-it-in-there-in-my-pocket-'cause-I-didn't..." He searched the room for the rest of his sentence.

"I-didn't-have-*three*-hands-and-I-needed-to-get-my-stuff-outta-here!"

Sunday said nothing.

"I'm *sorry!*"

Sunday shuddered. "It's *okay*, but what're we gonna *do*?"

Friday ran to get a dishtowel out of the drawer in the kitchen. Sunday ran a finger over the mark in disbelief. The sound of tap water running carried from the kitchen. Friday ran back in and gently pressed the wet towel into the mark. "Maybe this'll soak the ink up."

They hovered over the cloth for a moment. He pulled the rag away from the gold fabric. Sunday whispered, "Oh, no." *It's still there.*

She ran to the kitchen for the dish soap. Friday draped the cloth over his hand when she returned. She zoomed in on the single bead of dish soap forming at the bottle tip until it fell in slow motion onto the cloth. Friday clapped his hands shut and scrubbed the cloth together until it was sudsy.

He scrubbed the mark hard that time. He pulled the washrag away again. No change.

"*Toothpaste!*" he yelled, throwing his fist into the air.

He spun on his heels and took off to the bathroom. He returned with a white blob on a dry corner of the cloth. He rubbed at the wet spot again. He pulled the rag away. They eyeballed the evidence.

Nothing's working. The line won't even smear.

"What about a little bit of bleach?" Sunday said, grasping at straws.

"No way. Bleach'll make a big white spot over the whole thing…"

The truth pressed Sunday's heart into her throat. They had rubbed and scrubbed desperately, but the mark was not coming out.

Each time she glanced down, the mark seemed to grow longer and longer. She was becoming frantic. *Think of something. Think of something!*

An idea sprang to Friday's mind. "Here, grab your side. Let's see if we can turn the blanket. It's all one color. They won't know we didn't lay the covers right."

They tugged and adjusted and pulled and layered, but it was no use. The comforter was a fitted cover and designed to be draped one way.

Sunday whined, "We can't turn it; we can't fold it; we can't wipe it; we can't scrub it out. And now, because we did all that scrubbin' there's a big wet patch!"

We're doomed.

Like mirror images, they turned to each other and dropped their shoulders, the same long sigh escaping their lips. After one last lingering stare at the giant mark surrounded by a big wet patch in the center of a sea of gold, they slunk down the hall and into their separate rooms to wait.

On the edge of her bed, Sunday breathed deep, pulled herself into her body cavity, and blew herself out to the ceiling in the farthest corner of her room. She floated there, thinking about nothing because there was nothing left for her to do.

The low rumble of Chester's car as it rolled down the street yanked Sunday back into place on the bed. Instead of the usual mad scramble for last minute straightening, Sunday was a rock. She was petrified. She couldn't move.

The car pulled into the driveway. The steel door slammed shut. The front door opened. Wednesday spoke. Sunday heard Chester lumber down the hall, his bedroom door open, and his bag drop.

He boomed, "You sons-of-bitches! What the fuck did you do to my room?"

Silence.

"Whoever fucked up my room better get in here."

Sunday shot up when he stomped back down the hall. He swung her door open wide, and without a word he leaned in, his narrowed eyes piercing into hers. He pointed at her and motioned for her to follow.

Sunday's knees almost buckled with that first step. She quickly recovered, and when she stepped through her father's bedroom door, he walked to his dresser, opened the top drawer, and pulled out the gloves.

They were his driving gloves, leather ones with no fingers, piping around the holes, and Velcro on top. He put them on whenever he was going to teach them a lesson. Sunday tried to stop it, but a whimper expanded her throat and escaped her lips.

He pumped his fists opened and closed tight in front of his belly. "What the fuck happened here?"

She tried not to cry. "I-was-doing-my-homework."

She winced when he dropped his arms. He boomed, "What the hell are you doing in my room?"

She stopped herself from cowering, and the words tumbled from her mouth. "It-was-colder-in-here-so-I-was-doing-my-homework."

Friday stepped to the doorway, but before he could say anything, Chester snapped, "This is none'a your goddamn business," and slammed the door in his face.

He turned back to Sunday to listen to the rest of her plea. "An'-I-guess-my-pen-marked-on-the-bed."

"You guess." His voice grew louder with every word. "You *guess?*" he yelled, "You guess what? You can't fuckin' see that mark?"

She was done for. She dropped her head. "Yessir."

She snuck a final peek up from behind her tiny glasses. His jaw jutted forward. He was seething mad, and he was red. She didn't expect the first swing. *Pop!* Right on the side of her head, where her ear met her jaw. Her head jerked to the side and down, and her glasses flew from her face. *It sounds like a basketball bounced off the gym floor.*

He pounded on her head and her neck and her shoulders.

She cried out, "I'm sorry, Daddy! I'm sorry!"

I'm not supposed to cry! Stop crying! I can't help it!

Her hands flailed as she tried to cover her head and neck.

"I didn't mean to! I'm sorry! Daddy, please!"

He didn't stop. With every blow she was shoved farther into the corner between the wall and the dresser behind the door. He dropped his fist with the force of an anvil in free-fall straight on the top of her head. A shock of white light burst from her eyes. She collapsed backward against the wall. She slid to the floor. *Please, God...I'm sorry.*

The world went black.

Sunday floated to the ceiling, away from the painful blows. She saw he was too tall for his fists to reach her crumpled body. So he kicked her instead. He kicked her with those big black boots. She saw the black rope laces whipping forward, snapping against the big knobby toes. He told her once there was steel in there.

She saw herself balled up in the corner as he kicked her over and over, up and down her lifeless body. He wheeled his leg back again and *CRACK*! Sunday was shocked back down into the corner in an instant by the snap of her ribs.

She sucked the air like she'd been holding her breath underwater for ages.

Still, he didn't stop.

She transformed into an animal, twisting and turning, trying to get away. She couldn't get out of that corner. He kept kicking. The blows landed up her left side and back down again, over and over and over. Every kick felt like a flash of lightning through her core. He kicked her as hard as he could. He gave it his all. He never missed. There wasn't enough room in this body for her any longer.

Stars floated in her eyes until the world faded to black again. This time she didn't fly away. It was just black.

More than a few minutes passed before the bang of June's fists against the door snapped her awake.

She could only move her eyes now, barely enough to catch sight of the door. Her daddy leaned into the wall, one hand holding up his weight, the other holding the door shut, keeping her momma out. He was heaving. Sunday couldn't feel anything anymore.

Here parents screamed at each other through the door. He started kicking again, yelling through gritted teeth with every kick, "Fuckin'…Virgin…Mary…God…damnit…*fuck*…the Virgin Mary…and fuck Jesus, too, the little bastard!"

June screamed back, "You're gonna kill 'er, Chester! You're gonna kill her! You can't kill her!"

With that, he let go of the door. June stumbled forward into the room, almost falling straight onto the bed.

Pacing, he yelled, "You're goddamn right, I'm gonna kill this bitch! She tore up our room!"

June stood and straightened her skirt. As she smoothed her hair she calmly repeated, "No, Chester. You can't kill her."

She reached around her husband to pull the door away from the corner, where the little girl lay in a pile. She spit, "You better getcher ass outta here."

Sunday rolled onto her good side and reached for her glasses. She pushed up onto her knees as best she could. She swayed as the room spun around her when she stood. She reached for the wall to steady herself. They both stared at her as she hobbled out. She stole a glance in her father's direction. He stood there, heaving and flexing his fists. June closed the door behind Sunday.

She strained to understand their muffled words as she limped down the hall. June mumbled something softly and Chester yelled back, "Goddamnit, we can't have anything nice because we got all these goddamn kids."

She raised her voice, too. "Well, Chester, I didn't have these kids all by myself."

Sunday smelled hamburger frying in the kitchen, where Wednesday had begun preparing dinner.

Sunday collapsed into her bed. She tried to raise her head toward Monday and Tuesday. They sat across from her on the bottom bunk of their new set of beds, their backs against the wall, their knees up and their arms wrapped around them. Their chins rested on their knees. Monday's face was wet from crying. Tuesday's was not. She just sat there with huge eyes, staring back at Sunday. Her head, too heavy to hold up anymore, dropped back onto the thin pillow. Monday started to cry again.

Everything hurt. Big red lumps began turning purple and blue on her arms before her eyes. She couldn't move. Breathing in hurt. She lay on her good side, staring back at her sisters through swollen lids. *If I breathe real quiet, it won't hurt. That helps a little. My head hurts so much. And my neck hurts so much, too.*

Friday crept in and knelt down on the floor by Sunday's side, his face inches from hers. He was crying, too. He reached for her hand, and whispered, "I'm afraid to touch you."

He eyed their sisters, and then searched the room. Something on the dresser caught his eye. He stood and padded over, picked up the brush sitting on top, and came back to sit gently next to Sunday. He brushed her hair softly and cried.

Sunday whispered back, "My hair doesn't hurt."

They exchanged a faint smile that gave way again to their frowns.

June stepped into the doorway, her hands on her hips. Her eyes moved over each of her children's faces, Sunday's last. June fixed her gaze there on her face, and then her eyes traveled slowly over every other part of the girl. She didn't say anything. She turned toward the kitchen to take over making dinner from Wednesday. Sunday fell into a deep sleep, with Friday still brushing her hair.

She awoke with a start when June sat down on the bed. Morning light was already beginning to seep into the room. No one else was there. Sunday lay stiff as a board, not daring to speak. *Momma never gets outta bed before us, unless we're late.*

June didn't say anything for a long time. Sunday scanned her mother without moving a muscle. *She doesn't have the belt.*

Her eyes rested at her momma's knee, where the bottom of the ruffle on her white cotton nightgown fell. *Momma's knee looks puffy like a cloud. She said the baby weight makes her knees fluffy.*

Without so much as a tender note in her voice, June said, "You know this is your fault. You're not supposed to be in our room. There's no need for you to go tellin' anybody what you've done."

June pressed her hands hard into her thighs. When Sunday remained quiet she stood. "Now getcher ass up and get ready for school."

She called from the hallway, "You girls have any leotards or turtleneck sweaters clean for your sister?"

Sunday leaned up and swung her legs over the side of the bed. She studied the giant purple lumps that swelled up overnight. She tried to breathe deep, and the pain crippled her. She pressed both hands against her left side and felt her middle swollen fat. She squeezed the other side of her rib cage where the bones lived just under her thin skin to compare one side to the other.

She stared at her closet, afraid the turtleneck would make the pain worse. She stood, and slid the door open. She pulled one down from a hanger and up over her head. She was relieved to find the compression of the sweater eased her breathing. She sat back down on the bed to rest and wait her turn for the bathroom.

She smeared the toothpaste on the brush and raised it to her mouth. She tried to open wide, but her jaw hurt too much. *They're gonna know I didn't brush.* She couldn't leave without at least covering her tracks first. She licked the brush instead. *There. If they check, it'll smell like I did.*

She made her way down the hall toward the kitchen, trying to pinpoint the pain in her face. *Right by my ear.* A high-pitched ringing assaulted her ears. *I wonder if anyone else can hear that.*

Wednesday handed Sunday a bowlful of oatmeal, and she sat down at the table to eat. No one said anything to her, but she detected something near enough to fear in each of their faces. When Sunday tried to meet any of their eyes, they averted their focus down to their own bowls instead. She opened her mouth only enough to get the spoon in. Sunday was glad oatmeal was soft. It would have hurt to chew.

At school, nobody dared to look at her through the morning, and nobody said anything. They pretended not to see how much she hurt. Sunday was glad of it.

By recess, the other kids seemed to have forgotten her condition completely, and Sunday joined the line for double-dutch. Sunday's teacher, Mrs. Rourke, stood next to the line observing the game.

Sunday was up, and she jumped in. Immediately she regretted the decision. She could feel her swollen body pressing into her lungs, her ribs stabbing into her side. She couldn't mess up the game so she closed her eyes tight, counted her ten times, and jumped out.

She limped to the school steps and bent down to catch her breath. That hurt too much, too, so she eased herself down to sit. Mrs. Rourke headed toward her, walking with one hand shielding her eyes from the sun.

Mrs. Rourke's long black hair was parted straight down the middle and pulled into a loose ponytail in the back. Her nose humped at the bridge. Sunday thought she was beautiful. She resembled Hiawatha, another Indian princess. She'd always been pleasant toward Sunday. She praised the girl on her writing, and always told her she should keep it up.

Mrs. Rourke stopped in front of Sunday and crossed her arms. "Are you okay, Sunday?"

"Yes, ma'am."

"Do you feel all right?"

"Yeah."

"Is anything going on?"

"No, ma'am."

"Okay…well, let me know if you start to feel bad, okay? We'll go to the nurse."

Sunday nodded. All she could think about was the warning her mother had given her that morning. *There's no need for you to go tellin' anybody.*

The last thing Sunday needed was for her momma to get a phone call from school today.

"You're sure you feel okay?"

"Yes, I'm fine."

Sunday avoided her for the rest of the day. Mrs. Rourke didn't seem to mind.

That evening, her sisters and brother tiptoed by her, and whispered when she was within earshot. No one asked her to help cook dinner or do her daily chores. Nobody said a word about what happened the evening before.

She went to her room and pulled her pillow to the floor in front of the bottom bunk to make a desktop. She did her homework alone until she was called for dinner.

June made Spanish rice. Sunday was glad of it. As Sunday dissolved the soft rice and swallowed the juicy morsels of ground beef without chewing she gave silent thanks.

Momma's good at that. If one of us is hurt, she makes sure we can eat. She makes soup and beans and fried potatoes and cornbread. Stuff like that with little pieces you can eat when you're hurt real bad. Maybe that's how she loves us. It's nice of her.

The next day, if it weren't for the dull, lingering pain, you would think nothing had ever happened. And though Chester and June never did anything for their children's birthdays, a few weeks later two unwrapped leotards and a brand new turtleneck were set on the counter for her birthday.

Shortly after that, the ringing in her ear seemed to fade.

Sunday never went into Chester and June's room without permission again.

...

Sunday now scoffed at the notion that easy-to-swallow food had been the key to her heart back then.

The same girl she'd barely noticed at the entrance of the Adolescent Ward appeared in the doorway of their room. Sunday jerked her hand away from the gold bedspread and sized up the girl with the "don't-mess-with-me" swagger as she sauntered over to the small stand next to her own bed.

The girl was taller than Sunday, but that might have been thanks to the tight honey-gold rings standing up so high from under the pair of black plastic clips on the top of her head. She was definitely bigger than Sunday. Her shoulders were broad, she was bustier than her, and she bore wider hips and longer legs.

The girl pulled a book from a stack, and sat down on her bed and eyed Sunday over the top. She leaned back and opened the book.

A voice came over the loudspeaker above their door. "Please report to the nurses' station for your medication. We'll see you all in the group therapy room afterward…I repeat, please report to the nurses' station immediately."

The girl slammed the book shut and sighed. She slid off her bed and stepped toward the door.

She called over her shoulder, "I'm Bo. You coming?"

Sunday nodded, and followed her roommate back down the hall.

The Horse Thief

THE MEDIATING THERAPIST flipped the light switch off and on three times, quieting the circle of patients in the center of the room. As she strolled toward the group she smiled and made eye contact with each patient. As her eyes passed over Sunday, she quickly darted her gaze to the floor. The woman settled herself into the last empty chair and began the meeting. "Does anyone want to open with anything today?"

A boy said about the girl sitting next to Sunday, "She changes the channel every time I'm tryin' to pick something on TV."

To which the accused shot back, "Well, you always take my milk."

The mediator volleyed her attention from the girl to the boy. "Good. It's good to get your grievances out in the open. Now, how does that make each of you feel?"

Sunday glazed over. *This is supposed to help me get normal?*

According to the therapist, switching the TV was somehow related to why the girl was sent to Rose Village in the first place, though the connection was completely lost on Sunday. The girl's name was Bonnie. She said she was sent here because she wouldn't clean her room. *Did I miss something? Who wants to live like a slob anyway?*

"I should be allowed to do what I want. Nobody's gonna tell me what to do."

It's not your room. Bet you didn't pay for that place...or anything in it, for that matter.

Bonnie said she was gonna teach them. So she tried to hang herself.

133

Sunday stared straight forward to avoid rolling her eyes. She thought the whole thing was ridiculous. *Well, you're here. Guess that didn't work out so well for you after all.*

Instead she focused on how Bonnie might have tied the rope, and where she would've strung the noose up. Her thoughts wandered to Monday...the time they'd strung her up for being a "horse thief."

I must've been, what, six? So Monday was probably five then.

Sunday tried not to chuckle.

...

The first thing Chester did after the Minors moved into the house on Niagra Drive was string up the clothesline. He dug two deep holes, poured concrete in them, stuck two big metal bars shaped like giant capital Ts, one in each of the holes, and then waited impatiently three days for the concrete to harden. Last, he hung two thick metal wire lines between.

The second thing he did was to build Crybaby a doghouse. He erected the shelter at the end of the clothesline so Friday could easily loop the dog's leash around one of the wires and run her on the line four times each day, up and back, for exercise. Friday never let any of the girls do the chore. His bike, the dog–these had been boy things reserved for Friday only; no girls allowed.

After Friday ran the dog up and down the line one afternoon, Monday, Friday, and Sunday grew bored and decided to build imaginary forts.

It was the Old West, and they were staking out their territory and plotting their homesteads. Monday chose an area closest to the clothesline right next to Crybaby's doghouse, and dug a "moat" in the pea gravel to set her property line. She claimed Crybaby was her horse, not to ride–she was too big for that–but a "miniature show pony" is what she called her.

An argument ensued. Crybaby was rightfully Friday's horse. Monday called finders keepers, so Sunday became the sheriff in order to settle the matter. Friday filed a formal complaint. "There's a horse thief among us, and she's stolen my horse!"

A brief investigation proved to Sunday that, sure enough, Monday was in possession of the horse. The children agreed everybody knew that in Texas you take care with horse thieves. You stop 'em in their tracks. They've got to hang. Standard procedure called for a trial and sentencing.

Somebody went into the garage and got a piece of their daddy's rope about six feet long. Sunday couldn't remember which one of them, but Friday fashioned the noose. The other two stood by as he carefully prepared for Monday's reckoning, in a manner only Chester could rival.

He laid the rope flat on the ground and carefully straightened it inch by inch with the same focus as their daddy when he pulled his lawn tools from the garage and set them out in a perfect row. The boy curved one end into a giant C and stood back to examine the rope exactly like Chester would. Once he was satisfied with his work, he curved the bottom of the C slowly backward to form an S. He stood up again and eyeballed it. He inched the curves so that the capital S transformed slowly but surely into a lowercase s before their eyes, and laid the remaining rope out to the side in a perfectly straight line. He eye-balled the clothesline and then his s again, calculating the distance from the line to the ground in his head, the same way his father would figure how much electric cord he'd need to take the mower out all the way to the edge of the lot. Friday adjusted the S so the end was a few inches longer and realigned the top and the bottom of the s just so. Afterward, he carefully flattened out the s until there were no more than three inches between each section of the letter. He struck and pinched the center of the S with the precision of a cowboy snatching up a rattlesnake by the back of the head and squeezed until the loop took the shape of a bowtie. He slowly began wrapping the long end around the middle, once, twice, three times, until there was one loophole about four inches around on one end, and another about eight inches around on the other. He reached for the long end of the rope and threaded it through the larger ring, and examined for imperfections. He pulled the loose end down and pinched it against the wrapped section, and worked the tiny loop out with absolute care until it was big enough to fit over Monday's head. He held the knotted rope up and eyed the hole, then Monday, then the hole again. He squeezed and pulled, adjusting until the noose was tight. And as he slid it over Monday's head and down around her neck, Sunday was sure their daddy was the one who'd taught him how to tie such a knot. She threw the other end over the clothesline.

"Any last words before we pronounce sentence?" Sunday announced to an invisible crowd.

Monday lifted her chin high, and called out her truth. "Yeah, I do. Crybaby was a wild mustang on my ponderosa when I got here. I'm not guilty of stealing. I'm guilty of claiming property on my property. It's not against the law to pick apples off the trees on my property, so why it's against the law to keep horses on my property, I do not know."

Friday protested. "Because everybody in town knows that Crybaby's my horse. Go on, you can even ask the sheriff." He nodded toward Sunday.

The sheriff pursed her lips and nodded solemnly with closed eyes. "Yep. I'm afraid it's true. Crybaby's his horse."

Monday accepted what was just and fair in the land. "Okay, sheriff, what's the sentence?"

Friday and Sunday shouted in unison, "She's gotta *hang!*"

The two pulled down on the rope slowly, drawing their sister up on the clothesline. Monday cleared the ground by about two inches and started kicking. She wasn't screaming, only kicking. The other two thought the theatrics were part of her act.

Sunday guessed that was about the time June stopped staring at them through the kitchen window, arms crossed, like she always did.

She came running. "What the hell are y'all doin' out here?"

The two immediately let go of the rope. Monday collapsed to the ground, coughing.

Friday explained, "We were playing horse thief."

"What?" Confusion clouded June's face.

He repeated, "We were playing horse thief."

Sunday jumped in. "Monday stole Friday's horse, and this is Texas so we had to hang 'er."

The haze of June's confusion gave way to familiar frustration at her wheezing daughter, who tugged at the rope around her neck. "Is that true?"

"Yes," Monday croaked.

"Are you a fucking idiot?"

Sunday saw the perfect ring of a purple rope burn across the front of her red and pink neck. June bent and yanked the rope from around Monday's head. She pushed the knot down to the end and started swinging.

Monday was first for "being a fucking idiot for letting them hang her in the first place"; Friday was next for letting all the neighbors see them. Sunday was last as June growled through gritted teeth, "And *you* for instigating this *shit*."

She beat them with that noose until no one could stand. She heaved and stared at her children on the ground, smearing their tears into the gray dust on their red, puffy cheeks with the backs of their hands. She dropped the rope. As she trotted to the door with her hands covering her face she mumbled, "Look what you little shits make me do. I don't know what you people want from me."

Monday lifted her head to call out behind her momma, but nothing emerged from her throat. Nevertheless, her voice echoed in Sunday's head. *We just want you to love us.*

. . .

Staring at the wall above Bonnie's head, Sunday imagined that June was probably watching the whole time. She wouldn't be surprised to find out there had been some sly amusement gleaming in her momma's eye, standing there observing through the window as they hung their sister. June's realization that the neighbors might take to gossiping about two of her kids hanging one of the others was probably the only worry that forced her to end their game.

A pang of shame washed over Sunday as she recognized they could've actually killed her sister. *We were only kids. We thought it was a game.*

"Sunday." Her name reached her ear, but she was locked in.

"Sunday." She turned her head to the source of the sound. "Sunday, do you have anything you'd like to add here?"

"No."

The therapist stared at her, but Sunday didn't speak. She wasn't interested in making some kind of connection with Bonnie's plight. The therapist checked her wristwatch. "Okay, well, I think that's a wrap for today."

The Padded Room

EVERYONE ROSE AND milled toward the door. Sunday scanned the room for Bo, and fell in behind her. The group herded over to the nurses' station for their mid-afternoon dose of Thorazine. Her anxiety made the pill hard to swallow. This was the first time Sunday had ever taken an antipsychotic–and the last time she felt any real emotion during her stay at Rose Village.

She shuffled forward in the medication line and her throat began to close. *Why do I have to take this? I'm not hurting anyone. I'm not hurting myself. They don't let us smoke, so not like I can burn myself anymore.*

The long line of people leading from the nurses' window made clear, however, that no was allowed to skip medication. Bonnie was the only one who stood to the side. Olly spoke quietly with her at first. She shook her head, and seemed to plead with him. Olly responded with a nod and Bonnie's voice rose a notch. "Pleeease, I don't *waaant* to…" Olly waved over the other orderly when Bonnie fearfully glanced back toward the line. Before another second passed the pair of orderlies were aligned against her. She moaned, "Noooo…" and began to fold into herself, backing away. They darted out and snagged her by the arms. She began to cry and went limp, causing her legs to drag. And when they lifted her off the ground she flew into a rage, kicking and screaming. They carried her through a door Sunday didn't recognize, and the silence in the room resumed, save the sound of feet shuffling in that long, long line.

They're not helping anything, the pills. They're not gonna make anything better.

139

Sunday wasn't interested in causing a scene. She wasn't angry. *But it's not right.* She needed to understand. She wanted an explanation, an answer to her question: *Why?*

Sunday stepped in front of the window as the nurse slid two paper cups across the counter, one with water and one with little orange pills printed with black letters and numbers. "Here's your medicine."

It was a split decision. "I don't want it."

"You have to take your medicine."

"Why?"

"Your medication'll help keep you calm."

"I'm already calm."

"Well, you'll either have to take your medicine or you'll have to go into isolation until the doctor can evaluate you and determine whether you need the medicine or not."

Sunday didn't realize that isolation meant something different here; sounded to her like she simply needed to go to a waiting room until the doctor could see her, the same as waiting on the edge of her bed for the next instruction. She thought she'd been given a choice. She thought that was the way things worked, and she wanted to follow the rules. She examined her options.

Well, there's nothing else in here for me. I've got nothing to lose by waiting for the doctor to evaluate me.

And she made her move.

"Okay. I can wait to see the doctor."

"Well, all right. You'll need to wait over there."

She stood to the side as the same burly orderlies, Oliver and the menacing somebody she'd seen grabbing Bonnie, slogged toward her.

The menace asked her, "Do we need to do this the hard way?"

Hard way? "No?"

"Okay. Well, come with us." The menace wrapped his hand around her elbow.

She tried to pull away. "I'm not gonna pass out or anything."

"I'm just showing you the way."

"I can walk on my own."

He let go of her.

They escorted her through the mystery door and down a hall she'd never been down before. The corridor was yellow, but not like the pale color of the Adolescent Ward, more like the yellow of walls in a house full of smokers that hadn't been wiped down in decades.

Screaming, crying, yelling, bumping, and thumping carried from the rooms down through the hall. She couldn't see into them. There were no windows except the small four-by-six-inch openings a little above eye level.

Where are we going?

They stopped at the second to last door. The menace spoke. "Here we are."

"This isn't my doctor's office."

"No. This is isolation."

"I thought I was going to see my doctor?"

"No. You are going into isolation until he can see you."

"Well, how long do I stay in there?"

"However long it takes."

"How long is that?"

He didn't answer. He only opened the door.

The three of them walked in, and without a word, Sunday petitioned for something more from Oliver. He looked embarrassed, but he didn't offer up anything.

"What if I have to go to the bathroom?"

"Someone will come and get you."

"How about a chair?"

"No. This is it. That's all there is."

"There's nothing *in* here."

"That's so you won't hurt yourself."

Hurt myself? How was she supposed to respond to that?

What is normal? What do these people want?

They walked out and closed the door behind them. She stared at the knob until she caught the sound of the faint click of a lock.

The walls and floors were covered with thin gray pads–like the ones in a service elevator or used to cover furniture when you're moving. She followed a stripe of cream stitching across the floor to where the pads curved up the wall, and curved again at the ceiling, and across again to the single thick seam that ran down the center above her.

What now?

She chose a place along the wall to the right of her and sat Indian style to wait. *What's the point of this? What am I supposed to do in here?*

She listened to the sounds of screaming and thuds coming from the other rooms. She thought Bonnie's voice was somewhere among those muffled cries. *Are they expecting me to go crazy?*

The confined space bore no clue as to the hour or how many minutes had passed, but every so often someone, a different person each time, would stop by the little window in the door and stare in.

This is stupid. I've spent my whole life sitting on the edge of my bed waiting for the next thing. If they think this is supposed to drive me nuts or something–

A nurse opened the door.

She asked, "Are you okay? Do you need anything? Are you hungry?"

"I gotta pee."

"Okay, I'll send someone to come get you on the next restroom round."

In the time that passed before two nurses came back for her, she counted the gray stripes between the cream stitches on each wall. There were ninety-six stripes on the wall in front of her and ninety-six on the wall behind. There were one hundred and eight to her right and forty-eight more on either side of the door. There were twelve short ones above it.

She'd begun counting the backstitches on the line closest to her when they finally returned. *One hundred and thirty-four, one hundred and thirty-five, one hundred and thirty-s–*

"Sunday?"

"Yes, ma'am?"

"Do you still need to go to the bathroom?"

"Yes."

"Okay, come with us."

The pair escorted her to the facilities, and when she was done one nurse asked, "Are you ready to take your medication now?"

Sunday examined the chessboard once again, carefully considering her next move. *If I gotta choose between taking some pills and being alone in a gray room bored to death, then yeah, I'll take the medication.*

"I guess so."

As the three of them walked back to the nurses' station Sunday tried to make sense of what just happened. Nothing had changed. There was no point in telling the truth here. After everything she'd been through, all the decisions she'd made, the truths she'd told, and the trust she'd given to the adults around her, nothing's changed. She still had no choice. Or at least, the choices she made had made no difference in the long run in the odds of making it out of her hell.

I am still being punished for no reason.

Her life still amounted to a bunch of people telling her what she could and could not do, with no regard for what she wanted, what she needed, and whether or not they could actually help her.

Still, takin' a bunch of pills has gotta be better than sittin' in a room by myself counting stripes. She dropped the pills on her tongue and washed them down with the tiny paper cup of water. *This isn't fixing anything.*

Dr. Faus never came to evaluate her, and he never mentioned the incident in any private session.

Thorazine

DAYS TURNED TO weeks and weeks to months as Sunday floated along in a drug-induced haze. She was vaguely aware the monotony would have normally grown tiresome and frustrating over time. Somehow she experienced neither effect, only a strange sense of nothingness. Of course, after her stint in the gray padded room she was resolved that no amount of argument would change things; she was too tired to fight anyway. So she followed the rules day in and day out: eat when you're told, sleep when you're told, watch TV when you're told, take your meds when they tell you to, stay in a group when you go somewhere, go to group when they call, and when they ask if you're having bad dreams…tell them no.

No one ever explained the conditions for release. There was no goal to reach, no incentive to improve oneself. And though occasionally words of commendation came from the nurses' station toward the group as a whole no announcement of anyone's release ever came. Rumors also fluttered through the halls about this boy successfully sneaking out to the icehouse down the street or that girl trying to hide her meds for weeks so she could take them all at once to end her extended stay. Nevertheless, none of the patients actually had a clue what to do to get out. And no one ever talked about how. Sunday felt like a cow being herded from one enclosure to the next.

She'd been informed her education placement test results put her above their highest class levels, so she was asked to spend the free time in her room. Private therapy became a series of endless variations of the same exchange: "Are you experiencing any bad dreams?" to which the correct response was, of course, "No." Group therapy was a joke, and Sunday did not participate. She couldn't identify with most of what the others shared, and telling anyone the truth never really got her anywhere anyway.

Besides, group sessions only seemed to serve one purpose—it was a chance for the others to complain about their parents and their lives and how nothing was fair. She was never allowed to complain growing up, or express any opinion, for that matter, without facing the threat of grave punishment.

Boys whining about mowing the lawn or having to help change the oil on the car...Ha! Try getting a wrench to the face when you handed your father one that was a millimeter too large. Or try getting whipped with an electric mower cord because you didn't reel it out fast enough–or in fast enough that your daddy didn't nick the line. Girls so put out for having to do dishes after school because they needed time to relax... Puh-lease! Try being beaten with a wooden spoon until it snapped because a dish was accidentally dropped. Kids skipping school, saying class was "stupid" because they never let you explore your "artistic" side... Artistic side? What the hell is that? And who said school was about art anyway? School was almost the only place to escape from home.

Sunday couldn't relate. She viewed the sessions like a setup of sorts. The other girls spent their free time gossiping about the "weird" ones from group while the boys played chess and fought over the T.V. She was acutely aware that *she* was the "weird" one, and she wasn't about to become the latest object of their disaffection.

So, Sunday kept to herself, speaking only when spoken to and turning on the TV when everyone else was away in class. She didn't laugh. She didn't cry. Sometimes she could barely find the energy to breathe. At any other time, in any other place, she would have been anxious not being told all the rules of the game, but in this case she wasn't. Emotion no longer held a place in her equation save the occasional twinge from a familiar gesture or phrase reminding her of life outside the hospital–a life that seemed galaxies away now. And the Thorazine took care of that, too.

Although those pills do make it easier to remember some of the harder things...

THE TRUTH ABOUT SUNDAY MINOR

The Destroyers

IN THE NEXT group session, Sunday slumped into the seat she'd assigned herself the third time she'd been. A boy named Arnold was called, and he repeated what he always did when one of the therapists called him by his name: "Name's not Arnold. It's Cutter."

And from that point on, the therapist reacted the same way she did every time he said this: She didn't call him by any name at all. "Do you have anything to share with us?"

"No."

"M'kay. Well, how about you, Lizzy?"

Nine-year-old Lizzie automatically began to well up with tears. A teenager named Blain squeezed into the chair with her, patting her knee. "You're gonna be all right."

Lizzy cried any time she was asked a question, but Sunday never learned why. The girl never could put her feelings into words. Sunday was acquainted with the implications of not being able to say something, and Blain was considerate to comfort her. Either way, the crying happened every session, so there must be something underneath. The mediators seemed mean, like they were picking on her, but Sunday couldn't bring herself to come to the little girl's defense.

Cutter spoke up for her this time. He shot back at the therapist, "Why don'tcha pick on someone your own size? Leave 'er alone. She's a little girl, and you keep pick, pick, pickin' at her. Can't you understand she doesn't wanna talk about it?"

He turned to Lizzy as she sniffled loudly and dried her tears with the sleeve of her shirt. "I know how you feel. It's why I do what I do. I just cut myself a little bit. That's the only way I can stop thinkin' about what's goin' on around me."

He shared with the room, never taking his eyes off the quietly sniffling girl, about how he would sit in his room, slip the pocketknife out of his back pocket while his parents raged at each other downstairs, and nick the back of his knees. "It don't hurt that bad. And the cuts don't bleed a whole lot."

He said at least it drowned out the fighting.

Sunday thought he was bizarre for slicing himself up for no reason. *Because other people are fighting?*

His habit reminded her of the way Chester would get so mad at himself when he made a mistake. He'd gotten that way in the garage once when he'd scraped his knuckle on an engine block–Sunday and Friday had been the ones assigned to help that afternoon. He burst into such a rage over hurting his hand that he lunged into the brick wall and began beating his forehead against it. *Thud, thud, thud...*

Chester turned around, and a single drop of blood trickled down to his brow. Sunday was shocked. Friday stifled a nervous laugh. Their daddy beat him with a wrench for it, yelling at his son, crumpled and sobbing on the garage floor, "You think that's funny? That'll show you funny."

Chester would kick the cabinets over and over when he stubbed his toe in the kitchen, say. Or when he banged an elbow on the corner of some surface, he'd beat his elbow against it until he cooled off. *So stupid.*

She glanced back at Arnold the Cutter, just like her daddy, hurting himself over nothing. For the first time in years, Sunday remembered when she and her brother and sister formed their secret society. *At least we had a reason to hurt ourselves.*

They called themselves The Destroyers.

At least your parents weren't whaling on you.

...

That day, the day The Destroyers was formed, Friday was up for asking if the group could go on a walk. He finished reciting everything they'd done, from dishes to laundry to weeding, before asking, "Can we go for a walk? Momma won't be home for awhile, and Tuesday's down for her nap."

"Yeah, go 'head." Chester didn't come out from under his car. "Be home before dark."

As they headed out of the garage, their daddy added, "Wednesday, you stay back. I'm gettin' a headache."

They were free until dark. No supervision, no rules.

Friday, Sunday, and Monday stepped outside. The sprinkler spit across the lawn, and the sun was still high. The grass seemed to sizzle and steam.

They set out across the yard and down the street on the way to nowhere in particular, talking about how they ought to form a club. With destinations unnamed and missions undetermined, they figured they ought to be called The Explorers.

At the end of the street they crossed a field, and a ten-minute hike brought them to where a house was being built. The construction site was perfect for The Explorers. Only the frame had been erected and the windows installed. Buckets of paint, tools, and drywall were lying all around, probably for the next day's work. As fate would have it, Monday started pacing. "I need to go to the bathroom."

She bounced in kind of a cross between tip-toe and show pony high-step. "I gotta go!"

No way were the three going to abandon their first exploration. They circled up to make a plan, Monday rocking side to side all the while.

"Well, this *is* a house..." Friday said.

Sunday finished his sentence, "...and there *has* to be a bathroom in here!"

151

They surveyed the foundation, pointing out the living room, the kitchen, and the hallway. Monday ran over to a far corner and called out, "Over here!"

In order to educate the builders on exactly where she thought the toilet ought to be, she pulled down her pants, squatted, and took a big shit. Crisis averted.

The three broke into uncontrollable laughter, doubled over, rolling on the ground, tears streaming down their faces, they were laughing so hard.

Sunday jumped up and yelled, "The stink!"

She began a fit of mock coughing and gagging, sweeping her hand through the air. "We need some air in here!"

She picked up a hammer and ran to where Monday had punctuated her statement. She smashed the glass in the bathroom window. Friday and Monday laughed even harder. Egged on, she ran to the other windows, one after another, and smashed them all.

By the last window, Friday was already standing over an open bucket of white paint, paint stick in hand. He shouted, "It's their own damn fault for not having their priorities straight! We need to leave them a note!"

He dipped the paint stick, and with paint dripping everywhere, he smeared the foundation with every bad word he could think of, starting with SHIT.

The children's frenzied peals of laughter eventually calmed to sighs. They collapsed in a circle in the center of the house, and talked about the day's work there at the exploration site. They knew what they had done was wrong, but for once, they didn't care. There was not one ounce of remorse, no hint of shame… just satisfaction.

The sun finally touched the tops of the trees off in the distance, and Chester's warning sounded off in Sunday head: *Be home before dark.* They stood, stretched, and headed for home. On the way back, they debriefed on the mission's events.

Friday concluded, "We're obviously way more than explorers, you know."

Sunday chimed in, "I mean, we did a lotta hard work today; we didn't only look at stuff."

Monday shot her fist into the air with a skip and a shout. "We *destroyed* it! We're the *Destroyers*!"

The Destroyers were born.

Wednesday later joined them on a couple of expeditions, but she said their treks were boring and that The Destroyers was a stupid idea. "All you do is go up and down the street. And why would I wanna sit around some stupid house that's not even finished?"

After that, she decided to stay home, and Tuesday was too little to go. So Friday and Sunday were left to plan everything out each week. They also decided they were the bosses of Monday. She said she was okay with that because she couldn't think of any good ideas anyway.

"I don't care as long as I get to do what I want and I don't have to sit around the house cleaning something."

Some two months later, while June was at work and when the children finished all their chores, The Destroyers stepped barefoot out the back door, walked down the street, and cut across toward the opposite side of the open field to a nearby development—one they hadn't visited before.

The grass was high, and none of them could see the ground. Sunday stepped down hard on something, and picked up her foot to take a gander. She burst into laughter. "It's a door! The door…" she choked out between belly laughs, her knee raised high, "…is stuck on my foot!"

Monday clutched herself, and leaned back in hearty laughter, too.

"Look at my big giant shoe!" Sunday lugged the door like a snowshoe, whining, "Now I don't have matching shoes. I only got one shoe. The *tragedy*!"

Friday raced to Sunday, grinning hugely, and lifted his leg high. He stomped on the door with all his might, and a jolt of pain knocked the smile clean off Sunday's face. They both inspected the door. There it was, the massive rusty nail protruding from the center of her dirty footprint.

She dropped to the ground and pulled her foot up close for inspection. She saw the single puncture, and one fat round drop of dark red blood welling up from the hole. Friday dropped to his knees beside her. She mirrored the horror in her brother's face.

Monday ran up. "Oh, God! You're bleeding! You're gonna die!"

Sunday stumbled over her words. "No-I'm-not-I'm-gonna-be-okay-we'll-just-go-home-and-wash-it-off-it's-fine! It's fine!"

More than anything else, Sunday was afraid of what her momma would do if she found out. June wouldn't stand for one of them dying. Everyone would be in trouble if that happened.

Monday and Friday each slung one of their sister's arms over a shoulder, and hoisted her up. Sunday wasn't sure if she was limping because her foot hurt or because she knew there was blood. The threesome hobbled back to the house and straight to the water spigot. She examined the wound. *Same as if I stepped on a piece of glass.*

They slipped into the backdoor and froze, listening for their father. Luckily Chester was still out in the garage working on his car. They stowed down the hallway and into the bathroom, where Sunday climbed into the tub. On tiptoe, Friday reached into the medicine cabinet, passing over the white bottle of rubbing alcohol, and opting instead to pulled down the big brown container of peroxide their parents kept for themselves. They used alcohol on the children, which always burned so bad. The peroxide never made their momma and daddy cry, so they estimated the brown bottle must be better.

Friday poured half the bottle over his sister's foot. The three sat in silence as the bubbles oozed from the hole in Sunday's foot, all the while carefully listening out for any footsteps.

Sunday whispered, "You think Momma and Daddy are gonna notice all that's gone?"

"No. It's gonna be fine." Friday turned to the faucet and refilled the bottle with tap water. "They'll never know." He slipped the bottle back onto the shelf, and carefully arranged the row exactly the way it was before.

Sunday all but forgot the dull throbbing in her foot until the next day in P.E. class. It was hula-hoop day for her grade, and she'd gotten to bring the one Momma June bought for her and her sisters and brother to share last time she came to visit.

As Sunday swung the hoop around her ankle, she gawked at how fat her foot was. The top rose over the sides of her shoe like a loaf of baking bread rising up and out over the edges of the pan.

The P.E. teacher must have seen her limping because she appeared next to her in a heartbeat. "Honey, what's wrong with your foot?"

"I dunno." Sunday's mind raced through what would happen if her momma found out.

"Well, let's take off your shoe and sock. Lemme see what's goin' on."

Sunday peeled the shoe from around her swollen foot and rolled the sock over her red sausage toes. The teacher's head jerked back at the sight. "What happened?"

"I dunno." There was no way she was going to tell the teacher that she and her fellow Destroyers had been on their way to destroy another house in the development down the street from them.

"Well, honey, you've got a puncture wound on the bottom'a your foot!"

As the teacher traced a fingertip up the red lines running from the hole and up over Sunday's ankle a few other fourth graders gathered around.

They wrinkled their noses at the girl, and one said out loud, "Ew! What *is* that?"

The P.E. teacher pushed the girl's hip over until she lay on her side. "Might be tetanus," she said as she continued tracing around the back of her calf, and then back up around the side of Sunday's thigh.

Tetanus?

"Ewwww!" the kids jeered. "Sunday's got a disease!"

The heat rose from Sunday's neck into her face.

"Alll right, everyone. That's enough. Sunday doesn't have a disease. She's gonna be fine." The teacher turned to comfort the girl. "Honey, you're gonna be fine, but we need to get you to the nurse."

Sunday glanced around at her peers and stuttered, "N-No. I'm-I'm okay. I'm okay. We already-we put medicine on it."

The woman helped her up and handed her the stretched out sock and her shoe. "Oh, no, we need to look at that."

In the nurses' office, the two women lifted the girl onto the examining table.

The nurse analyzed the symptoms. "I think we need to call your mom because, sweetie, you need to go to the doct–"

"No! No, I told the teacher Momma put medicine on it already."

"Well, I think we better go ahead and call–"

"Well, they're not gonna do anything anyway. Look!" Sunday popped down from the table, waved her foot, and hobbled around, trying hard not to wince. "It's healing! You don't need to call her. We put medicine on it, I told you! You don't need to call her!"

The nurse guided Sunday back up onto the table. "Now, just lie here for a minute. We'll be right back."

She and the P.E. teacher stepped out into the hall, while Sunday pressed the growing panic back down into her stomach. *What is tetanus? Am I gonna die?*

They both stepped back in, and the nurse picked up a bottle of peroxide off the counter. "Let's go ahead and pour some more peroxide over it."

"That burns!" Sunday lied.

"I understand. We're only gonna use a little." She pressed Sunday's shoulder back. "Now lay down and put your foot back up."

Sunday couldn't help herself anymore. Tears sprang from her eyes.

"Sweetie, why are you crying?"

The nurse didn't realize what her momma was liable to do to her if she had to come up to the school to take her to the doctor. "I don't want to go to the doctor."

"What? Why not?"

Sunday couldn't tell her the truth; she searched for something convincing. *Doctors cut!*

"They're gonna *cut* me!" *Yeah, that should work.*

"Oh, honey. Now doctors don't *always* c–"

"What the hell is going on here?" June shouted from down the hall.

Sunday froze.

The nurse opened the door and leaned out. "Mrs. Minor? We're in here. Come on in."

June stepped in, scanned the room, and barely glanced at Sunday before resting her eyes on the nurse. Her tone transformed into the one she took on with dear strangers only. "As I asked the young lady at the desk, what on *earth* is happening here?"

"It seems Sunday's hurt her foot. We've doused the wound with peroxide, but she needs to see a doctor."

June bristled again. "She doesn't need a doctor. The only thing they're gonna wanna do is give her antibiotics, and she can't take them. She's allergic to penicillin. They're gonna do the exact same thing as you." She whipped around to face Sunday. "Get up."

The nurse matched June's icy tone. "Ma'am…judging by the red lines on her leg we believe Sunday may have tetanus. She definitely needs medical attention for that. Do you need help getting her out to the car?"

"No. She can walk. But thank you for your medical recommendation."

Sunday popped down from the table again to attempt the same dance she did before. "Yeah, I can walk. See?"

June nodded. "See? She's okay to walk. She can make it out to the car."

All the way to the doctor's office June screamed at Sunday, red faced, the veins in her neck popping out. Her knuckles were white, she was gripping the steering wheel so hard. "Goddamnit, Sunday. I'm tryin' to get the house cleaned! I'm sewing clothes, I'm cooking, I'm doin' laundry, I'm cleanin'! How am I supposed to get anything done when I'm runnin' back and forth to the school for you? And you know your father can't *stand* when I drive!"

Sunday pressed herself against the car door, in case her momma started swinging at her. And after she got a shot at the doctor's office, her mother screamed all the same things all the way home.

As soon as they arrived, Sunday hobbled straight to her room, where she waited in her assigned seat on the edge of the bed.

In less than two minutes June appeared in front of Sunday, wrapping the soft end of the belt slowly around her hand. "Bend over."

Sunday had been taught to keep her hands at her sides when being whipped. After a point, however, hands seem to develop a mind of their own. Sometimes they crept up and over her backside to buffer the blows. The sting on her hands would become so bad she would curl them under herself to keep them in place. Sunday lay crossways on the bed and tried not to let them move this time.

June screamed between lashes, "You got hurt [*crack*] and somebody else has to tell me? [*crack*] How do you think that makes me look [*crack*] when you don't even tell me you been hurt? [*crack*] Goddamnit, Sunday! [*crack*] Those people are gonna think I don't take care of my kids!" [*crack*]

Sunday curled her hands tightly under as June continued to swing, but as she slipped them underneath herself she slid to the floor and landed on her sore foot. A shriek erupted from her throat, but the cry didn't stop June. She kept whipping [crack] and screaming, "Y'all do whatever y'all can to make us look bad!" [crack]

Sunday wished for a split second that they'd never thought to go for walks, and that they'd never decided to be The Destroyers. But only for a second.

The Destroyers' walks were never so exciting as the first one, and the "snowshoe expedition" counted as a disaster. After that, many times, they weren't allowed to walk anywhere at all anymore on of account of it costing a trip to the clinic. Thus, The Destroyers began to serve a new purpose–a purpose Sunday was sure had kept them alive.

See, on the days they weren't allowed to walk, they got together in the backyard to talk. Eventually the conversations turned to getting in trouble. They talked about getting slapped and pinched and dragged, and the hair pulling, the pushing and shoving. When their momma went crazy, she grabbed whatever was closest: a brush, a spoon, a belt, it didn't matter.

Sunday recalled the first time her momma grabbed a paint stick. She made all four of them stand with their legs spread apart wide. She slapped the paint stick back and forth between their thighs fast and hard–*bap-bap-bap-bap-bap*! The insides of Sunday's legs stung for days, especially in the sweaty heat of summer.

Her daddy told June one time nobody ever needed anything outside of a firm backhand or good wallop with a fist. He said their hands could deliver all the punishment they needed. So June would go lighter on the children when he was around by doubling over the belt. The times he wasn't, she left that belt buckle swinging free. And it was the *worst* when she made the children get the belt for her.

Once when Friday was in trouble, June commanded, "Go get the belt."

He slinked away, and returned sheepish and meek, with one of her soft, thin cloth ones in his outstretched hand.

"You know what belt I'm talking about," she growled.

"I can't find it!"

"Nice try. You better getcher ass back in there and find the belt you're lookin' for. If I have to get up…If I go in there and find it, I'm gonna tear you up."

She's gonna tear him up anyway. Because in the end, Friday always ran. His sisters gave up a long time ago on trying to tell him to stay in one place. He said he couldn't stop himself. *Momma gets so mad when he runs.*

From the top of their heads to the heels of their feet, all was fair game when June was after them. Better to stand still with eyes squeezed shut, waiting for the punishment to be over.

All of this was a part of The Destroyers' discussions in the backyard. The conversation almost always turned to what they ought to do about it, but only after their mother almost killed Monday did The Destroyers' *new* purpose surface fully for the first time.

Sunday was washing dishes, and Monday was in charge of drying. Both her sister's tics were going strong at the same time because she was nervous about drying the dishes with her momma hovering so close.

June was on the other side of the kitchen stirring a pot of beans with the big wooden spoon. Sunday handed Monday a glass and turned back to the sink. *Crack!* The glass hit the floor. Sunday didn't see what happened, but she knew how. Monday had squeezed her eyes tight and flung a snap.

Sunday and June whipped around from their posts as Monday bent down, frantically picking up the pieces, squeezing and snapping and shaking her head, crying out, "I'm sorry, Momma! I'm cleanin' it! I'm sorry!"

Time tapered to the pace of a slow motion reel. *Dear God, please keep my mouth shut. Please God, don't let her turn on me.* Sunday, frozen, stared as the scene played out before her. She saw everything.

"What the hell is goin' *on*?"

Squatting on the floor, Monday explained between tics, "I dropped a glass, Momma. I'm sorry. I'm cleanin' it."

June wheeled back and lunged toward Monday. Spoon in hand she began beating her with it.

The whole time, Monday kept tic-ing. Squeeze, *snap!* [*whack*] Another blow to the head with the spoon. Squeeze, *snap!* [*whack*] Another blow to the head. She picked up the pieces of glass–squeeze, *snap!* [*whack*] A blow to the shoulder. And carried them to the trash–squeeze, *snap!* [*whack*] Another blow to the head. Back to the floor again. June followed her, wheeling blow after blow. The wooden spoon rained down over Monday's head and on her shoulders over and over, while her momma screamed, "Stop it! [*whack*] Stop it right now! [*whack*] You better stop that snapping!" [*whack*]

"I can't, Momma, I can't!" Squeeze, *snap!* [*whack*] A blow to the face. "I'm *sorry!*" Squeeze, *snap!* [*whack*] Another blow to the back. "I'm *cleaning* it!"

Monday shot up at the same time the wooden spoon came down, and it *snapped* over the top of Monday's head. The pieces clattered to the ground. June's eyes narrowed and her nostrils flared like a raging bull. June bent slowly to the floor without ever taking her eyes off her target. She instinctively reached for the thickest splintered piece with the sharpest point. She rose slowly until she was towering over the girl. She stared down at the wooden stake in her hand, and tightened her grip until her knuckles were white. She'd gone mad. She sneered at the girl, and raised her hand high above her head, the sharp end pointed down at Monday, and inhaled deep. She held the air in for an eternity, it seemed.

Monday screamed, "*No, Momma! No!*"

And the instant Monday realized what was about to happen, June did, too. The blood in her face drained, leaving her a ghostly white. Her eyes glazed over, her shoulders slumped, and she dropped her arm to her side. She released the stake, and it clattered to the floor. Then she walked out.

Sunday wasn't positive how long she'd been holding her breath, but as soon as the hem of her momma's skirt disappeared around the corner, she finally exhaled and dropped to the floor next to Monday. She picked up the pieces of the spoon and walked over and dropped them in the trash.

Sunday was acutely attuned to the fact that she came close–*too* close. Her momma was going to stab Monday. She was going to kill her. No telling what stopped her. What was more, she didn't know if, next time, anything would.

What can we do?

This had been the first question raised the next time they met on the back patio. None of The Destroyers offered an answer straight away. *We have to find a way to make it through.* They thought about how to endure the whippings. They agreed they'd never be good enough to avoid punishment altogether. And they sure couldn't stop her. *What if Momma slapped you? Would you be able to not cry?*

These questions evolved into more questions, and eventually into an answer. Maybe the only way to survive was to get really good at being able to take what their momma was dishing out. *We need to do endurance contests.*

The Destroyers listed the most regular punishments, and ways to practice enduring them. Over a short time, they created new contests when June came up with new punishments or revived old punishments they'd forgotten about, and pretty soon the list included as many forms of punishment as they could think of.

The rules of their game were simple: 1. Anyone can start a contest whenever they want, and the other person always has to accept. 2. Whoever starts the game picks the punishment. 3. The one who starts can't do anything else until the other one strikes back. 4. You can call 'times' if it hurts too much.

The unspoken agreement was that no one could use a weapon of any kind, ever. Too many times their momma grabbed whatever object was within reach, and whaled on them with it until she'd grown to weary to swing anymore. Sometimes June would even sit down and take breaks in between beatings. She was so much bigger than them. Sunday couldn't figure out why she even thought she needed something to help her. They were so small next to her. They drew the line right there. No weapons, ever.

In the unwritten footnotes, they also agreed to only hold the contests at the house. For the Minor kids, horsing around, wrestling, fighting, the contests…they were all the same–no anger, no grudges, just "plain ol' survival of the fittest." Sunday had learned about the concept in science. Darwin came up with the line a long time ago, and Sunday and the others were only practicing what he preached. The kids at school would never understand The Destroyers' games to strengthen, not hurt one another. Better to keep their games to themselves.

They tried to anticipate the myriad of things that might occur during any one of their momma and daddy's given tirades. Face slapping, hair pulling, pinching, choking, fisted punching–those were the main ones. They thought if they practiced, they could eventually take whatever their momma and daddy could dish out without shedding a single tear.

Occasionally The Destroyers agreed getting some practice in for schoolyard things might even be good, too. Take Indian burns, for instance.

They'd traded stories about the new tactic all the way home one afternoon. Monday was the one who got into the most fights. She stuck up for everybody. If other kids were teasing someone, or a bully was extorting lunch money from the little ones, she was always first to jump in and handle the situation. So naturally, she was up for adding Indian burns to the endurance list.

June was home so The Destroyers couldn't go for a walk anyway. They opted for the regular spot on the back patio when Monday called it: "Indian burn contest!"

Sunday hollered back, "Circle up! Indian style!"

The three of them, Sunday, Friday, and Monday, sat down cross-legged on the concrete.

As they settled in, Monday explained one more rule, since this was their first time to do this one. "For this contest, we can only use one hand. That way the skin won't rip."

The other two nodded in agreement.

"I pick Sunday!" And the contest began.

They'd finished round one when June stepped out to check on them. "What the hell are y'all doin'?"

"Indian burns," the three chimed in unison.

"Oh, I've played that game before. Me and your daddy both learned that in grade school!"

She bent down and scooted into the circle with them. "Let's see how the kids are doin' it these days."

"Okay, you can play, too!" Friday lit up, forgetting completely the main reason they were doing these things was because of her. He always brightened when his momma did stuff with him. Sunday guessed that to him, this seemed to be as good a time as any. None of them would dare tell her "no" anyway.

Friday's turn to Indian burn the girls. He grabbed Monday by the hand to steady her arm, and grabbed her wrist with the other, and twisted. She twisted hard enough to leave a red mark, and a faint purple ring.

"Ooo, look at my fancy purple and red bracelet!" Monday cried, doing a fair job of playing tough.

"See, Momma? We twist each other's arms like that! Is that how y'all did it in school, too?" Friday held his breath, anticipating her approval of a job well done.

"Yeah, I suppose you did all right. Except when we were kids, this is how we did it." June grabbed Friday's arm from across the circle, and yanked him toward her as hard as she could. As she twisted hard with, not one, but both hands, his smile twisted into a grimace, and he squirmed.

Sunday saw the twinkle in June's eyes as she chuckled. "Now that's how ya do an Indian burn."

Friday didn't cry about it, but he sure wasn't beaming anymore.

"Now you." She grabbed Sunday's arm, and as she squeezed and twisted, Sunday's mouth widened and her eyes squeezed tight. She didn't dare cry out.

June was glowing with pride at her accomplishment. "Monday, your turn."

Her eyes gleamed as if she'd won a prize, as Monday squeezed her eyes and flung a snap with her free hand. Afterward, their momma insisted each of them do it to her. They didn't dare double-hand twist. They stuck to their own rules. June laughed at them as she popped up from her seat in the circle. "None of y'all have the muscle it takes to be tryin' this kinda thing," she said, and walked back into the house.

Over the following months, when one of the children was caught doing something related to their hands like bad penmanship or fluffing the good pillows the wrong way, June would grab one of the children's arms and twist hard enough to make their wrists swell up and for tiny red dots to rise. The dots usually took a few days to scab over and flake off. The Destroyers adapted quickly. Friday figured out that the best way to handle her dole was to go limp, twist a little with her, turning under her arm, and slip free, and he showed the girls how.

Now, the choking contest...that was the only one that took two hands. Sunday was pretty sure they almost killed each other when they did it, so no one called that game too often. They kind of liked the contest, though–and practice makes perfect–so once in a while Monday would call for choking practice.

The first part was to get on your knees so you wouldn't have too far to fall. Next, you started breathing in and out as deep and as fast as you could. Friday called the heavy inhaling-exhaling "hypervennalatin." Last, the other person would squeeze you by the throat until you passed out. The other person would lay you down gently so you wouldn't hurt yourself, and when you first started waking up, you couldn't tell where you were or how long you'd been asleep. You didn't know how you got there. You could feel your body tingling, before shaking yourself awake the rest of the way. Friday called the tingling and shaking "convulshins."

This was practice for when June would lift them off the ground by the head to keep them from screaming. She'd done it to Sunday a couple of times, and to both her sisters and to Friday, too. Although, when June tried to do Wednesday the last time, the girl'd grown strong enough to rip her momma's hands from her mouth. She shoved her momma hard. June never tried her again. It never happened to Tuesday at all.

...

Sunday remembered she liked the tingly feeling she got when they played that game, but to win, you had to shake. They'd all agreed the tingling and shaking must have been because they'd squeezed the oxygen right out of each other. So if you didn't shake, you didn't get all the oxygen out, and that wasn't fair. You didn't do the contest all the way, so you would lose.

Survival of the fittest, I guess. Flying away never worked. Leaving your body was only temporary. What do they say? If you can't beat 'em, join 'em? I guess that's what we did for each other with those contests. The only thing The Destroyers never had a contest for was fire—

Bo shoved Sunday's shoulder. "Hey. Session's over. You just gonna sit here by yourself?"

Sunday rose without a word and headed to the Adolescent Ward with the rest of the herd.

No Contest for Fire

AFTER THE CATTLE call, Sunday was left to her room again while the others collected their things for afternoon classes. *There's no way we could have done something with fire. There's no way to make that safe, no way to practice without getting burned.*

. . .

By the time that lesson was learned, although the endurance training paid off to some degree, all three of the middle Minor kids had outgrown the childish games of The Destroyers. Sunday was only ten, but they were all seemingly tough enough by then.

Besides, several months'd gone by since the move to Rock Knoll, and the new house took more time to clean. That house was Chester and June's dream house–a "real vision" is what Chester called it–centered in a cul-de-sac, which the real estate agent told June was first designed and used in city planning in Egypt. The notion struck Sunday as funny all these years later: *"Cul-de-sac" is nothing but a fancy word for dead end.*

Yes, that house with the giant oak tree out front, its *two*-car attached garage, a sprawling living room and den, and spacious bedrooms was a dream–for their parents. For the kids, bigger and better meant greater scrutiny of their maintenance and harsher punishment when they hadn't taken the utmost care.

The children had already begun to grow more withdrawn, even from one another, escaping into their own interests in their limited spare time.

During the occasional lull, Wednesday could be found with her nose in a book while she sharpened her "talons."

Sunday liked to brush her hair. By that age, she hated the pixie cut her mother gave her every few months because she thought her haircut made her look like a boy. Somebody told her that brushing made her hair grow faster, so that's exactly what she did.

When she wasn't assigned to some remedial handwriting or math problem task by her mother, Monday could usually be found separating nuts from bolts and screws into mason jars while her daddy worked on his latest hotrod or built things out of this and that.

Sunday knew Friday had taken to carrying around a few matches in his pocket. They were kitchen matches, the ones that came in the big box with a blue diamond on the top. Friday couldn't get away with carrying the whole box, so he snuck several at a time into his pockets while he was doing the dishes, and then stowed them in the bottom-most cigar box in the collection gifted to him by Grampa Herbie whenever they visited him and Gramma June and neatly arranged along the back of his closet. The others each an assortment of various things like those art supplies and his plastic army soldiers. One box remained empty until he got his bicycle. In that box, he stowed the two blue shop rags Chester begrudgingly handed over when Friday asked. Underneath the others, that purloined stockpile of matches would be the last his parents found if they went snooping.

Sunday saw her brother taking out those matches now and again, and he admitted that he occasionally tried to set tiny fires in the grass alongside their daddy's precious dream house. He figured out how to strike two of the red tips together to get a spark, and if he struck the matches close enough, sometimes a few blades would catch. He said it was just for fun. Afterward Sunday and Monday would help him pull up the patches of burnt grass so Chester wouldn't find them while working in the yard. Sunday could only guess they missed a little bit of grass from one of his tiny fires.

That day, June sat at the table thumbing through her *Prevention* magazine while Sunday did the dishes in the kitchen, and Chester banged around in the garage, pulling out all the things he needed to get ready to work in the yard.

The sounds of the scythe coming down off the wall, the rifling through drawers searching for the sharpening file, and the thud of her father's feet out of the garage to the driveway were familiar ones. As she expected, he lumbered back in and rolled the mower out. Then the clang and clatter died. *He's probably taking extra care laying the parts out in a perfect row on the sidewalk in the order he would use them, like always: first the file, next the scythe, and after the electric extension cord, the mower, the hose, until finally the stack of blue shop towels to wipe down his equipment when he was finished... He's usually back by now to pick one of us to help...He must be examining things extra close today.* He was always examining things, planning his course of action, and making perfect his preparation. He took inventory so there would be no interruption before a task was complete once he started. He hated interruptions. *Today he's taking too long...*

BANG! Sunday stiffened and turned toward the garage door. The mason jars crashed to the floor, and all the nuts and bolts within them scattered.

Friday screamed, "No, no, no, no, nooo!"

Chester stomped across the garage.

What's he dragging?

The door swung open with a *swoosh*. He lifted Friday by the armpit and threw him into the kitchen. He lunged in after him, picked him up again, and threw him back down. All the while, Friday cried out, "No, no, no, I'm sorry, I'm sorry! I won't do it!"

June jumped up and rushed toward her son.

Chester pushed her backward and boomed, "Wait a goddamn minute. He's tryin' to burn the goddamn house down! This little motherfucker's been settin' fires to the house, the little cocksucker!"

Friday pled from the floor, "It was an accident!"

Chester fired back, "An accident? A goddamn accident? *Five times* an accident!"

He pointed an angry finger at June. "Goddamnit, you better deal with this son-of-a-bitch or I'm gonna kill 'im."

He spun on one heel and stomped back out to the garage, slamming the door behind him.

June seemed bewildered.

She stared at Friday. The girls stared at her. If her momma didn't come up with something to do to him, Chester would surely hold true to his word.

The lawnmower revved, breaking the spell. June snapped her mouth shut. Sunday ran to Friday. Monday stared on from her place next to June.

June screamed, "All of you! Go to your room!"

Sunday jumped up and followed Monday down the hall. Friday fell in behind the girls, but June clotheslined him. "Not you."

His wide-eyed sisters sat in their assigned seats on the bed in their room, completely silent, listening hard.

"Goddamnit, Friday! We buy this new house, and try to give you a nice home to live in, and you're tryin' to burn the whole thing down!"

Friday pled with her, "It was an accident! I didn't mean to!"

"I'll show you what it feels like to burn!"

"I'm sorry, Momma, please! I'm sorry!"

"Maybe this'll teach you to play with fire!"

They struggled in the kitchen, their bodies banging against the stove while Friday tried to break free.

He cried out again, "No, Momma, please! I'm sorry, I didn't mean to! *Pleeease!*"

Then, he screamed.

He cried out like Sunday never heard him cry out before. His cry sounded like an animal's. It was the sound of pure pain. He

172

screamed for too long. She smelled the same sickeningly sweet aroma of rotten barbecue that she'd smelled years ago at the doctor's office when her tiny mountain range was brought down. Tears sprang from Sunday's eyes. *I can't do anything. Momma's holding him there against the stove...and...I can't do...anything!*

And as quickly as the ordeal began, it ended. June snarled, "Get outta my *sight*."

June heaved a great sigh, and slammed the garage door behind her. The girls studied one another's faces for a moment.

Monday's big glassy eyes fixed on the doorway and she whispered, "Do you think it's over?"

"I think so."

"Go check on him."

"Okay."

Sunday slipped down from her seat and crept to the bedroom door. She peered around the corner to make sure the coast was clear. She tiptoed down the hall. Monday followed close behind. As she slipped into Friday's room, Monday continued on toward the kitchen. Sunday fell at her brother's feet so she could peer up into his face.

He was sobbing, but no more cries were coming out. He lifted his head from his balled up hands to console his sister. He whimpered, "It's okay. It's not that bad."

"Show me."

They both peered down at his hands. He uncurled them slowly, painfully, and stopped when they were halfway open. Sunday gasped, and fat tears rolled down her cheeks.

There was a row of broken blisters in each of his palms, and another row across his knuckles, as if he curled them up and pulled them away from the coil.

Monday crept into the room, and dropped to the floor beside Sunday. She began crying, too, as she pressed a cold wet rag to her brother's burned hands. The three hugged each other tight, and cried.

Friday whispered over and over again, "It's okay, it doesn't hurt that much. It didn't hurt that bad. It's gonna to be okay..."

Later that evening, the Minors went to their Gramma and Grandaddy Paw's house for a visit. Gramma noticed Friday's hands immediately. She asked him loudly, glaring across the room at his momma, "Boy, what happened to your hands?"

He opened his mouth, but nothing came out. He turned away so he didn't have to face her while he lied. "I been workin' in the garden."

She deepened her glare at June. "You shouldn't be workin' that boy so hard."

With a wave of her hand, June talked about how "her boys" kept the yard perfectly manicured.

In the night, when everyone else was asleep, Sunday heard Monday slip out of bed and go down the hall into the kitchen, the cloth drawer roll open, and the suction from the seal around the door separating slowly from the fridge. Monday poured from her daddy's pitcher of cold water, and padded back to Friday's room to wrap his hands. He murmured, "It didn't hurt that bad..."

And no one said a word about his hands after that. Sunday periodically saw Friday picking at them, pulling off the dead skin, causing that terrible scream to pitch in her head again as images of his hands and his afflicted expression flashed through her mind. *The burns are almost gone...and nobody'll know. Nobody'll know we were bad, that Friday was setting fires.*

· · ·

No. There are no contests for that.

Sunday couldn't understand why her gramma hadn't done more. She was right there. She knew Friday's hands couldn't get like that from working in the garden. Gramma was exactly the same as Miss Doddy and the First Lady, and every one of her teachers. They all for some reason...just looked the other way.

Strange that Sunday could see so clearly now how alone they were. And strange that she felt nothing about her childhood in that moment.

And these people...This place...All this medication...They aren't helping either. I'm doing nothing but sitting here. I gotta get out–

Sunday didn't hear Bo come in, but she must have seen something in her expression.

"You all right?"

Maybe something she thought she detected in Bo's voice, a genuine concern she hadn't sensed from anyone in months, was what made her say it.

"No."

Finally a Friend

....

BO APPEARED ABOUT as shocked hearing the word as Sunday felt saying it. She eyed her roommate carefully before sitting down next to her. They'd never spoken more than a few words at a time to each other. Sure they shared an unspoken understanding, but now…now they were actually going to talk.

"No? Well…what's wrong?"

Sunday hesitated. "I dunno…everything…" She changed her mind. "Nothing. Nothing's wrong."

"Aw, c'mon, man. I can see it written all over your face. What's happening?"

Sunday set up a diversion. "How'd you get sent here anyway?"

Bo heaved a heavy sigh and rolled her eyes, "Well…let's put it this way. Shit wasn't goin' my way…and I decided to try and take a stand…and then shit got worse. So. Here I am."

Sunday nodded and chewed the inside of her cheek. "You think you'll get out of here soon?"

Bo chuckled. "What do you think? There ain't a way outta here, 'cept time."

"What do you mean?"

"Man, I got one more year. I'll be eighteen. They can't keep me in here after that. Fuck 'em. I'm out. And, man, when I rise above all this shit…I tell you, back home…they're all gonna wanna be the ones to come to me. Fuck 'em."

Silence settled over the two of them. Sunday never witnessed that kind of confidence, and she couldn't be sure exactly what Bo meant, but she liked the way her words sounded.

Bo spoke up. "So how was it?"

"How was what?"

She smiled and waved her fingers ominously. "I-so-la-tiooon."

Sunday half-smiled. "Boring. Nothing. You just sit in a room until they let you out."

"Hmph. That's not what Cutter said."

"I dunno. A couple people were going crazy in the other rooms."

"Oh, yeah, I heard all about Bonnie, too. Olly and that other guy were blabbing outside our door about the whole thing. They found out about all the pills she was stuffing under her mattress so she could scarf 'em down and kill 'erself. They were whining about how too many of us are tryin' to *get brave* in here and they don't have enough people to be dealing with this kinda shit, blah, blah, blah...She had a helluva come down, I guess."

"I dunno what their problem is. All I did was sit there. They made me take the medicine, and that was it. I got out."

"Maaan. You beat the system, huh? Well...sort of...Well, hey. Everybody's going bowling. Rules are rules. If one of us doesn't go, none of us goes. So c'mon."

Sunday was relieved. She couldn't be sure, but maybe she was actually happy to have finally made a friend.

A Taste of Freedom

BECAUSE SHE WAS smart and excluded from classes, and because in therapy she shared nothing, *and* because there was no money coming in from anyone on the outside to pay for the rare field trip, Sunday didn't do much apart from eat, sleep, and pretend to watch TV. And while some of the kids played chess or ran the pebbled paths of the inner courtyard, she mostly kept her distance. With the pharmaceutical regimen of this three-part program of hers rendering her all but numb, she didn't feel like doing much of anything anyway. So bowling with the group, when Bo specifically asked her to come, by default, was her only form of "fun."

Bowling was okay. Not as fun as getting out might be. Or riding a bike. Sunday's heart swelled when she thought about riding. No rules, no consequence, just the wind whipping through her hair. That was *real* fun.

Sunday only rode a bike once. And between her turns on the lane down at the Rose Village bowling alley, she thought about that bike and the first–and last–time she rode it.

· · ·

They were still living on Niagra Drive. It was a few months before the Minors moved to Rock Knoll, and not long after the first time she remembered being raped by her father. She was eight years old.

Chester never fully approved of June driving because that was a man's job. He admitted that sometimes there was no other option, but otherwise, he made his opinion on the matter clear. So she wasn't surprised when he told June on the way to the store one day, "If a woman needs to go somewhere, a man's gotta take 'er. If that woman does what she's supposed to, the man'll make sure she gets to wherever she needs goin' to…That boy's gotta learn how to get around sometime."

Only her and her parents went on this trip, and she had no clue how what her daddy was saying was related to whatever the store clerk was loading into the trunk. Chester had pulled in backwards around the back of the strip mall, and the children weren't allowed to get up from their seats, facing forward only in the car, so she couldn't see. Her daddy backed into the driveway when they got home, too. He never backed in.

He turned off the engine and grumbled, "Go get the boy."

June asked, "You want the rest of the kids to come out?"

"No. Just the boy."

He got out and leaned against the side of the car and crossed his arms over his chest and waited.

Sunday hadn't been given permission to get out of the car yet, so she remained there facing forward. She raised her head as high as she could to peer out at the door. Out of the house came June, followed by Friday. Sunday could tell he was worried. She bet her momma didn't tell him why he was coming out.

Friday stepped out from behind June and stood at attention in front of Chester.

"Friday. You're the second man of the house, and one of your responsibilities is to make trips if your momma needs somethin' or if you need to check on your sisters and whatnot. You need some transportation."

"Yessir."

"You need to be able to go places if 'n' when you're told so go on now, get it outta the trunk."

As Friday walked around to the back of the car, Chester threw the keys at Friday. They thumped him in the chest and dropped into his hand.

"Startin' tomorrow, you need to be able to do whatever errands your momma needs you to do."

"Yessir."

The key clamored into the trunk lock behind Sunday. Her brother lifted the lid, and he struggled to pull out something that seemed awkward and heavy. Only when he wheeled it around to the side of the car did Sunday dare turn her head. It was a shiny new bike, royal blue with a black banana seat. Friday pushed the bike by the sissy handlebars–the tall kind that curved out–toward his father and stopped squarely in front of him, awaiting the next instruction.

June prodded, "Well, what do you say?"

Friday nodded toward Chester. "Thank you, sir."

Chester nodded his approval. "Now. D'you know how to ride that?"

"Yessir."

Sunday was certain her brother never rode a bike in his life. She also had a good idea of what would have happened if he'd been truthful about that.

"Well then, lemme see you do it."

Sunday saw Friday glance nervously at the bike, and then at the ground. He climbed on, and wobbled across the yard.

"Jesus. Well, hopefully you'll get better before you get your damn driver's license."

Friday's voice wobbled like the wheels on his bike. "Yessir, I will."

He dropped a foot to the ground and turned the bike to face Chester again, awaiting the next instruction.

"Boy, this is your transportation. You have to keep it up. You need to wash it. Wipe the thing down after you ride. Keep the tires aired up. And if I see your bike layin' on its side or if you leave it in the yard, so help me…the goddamn thing'll be gone. Is that understood?"

"Yessir."

Chester leaned up, pushed himself away from the car, and headed toward the house. He stopped at the door and called out behind him, "You got thirty minutes. You need to get back on your chores after."

"Yessir."

"And Sunday. Get your ass outta the damn car. What the hell are you sittin' there staring at us for?"

Sunday lifted her chin and called out to him as loud as she could, "Yessir."

As her momma and daddy stepped into the house, Sunday leaned all her weight into the car door and heaved it closed. She made her way to the front stoop. Like some circus clown on TV, Friday wobbled across the yard again, stepped down from the pedals, see-sawed the bike around to face the other direction, and hopped back on to go back across to the driveway.

After about four or five of those awkward circles, Chester stepped back out onto the front stoop behind Sunday. "Lemme see how you're doin.'"

Friday nodded with determination. He pushed off again.

Chester snidely remarked, "Well, I guess you feel pretty safe makin' tiny circles in the grass, huh? At least it won't hurt if you fall."

"No, sir."

"Wha'd you say to me?"

"No-sir-it-won't-hurt-if-I-fall-down-on-the-grass."

He wasn't wobbling anymore.

"Let's see you do that on the sidewalk."

Friday pieced together his question carefully.

"C'mon, boy, lemme see you ride."

He treaded lightly. "Well...how far...how far do I go, sir?"

"Jesus, do I have to spell it out?" Chester shook his head and waved his hand down the street. "I wanna see you go down to that third house."

Friday hopped on and pumped down to the third house. He popped back down off the pedals.

Chester yelled down the street, "No, no, no, no, no! You gonna sissy it around every time you gotta make a turn? Get back down here, boy, and do the turn right."

Friday pumped back down in front of the house, and as he turned into the patch of grass between the sidewalk and the street, the wheel slipped off the curb and both the bike and Friday slammed into the ground.

In a flash, Chester was at Friday's side, looming over him.

"Goddamn it! Can't take care of a fucking thing!"

Friday jumped and pulled the bike up off the ground. He grabbed the tail of his shirt and polished the middle bar furiously. "I'm sorry, sir. It won't happen again."

"Well, it goddamn better *not*! Now get back on that bike, boy, and lemme see you ride back down."

Friday straddled the bike. "Yessir."

As he readied himself to push off, his daddy popped him upside the head. "You get on that goddamn bike, and you ride it."

Friday dropped his feet back down to the ground, and staring straight ahead, he dared to ask, "May I go in the street?"

"What for?"

"So I can turn properly, sir."

Chester didn't say anything, so Friday explained. "The maneuverability is better."

Chester cocked his head to the side. "Lemme see what you're talkin' about."

Friday pedaled down to the third house, but this time, he curved right, down the end of the neighbor's driveway into the street. He was careful to stay as close to the curb as possible, and then curved gracefully back up his own driveway.

Chester blew out and threw his hands. "Well, if that's the best you can do, I guess that's all I can hope for. Hope to God you don't get hit by a car."

June stepped back out onto the stoop next to Sunday, waving Friday over with two dollar bills. As he wheeled the bike back to the steps, she ordered, "I need you to go on up to the ice house and get a gallon of milk and a loaf of bread."

Friday thought for a minute before he answered. "I don't have a basket."

"That's not my problem."

June bent and shoved the dollar bills in his hand. "Bring me back the change."

She turned her back on him, stepped in the house, and slammed the door behind her. Chester shrugged and headed toward the garage. Friday straightened the crumpled bills in his hand, keeping one eye on Chester until he disappeared into the garage. He shoved the folded money in his pocket and got back on his bike. He pedaled through the yard, over to the end of the driveway, and onto the street. He made a wide right turn and rode away. *How's he think he's gonna carry all that stuff home with no basket, no nothin'?* She waited there to see how the whole situation would all play out in the end.

About a half-hour went by before June stepped back out on the porch–long enough for any one of the kids to just walk down there and back already. June stood over Sunday with her legs spread apart, one hand on her hip, one shading her eyes from the sun. June squinted down at the corner and asked, "Where's your brother?"

As if she doesn't know.

"He went to the ice house."

"He's not back yet?" June dropped her arms to her sides and shook her head, turning to go back in. She mumbled to herself, "Well, great. I guess he got hit by a car. We're probably gonna have to take him to the damn hospital."

Panic struck Sunday's heart. She looked down the street at the corner. *Oh, my god, he got hit by a car and he's gonna die out there. He's probably already dead!*

184

Then, the second she thought her brother's life was over, she caught a movement out of the corner of her eye. Her heart leapt. *There he is!*

With a wide wobble and a slow, heavy pump, Friday struggled up the street toward her, balancing the bag of bread by the pinky finger of one hand and the much heavier gallon of milk on three fingers of the other. Sunday called out loud, "Momma, he's back!"

Friday made his way across the front yard, in time for June to step out and spit, "If it's gonna take you that goddamn long, we might as well get rid of that thing."

Huffing, but obviously exhilarated, Friday pled, "I'll get better, Momma! I'll get better. He said I was gettin' better!"

"Your father said no such thing."

She stepped down, jerked the bread and milk out of his fingers, spun around, and disappeared back into the house.

Friday and Sunday looked at each other, as the excitement faded from his face. He balanced the bike under his straddle and examined the palms of his hands, red from the strain. He inched toward the garage. He stopped halfway and stepped over the bar, carefully dropping the kickstand into place.

He walked in, and asked, "Sir, can I borrow one'a your rags?"

"What for, boy?"

"I've been out, sir. I need to wipe my bike down, sir, and polish the metal parts."

Sunday heard her daddy roll out from under his hotrod, and get up and walk to the cabinet where he kept his shop rags. "Here's two. Now, goddamnit, boy, those don't grow on trees. They cost money, you understand me? You won't get any more."

"Yessir."

Friday wiped down each handlebar of the bike as Sunday got up and walked inside.

Friday loved that bike, and he washed and polished it as carefully as Chester washed and polished his cars. He never left his transportation out in the yard, and always used the kickstand.

He kept his two rags neatly folded inside one of the cigar boxes he got from Uncle Herby that he kept stacked neatly underneath his box of art supplies.

Friday was the only one that got a bicycle. After all, he was the boy. Still, Sunday wanted to ride, and she waited weeks for exactly the right time to ask.

One afternoon, after Chester and June left for the grocery store, and Sunday couldn't pick up the rumble of her daddy's car anymore, she walked out front where Friday was polishing his bike. "How does it feel to ride one?"

"It's groovy."

Sunday chuckled. "You're not a hippy. You can't say *groooovy*. Momma and Daddy are gonna get mad if they hear you say that."

He stopped polishing to address her this time. "Well. Ridin' this bike's amazing."

Excitement washed over him. "The wind's in your face, and your hair's blowin', and it's just...just you...and just...you can pretend it's a car. Or you can pretend you're on a train or a bus and you're goin' someplace...like you're leavin'...pretend you're not coming back."

"Oh..." Sunday never thought about that. "Well, is it like that all the time?"

"Yeah, pretty much..." He raised his chin to the sky. "Until you get where you're going." He dropped his gaze back to Sunday. "Then you remember you gotta turn around and get back..." He smiled again. "But on the trip out, it's pretty much like you're grown. You don't have to answer to nobody. You don't have to ask anybody anything."

"Do you ever think about not coming back?"

"Yeah, but they'll find you."

"Well, I wanna ride your bike, okay?"

"No. You're a girl, and you're not allowed."

"Well, is it hard to ride?"

"Yeah, at first, a little bit because you think you're gonna fall off all the time. It's not that hard, though. All you have to do is learn to balance and you do that with your butt."

"With your butt?" Sunday giggled, and asked again, "You do it with your butt?"

Friday chuckled, too. "Yeah! I mean, all you do is move around on the seat 'til it feels right and you can tell you're not gonna fall."

"Can I try?"

"I dunno. You have a little butt."

She mocked indignance. "Heeey! I don't have a little butt!"

Friday teased some more. "What? You want me to say you have a *big* butt?"

Sunday was serious. "I have a butt that can ride that bike."

Friday rolled his head to the sky and back down. "You know if he sees you on a bike, we're both gonna get in trouble."

Hoping to appeal to his sense of reason, Sunday listed the facts. "They've only been gone for a little while. They're not gonna be back for a long time. I'm only gonna ride around for a minute. Pleeease?"

"He's gonna call you a queer if he sees you…"

"No, he won't."

"If he sees you on the bike, he's gonna think you wanna be a boy."

"Well, I don't."

"I know, but that's not what he's gonna think."

"I don't care. C'monnn. Gimme a chance to try'n ride it."

Friday sighed. "How long have they been gone?"

"I dunno. Fifteen or twenty minutes?"

"Okay."

He leaned the bike towards his sister. "You have to stay in the yard."

Sunday clapped her hand over her mouth. "Okay!"

"I'm gonna go in the house and get me a drink. I'll be right back."

187

Sunday grabbed the handlebars from her brother. "Okay."

As he went inside, Sunday stepped over the middle bar.

Sunday pumped from one side of the yard to the other like Friday did that first day. She would stop, get off, turn the bike around, and start again. She did that once, twice, three times. She thought to herself, *Well, pfft, how hard can this be? I didn't fall once!*

She thought she needed to practice her turns, and she remembered from Friday's first ride you couldn't do that on the grass or on the sidewalk, so she went for it. She swooped down the drive and into the street. And there on the open road, she instantly understood exactly what Friday was talking about. Riding a bike was like swinging, like flying away, only pedaling instead! Her hair fluttered and whipped around the back of her head. She coasted down to the corner. She realized she didn't have enough room to turn around at the end of the street. *Oh, no! How am I gonna do this? How do I turn? There's no driveways left!*

As she got closer and closer to the end of Niagra, she scanned the intersection, first left toward the store, then right. She spotted the high school. *Yes!* She quickly counted the curves in the driveway where it circled up and around in front of the school, and reviewed the exact steps to make the trip around. She eyeballed the downhill slope back out into the street. Without stopping, she made the widest right turn she could, and pumped hard toward the school.

All the while, she sucked in at the wind on her face and blew out, happy and free! *I can go! I can leave!*

She made the first curve, and an even wider left turn up into the circular drive. She whisked herself down to the end of the circle. She sailed down the slope back into the street toward Niagra. Without warning, a low rumble thundered in her ears. *Oh, God! It's Momma and Daddy!*

She didn't see the car. She didn't have to. She knew it was them. She stood up on the pedals like she'd seen other kids do. She pumped as fast and as hard as she could, not looking back.

She prayed they didn't spot her, and prayed that if they did, they didn't recognize her. She flew back toward Niagra, and judged the corner at her street. She couldn't make the angle. She couldn't tell how wide she should turn, flying so fast down the street. *I don't know how to use the brakes!*

She zeroed in on the house. She saw Friday standing in the yard scanning the block for her with his hands on his hips like her momma when she was mad. *He told me not to leave…Oh, no!*

Cuuurve, *BOOM!* Sunday slammed into the curb and the bike exploded into three pieces. All of it, and Sunday, skidded across the asphalt. She flipped up onto the grass, and instantly sat straight up. She swiped her tongue across the inside of her bottom lip, where she felt the cut and tasted the blood. She saw Friday break into a dead run toward her and his bike, now in pieces.

He must have recognized panic in Sunday's face, and shouted, "Are you okay?"

Sunday hollered back, "Momma and Daddy are comin'!"

He dropped down next to Sunday, and cried, "What did you do to my bike?"

She shook her head, "No, Friday, Momma and Daddy are comin'!"

"What?"

"Momma and Daddy are comin'! Help me!"

Sunday grabbed the handlebars where the front wheel was still attached, and pushed herself up on it. Friday scrambled for the other two pieces. The muscle car rumbled down to the corner, and turned slowly onto Niagra. The pair sprinted back toward the house.

They set the pieces on the floor in the garage. They ran into the kitchen as the car pulled into the drive. It was all over. That bike was in three pieces. There was no way around this.

They followed each other, like a solemn death row march, to their respective rooms, and Sunday sat down in her assigned seat on the bed.

The car door slammed. Only June stomped in through the garage. Chester stayed outside. Her momma clomped down the hall, ranting all the way to her room to get the belt, "I'll teach you!"

She was in Sunday's room in a flash. "Lay over the bed." She struggled to throw her girl's hands to the sides. "Bend [*whack*] over. [*whack*] Hands by your sides, [*whack*] goddamnit." [*whack*]

She lashed Sunday's legs as she slipped down the bed.

June screamed, "I said hands by your sides!" [*whack*]

Sunday slipped further, and the belt licked her backside and lower back.

"You're gonna mind me!" [*whack*]

Higher, the leather licked her middle.

Her momma screamed on. "You're gonna mind me and your daddy!" [*whack*]

She lashed Sunday across the shoulders, still screaming, "When we tell you to stay home, [*whack*] by god, you're gonna stay home!" [*whack*]

Sunday slipped to the floor.

June kept on until she swelled with exhaustion, and her arms dropped to her sides. She heaved a great sigh. "I don't know what you people want from me," she said, as she turned and walked out.

We just want you to love us.

Sunday raised herself off the floor and eased back into position on the edge of the bed to wait for her daddy. She listened as her mother clomped back down the hall toward her brother's room. She listened to her repeat every command, every threat, and every lash she'd just endured.

Chester stepped into Sunday's doorway and glared at her in silence, then he growled, "That's why we don't have nice things, goddamnit. You sons-of-bitches can't take care of a goddamn thing, and I'm not about to replace every goddamn thing you can't take care of."

As quietly as he'd appeared in her doorway, he was gone. The Minors never got another bike.

...

But that one ride–I was free.
"Sunday," Bo called from the ball return. "You're up."

THE TRUTH ABOUT SUNDAY MINOR

Prize Fighter

A T THE NEXT group therapy session, as Sunday slid into her chair in the circle, she wondered when she would never have to come back to that room. From the sound of Bo's explanation that day was a very long way out. As it turned out, though, this session would be Sunday's last. That session would also be the one in which she came as close to true empathy as she would in that room for the two that held the floor that day.

Adonai was a girl who couldn't have been more than fourteen. She was in for consorting with men that were twice her age, and sometimes older than that. Her parents said they didn't want anything to do with her anymore, that she was a disgrace, so they sent her to Rose Village. She said she knew the other girls made stuff up about her sleeping with the orderlies and the doctors. She said the stories weren't true, but she didn't care what anyone said anyway; she was used to everyone hating her. "I sleep with people who are nice to me, is all."

Sunday was no stranger to trying everything you can to do the right thing, to not make your parents mad, but still fall short. She understood that being sent to this reform school of a facility wasn't any different than having been cast in the role of outsider in any public school she'd ever attended. She comprehended her place among the weird ones, the ones who weren't normal, the same way she grasped that there was not a "normal" she would ever be able to "get back to" as Dr. Faus promised.

And though Sunday didn't agree with Adonai that the price was giving your physical self over in return, she possessed the same deep craving for kindness. Small kindnesses are what allowed room for the Minor children to breathe; Like the day Grandaddy Paw brought Crybaby in as a puppy; Or the cigar boxes from Grampa Herbie filled with popcorn and striped candies and the handmade purses and wallets woven out of the pink and blue dry cleaning bags Gramma June had collected from work throughout the year; The care Gramma June took in teaching the children how to decorate eggshell ornaments with sequins and glitter at Easter and the occasional birthday cake she would make for the children when she could; There were the compliments they got from aunts and uncles for their cleaning skills every time they stayed overnight, too. Nevermind they'd been taught the compulsion. Sunday also never forgot every compliment any teacher ever paid her for doing a good job. She needed those bright spots in her life in those days more than she'd ever realized.

Sunday wanted to tell Adonai she understood. Instead Blain was the person who raced to Adonai's side, encircling her shoulder and patting her on the arm.

A boy called Ray spoke for the first time in a long time. "Nobody's parents are ever nice. Not to each other and not to 'emselves. Nothin' left to do, but get even."

Keeping his eyes on Adonai, he waved a finger around the circle. "All these other kids, they don't get it. Fuck 'em."

"Language," the mediating therapist interjected.

Ray rolled his eyes. "*Forget* 'em. 'Scuse me."

He said to Adonai, "You just gotta get even."

In a previous session, Ray shared that he'd been sent to Rose Village because he beat up his dad. He saw him beat up his mom one too many times. His dad was raging again about his mom not doing the dishes often enough, not vacuuming and dusting enough. He told Ray he was a good-for-nothing ingrate who couldn't even take out the trash.

"That fucker can't even get a job, and here we are working and going to school and cooking and cleaning. Fuck. Him. You know what I did? That's right. I got even, didn't I? I waited 'til they were asleep. Got out the ol' H&B *bat*, didn't I? I showed *him* 'ingrate.'"

Ray had put his dad in the hospital for two months. That was two and a half years ago.

Sunday understood wanting to get even, though she'd never found the courage to act. And frankly, in her opinion, Ray had taken things too far. Her brother, though, when she was eleven and he only twelve, now, *he'd* shaken her daddy to the core. The stand he took lasted no more than a moment, but she would never forget it.

...

Friday always ran from his momma come time for punishment. And he ran from his sisters, too, when they were horsing around. But not Chester. He never ran from Chester.

There was no love lost between those two by then. He knew his daddy hated him, and at that point, Friday hated him right back. There was no reason to run. He stared out into space while his daddy punched or whipped him. On *that* day, however, her brother stopped just staring out into space. Friday fought back–maybe not outwardly, like a man his father's own size, but the way a twelve-year-old boy could. Sunday saw what he did. And her daddy saw it, too.

Friday was lying on his bed, lost in his sketchpad. He was breathing deeply and slowly, so focused on what he was doing he was oblivious to all else. Almost perfect. She'd have to catch him off guard if she were to have any opportunity of pinning him before he ran. He rolled over onto his side to get more comfortable. This was her chance. She pounced!

They were all over the room, tumbling, rumbling, rolling, grunting, and sweating. *He's not gettin' away this time!*

Sunday threw her full weight on top of him, and worked quickly to get her knees on him. She missed. She tried again to pin his shoulders when he was face up on the bed. He wiggled free. *Foiled!*

He tried to take off, but Sunday caught his arm and yanked down with all her might again, and he landed on his stomach. She went at him again, and managed to peg both knees into his back and leaned in with all her weight. She could feel him panic like a snared rabbit. Friday fought like his life depended on it. He would not be pinned.

Her daddy's voice shocked them into silence. "Both'a you! In the backyard! Now!"

He had walked in on them whirling like a couple of tornados. Friday's room was a mess. Sunday and Friday jumped to attention. Chester turned and walked out.

They followed close behind him, completely silent, not even stealing a glance at each other. They kept their eyes on their daddy, as he picked up his black racing gloves, the ones with no fingers, on the way out. *Keep your room neat and tidy. Dress-right-dress,* as they say in the army barracks. This lesson would be short and brutal.

Friday was called up first. Sunday couldn't say whether he went first because he was older or because the mess gave Chester a good enough reason to beat him up and he couldn't wait to do it.

Sunday stood on the patio, peering out through her glasses timidly. She watched as her father challenged her brother in the yard in front of her. Gloved fists up, elbows in, Chester reminded Sunday of a prize fighter. The stance of a boxer, dancing around his twelve-year-old son, taunting him, questioning Friday's masculinity. "You a little *cocksucker?* Can't wait to get a *pansy-ass* of your own, huh?"

Boom! The first right cross caught Friday on the left side of the face. Friday's head spun, and he shot his right foot backward, struggling to regain his balance. He pulled his foot back in, and turned back to face his opponent. He balled up his fists at his sides, but didn't say anything. Sunday was in awe.

Chester kept dancing around him, calling out slurs like "homo" and "faggot" and "fairy." Friday's fingers uncurled to hang loose at the ends of his hands.

Boom! Another right cross to the jaw. He recovered the same as before, but quicker, loosening his fists again.

That's when it happened. As he brought his head back to center and heaved a great breath through his nose, slow and strong, he leveled a steely gaze back at Chester.

For the first time in her life, Sunday saw Friday, there, present, and not a glimmer of panic in his eyes. Sunday threw a glance at Chester. Her father was visibly wrecked. Something stirred in her that she'd never felt before. *He is my brother. He is my hero.*

She even thought she might have seen Chester's chin quiver, but he shook off the shock before she could be certain. The anger pushed out his jaw again, his face turned the color of blood, and his eyes narrowed to slits.

Bam! An uppercut to the chin. Friday's head snapped back. He maintained that new determination, slowly bringing his chin down again, and this time, he took one step forward. He didn't say a word, but he looked Chester squarely in the eye. His arms were still loose at his sides.

Chester stopped dancing.

Friday had beaten him.

Intimidated by a child.

They stood there staring at each other for an eternity.

Finally Chester broke the standoff, "If you don't like the way I run things around here, get the *fuck* out."

He retreated to the garage.

. . .

Sunday didn't realize how far forward into the therapy circle she'd leaned until she nearly slipped off the front of her chair. She waved her arms to balance herself, catching the therapist's attention.

"Yes, Sunday? You have something to add?" Sunday thought she might have actually picked up on a hint of hope in the therapist's voice, but her constant glances at the clock on the wall behind her told her she was wrong.

Sunday shifted back in her chair, and hunched her shoulders in, "No."

"You have nothing to add? Nothing at all?" She sighed, and glanced at the clock again.

"Nothing."

The gossip girls' ringleader erupted, "Nothing? You got *nothing*?"

She whined to the mediating therapist, who was clearly as ready to be done for the day as Sunday, "She never has to say anything. At least Lizzy cries. We know *something's* wrong with her. Sunday *never* has to participate. It's not fair!"

Sunday stood up and cupped her mouth, and the therapist clutched the notepad in her lap as though it were the weapon she needed to save the group's life if Sunday blew up. Sunday thought carefully about what to do. She dragged her hand down slowly, surely over her chin and under it until she gripped her own throat. She raised her head to the ceiling. Almost a full minute passed. Then she decided. *No. There's nothing to say here. No reason to stay.* Sunday walked out.

Breaking Out

A S SHE TREADED slowly back down the hall toward her room, she listened to the nurses tittering on about some court cases up North, and not enough money or help. A change was coming down the pipeline. Her mind wandered back to that day in the yard when her brother somehow mustered the courage to make a change.

Sunday remembered laying down on the patio after her battered and bruised brother had stumbled into the house, certain that Chester was going to come back for her soon enough. Her last thought before drifting off had scrolled through her mind. *He is my brother. He is my hero.*

...

She didn't know how many times Friday'd whispered her name before she awoke.

"Do you like the way he's runnin' things?"

Sunday didn't have to answer. They stood up and walked out. They weren't coming back.

It was the first time Sunday ever ran away, and for the most part, the adventure was magnificent.

First stop on the road to their new life: the rock quarry. The sun hung low, but there was still plenty of daylight left. They walked down Rock Knoll and crossed over onto a familiar path that rose up and into the woods and curved right and down again. The path was overgrown with old mesquites and junipers and tall grasses that swayed in the breeze the way she thought wheat ought to. There were weeds and vines and tiny white and yellow flowers, like what she knew to be in what little of the Texas

Hill Country she'd been exposed to. The footpath was worn down enough to walk through, and in Sunday's mind the trail must have been forged a hundred years ago at least.

Along the way, Sunday didn't say much. To her surprise, it was Friday doing most of the talking this time.

"I'm tired of things, Sunday. I can't do anything right. How come he hates me so much?"

Sunday didn't say anything. What *could* she say, stunned as she was by someone in this world feeling the exact same way as her?

"Even if everything gets done, they're always gonna find something wrong. There's always gonna be a reason to be mad at us. They're always going to punish us."

Sunday pictured Friday standing in the yard again, staring down her daddy after that final blow. She wanted to be more courageous like him. She wanted to understand his secret.

"How come you could take those punches?"

"I sorta tell myself I'm not there."

What? He never said he could do that. Maybe he can fly away like me. Sunday didn't say it out loud. "Well, how come you didn't fall or cry?"

"I dunno. I pretend I'm somewhere else."

All of us wanna be somewhere else. She didn't say that out loud either.

Sunday wanted him to keep talking. She wanted to keep hearing his voice tell her all the things she thought about, but never said. Friday didn't usually talk much at all so when he *did* say something, they all tended to listen because it was probably important. She also knew if she asked too many questions, he would change the subject. He'd say, "Well, that's just the way they are"...or "That's just the way it is" and walk away. She couldn't take the risk. So the rest of the way to the quarry, she walked beside him and listened.

"Maybe we can stay with Uncle Vernon...Maybe we can ride in his truck when he's workin'...Maybe that man'll never know where we are."

Maybe we can.

The end of the path opened up into a great big familiar clearing. On the other side was the cliff that must've dropped more than twenty-five feet straight down into water so clear you could see fish at least ten feet deep. Below that was dark blue so Sunday was certain the watering hole was deep.

A gravelly path on the right side of the cliff wound down between huge limestone boulders and into the shallows. Some of the rocks along the way down were big enough to climb while others were too tall. The farther down the path, the less the boulders stuck out of the water, until they were only high enough to hop across them.

Today, they weren't going down the windy path into the shallow end. That day they were going to jump. Friday had made that leap a hundred times over, and before Sunday even realized he had left her side, she felt him whip past her. He hurled himself over the edge. He was flying! She ran to the edge to catch him as he hit the water. *Smack!*

She saw him surface. He cracked a big smile and waved her in from below. "C'mon!"

Sunday was afraid. *No. Today is the first day of our new life.*

She stared straight down into the water for a minute. She still couldn't see the bottom, but she noted where the boulders were, how they formed almost a perfect circle around the deep blue hole. *Bottomless, straight to the center of the world. I'll be okay.*

"C'mon! You can do it!"

I can do it.

"Jump!"

She backed up a ways from the edge to get a running start, and planted herself with one foot forward. She leaned into the front foot, and counted to herself: *One... two... THREE!* She shot out of her stance, and broke into a dead run.

Whooooooaaaaah! She stumbled to a stop, arms waving to balance herself just short of the edge. *I can't!*

Friday hollered up from below, "Do it!"

Sunday backed up to her start again...*One...two...THREE!* She bolted!

I'm doing it!

WAIT! It's not right!

She backed up a third time, and stopped herself short of the edge again. *I'm never gonna make the jump.*

She searched Friday's face down below for disappointment, but none was there. He was still smiling, waving her on. "This time! This time you're gonna be great! Do it again, Sunday! You're gonna do it!"

Enough is enough.

The fourth time, she shot out and...*and...I'm not stopping! I'm running! I'm in the air! I'm still running!*

Sunday fell through the air in slow motion, her arms flapping awkwardly, like chick taking flight for the first time, her legs pumping like an ostrich. *I'm doing it! This is what it feels like to really fly! It's better than swingiiiiiiiiiiiing!*

Crack! She hit the water hard.

She opened her eyes to darkness. She couldn't tell whether she was upside down or right side up. *I'm gonna drown before I get back up to the top!* She never did touch the bottom. *There's nowhere to push off from! I was right! It is bottomless!*

In a panic, she did the only think she could think of–she pulled her legs up into her chest and shot her arms straight above her head, hoping she was pointed in the right direction: up!

She kicked and pushed down the water as hard as she could. She saw Friday treading water overhead. *Almost there!*

She pulled her arms and legs in and pushed down hard again. She broke the surface, and sucked the air into her lungs. *I made it!*

Friday guffawed, clearly thrilled.

I didn't drown!

Sunday turned to him. "I gotta do that again!"

For hours, they swam, and dove, and splashed and laughed, and reminisced about other times they'd come down to quarry.

While the other kids went to the public pool during the summer, the Minor kids went to the natural pool. They weren't allowed to go to the public pool. For one, the public pool cost money. Two, they would need a ride. Three strikes you're out; simply asking the question might even be enough to send June into a fit of rage, whipping them and screaming about how what she did "was never enough for them." So they never bothered to ask.

A couple of times, Friday had brought Sunday there to teach her to swim. The first time, they started at the shallow end.

He told her, "Okay, now, lay back and try'n act like you're sleepin' and hold your breath."

He held her up with one hand under her back. "Remember, if you get nervous or scared or whatnot, you're gonna sink."

After Sunday got that down, the next time, he took her out to where the water was deeper and she couldn't touch bottom. He told her, "Okay. Nooow act like you're crawlin'. Keep pushin' down with your hands and feet...That's called the doggy paddle!"

The last time they'd gone for "swim lessons," he first set Sunday to doggy paddling, and next instructed, "Now...just put your arm out in front. Stretch your arms out one at a time. Pretend you're pushing the water outta the way."

Last, he told her, "Now stretch out your feet one at a time and keep doin' 'em like you're walkin' real fast."

That was it. Sunday had learned to swim.

And the day they'd run away, laughing, swimming, and splashing seemed like all they needed in the world. Time didn't matter. He was Sunday's brother, her hero, and she was his sister, and they were living life the way it ought to be lived. In that moment, Sunday thought this was the best first day of the rest of her life ever.

That was until Friday glided up behind her and whispered, "Get out of the water."

"No!" Sunday said, thinking he was kidding.

"Look."

His tone startled her. She followed his line of sight across the water and up the cliff to the edge. There, on the ridge, stood Wednesday...and their daddy. *She told.*

She'd led him directly there. *How'd she know we'd be here?*

Their father and Wednesday stood there, united, surveying the scene below.

Sunday was petrified. Reality suffocated her.

We haven't actually run away. Not so far. We just aren't going home.

Then, directed solely by fear, they eyed the opposite side of the cliff. She and her brother glanced at each other, and in that glance they formed an unspoken pact–they weren't going back. They swam away from the ledge with strong, smooth strides through the water. As soon as they reached land on the other side of the quarry they made a break for it, heading into the backwoods where they never went before. She didn't care. As long as they were getting away from them they were going to be okay.

Sunday felt like she'd awoken inside the scene of some horror movie, and the villain was approaching. The two of them were running so fast, they were unaware of the thick underbrush whipping against their faces, their hands, their arms and legs. Neither felt the rocks gouging the bottoms of their feet.

They hit a fence and fell to the ground, heaving. They listened for footsteps.

They waited there a while longer. As their breathing slowed, they peered back through the chain links at the plain concrete building there.

Friday huffed, "Must be the research center."

He once told his sisters he'd learned about the research center in science class. "They do all kinds of experiments to better humanity."

He started in again about the kinds of animals they used to help the scientists figure out how to make cures. Curiosity overtook any lingering worry that their daddy and sister might still be after them. They stood and walked the fence line.

As they moved along, the gap between the fence and the building closed, a row of outdoor cages came into view. Inside each cage was every different kind of monkey Sunday had ever seen plus some she hadn't. Some of them paced back and forth, and some lumbered in and out of the concrete doorways that led inside. Some simply sat there watching Friday and Sunday watching them. None of them, neither the children nor the monkeys, made a sound. The quiet was unnerving. It was like they connected as kindred spirits–caged animals. *Only we escaped.*

They walked on to where the fence met the access road of a highway. They plodded quietly along the road. Sunday examined her arms, counting the scratches. As she dropped them to her sides, Friday said, "We're on our way to Dallas."

Uncle Vernon lived there.

Not much time had passed since the pineapple upside down cake incident. Walking along the access road to Dallas, Sunday's stomach growled loudly, and Friday laughed.

Sunday laughed, too. "A pineapple upside down cake would be great right now."

"Sure would."

They linked arm-in-arm and he told her, "That time, after Uncle Vernon saw Daddy bein' mean to me, he told me later… he said if I ever needed a place to stay, all I have to do is get to his house. I just know he'll let us stay there together. We'll ride with 'im in his truck…"

Sunday finished his thought. "…Daddy'll never know where we are."

Friday repeated what he told his sister earlier that day on their way down to the quarry, but this time, there was something different about his voice, and in that moment their escape felt more real. They *were* running away. They *weren't* going home this time.

At least not yet.

As the sun sank down below the horizon, massive gray thunderheads loomed in the evening sky. Sunday was starving by that time, and after the day's events, she was exhausted. She could tell Friday was growing hungry and tired, too.

Nothing we can do about bein' hungry, but we gotta find a place to camp out before the rain comes.

The air thickened under the weight of the cloud cover, and traces of damp citrus drifted up from the limestone in the soil, compelling Sunday picked up the pace. Friday matched hers, both keeping an eye out. About a hundred yards out, across an open field, they spotted a row of new houses under construction. Without a word, they turned and started walking that way.

The frames reminded Sunday of their first Destroyers mission years ago. They didn't have walls or roofs yet, but there were piles and piles of broken down cardboard boxes of all sizes stacked around them. The pair began prying away layers, examining each until they came across the biggest one. They turned the box on its side, and while she held one end open, her brother ran to grab a stick, and he wedged it in to prop the shelter up. They squeezed themselves in. Too small. Friday eyed the boxes spread out over the ground, and picked one almost as wide, though a little shorter. He shoved it together with the first box, overlapping the ends.

"Perfect."

They crawled inside, and huddled there together to wait.

Lightning cracked, and the sky opened up. The rain poured down. Sunday and her brother sat Indian style, facing each other. Friday plucked a piece of grass out from between the boxes underneath his legs and start pulling it apart. For a moment, while he stared at his lap, she studied the deep blue rings spreading from the center of his swollen jaw. The rain poured down harder and harder.

Within minutes there was a full-out flood, it seemed. Somehow, they stayed dry enough inside. Lightning bolted down from the sky faster and faster, illuminating their little shack with brief strobes of daylight, startling Sunday. The thunder rolled again and again, louder and louder, until she was swallowed up in its rumbling waves.

Her brother looked up from his shredded blade of grass. Sunday saw that he could see the fear in her eyes, but he asked her anyway, "Are you scared?"

"Are you?" Sunday gave herself away.

"A little."

They stared up at the thin shelter and waited it a little while longer.

"You wanna go home?" he whispered.

Sunday's mouth hung open. No words came out. She didn't want to give up. *He is my brother. He is my hero. I don't wanna disappoint him.*

She snapped her mouth shut and shrugged, and she wrung her restless hands in her lap.

Crack! They both jumped out of their skin. The thunder that followed shook their cardboard tent. That was it. Friday took Sunday's hand and led her out into the downpour.

Fair Price for Reprieve

....

S OGGY AND DOWNTRODDEN, the pair trudged back the way they came, neither of them paying any attention to the fact that they were soaked through to the bone. Neither lifted their gaze from the ground in front of them. Sunday watched streams form through the soaked mud where no grass had been laid. Out on the road along the highway, the water rushed like a river down the storm drains. The rain poured, the thunder roared, and the lightning crashed all around them, and Sunday barely noticed. Neither of them spoke. She was afraid of stepping back inside that house. She silently prepared for what surely would be the last beating of her very short life. The gap between a life of freedom and their permanent hell closed again.

They reached the front of the house, but were not yet ready to face what was waiting inside. Instead they sat down on the step to muster the courage needed to go through that door. Out of the corner of her eye, Sunday caught Chester peeking through the shears out the front window. He dropped the curtain, and his shadow fall away. Sunday and Friday casted a knowing glance in each other's direction, and both heaved a hopeless sigh. The last thought of freedom slipped away, and with the tiniest of nods, they stood together, turned around, and walked back in.

No one seemed to be waiting. Only a single living room lamp was on. They plodded with heads down to their own rooms, where they waited for the verdicts to be read, their sentences to be doled. The punishment would have to fit the crime. That was the Minor way.

Sunday chose a place on the floor, not daring to wet the bedspread with her soaking wet clothing. She didn't change because she didn't want a pile of wet, dirty clothes sitting there, evidence of her crime, when her turn came up. She didn't want to stir her sisters anyway. She was never more hungry or cold or tired in her entire life. She longed to fall asleep and simply never wake up. She knew the end would never come that easy.

Finally, she heard her father's footsteps, slow and methodical. She strained to make out what he was saying to her brother. Friday didn't say anything back.

Silence. Then *crack*! The leather belt across bare skin. *One...* [*crack*] *two...*[*crack*] *three...*Sunday counted, [*crack*] *four...* [*crack*] *five...*[*crack*] *six...*choking off a crushing sob...[*crack*] *seven...*[*crack*] *eight...*[*crack*] *nine...*as each swing of the belt... [*crack*] *ten...*[*crack*] *eleven...*[*crack*] *twelve...*connected with her brother's flesh [*crack*] *thirteen...*[*crack*] *fourteen...*[*crack*] *fifteen...*He didn't cry. [*crack*] *sixteen...* [*crack*] *seventeen...* [*crack*] *eighteen...*They didn't speak. [*crack*] *nineteen* ...[*crack*] *twenty...*[*crack*] *twenty-one...*She kept counting, [*crack*] *twenty-two...*[*crack*] *twenty-three...*[*crack*] *twenty-four...*until it stopped [*crack*] *twenty-five...*Silence.

Chester started toward Sunday's room. With every footstep, the sadness crushing her chest twisted into fear, and fear into panic. He stopped in front of her door. It swung open.

"Strip," he snarled.

Friday appeared in the doorway. He cried out, "Don't whip her!"

"You willin' to take it for her, then? We got punishment to give out here, boy. It's got to be fair."

Friday didn't hesitate. "Yes."

Before Sunday could protest, they both turned. Chester loomed so large in the shadows over the boy who was so small at his side. Sunday caught site of the deep blue marks on Friday's pale back, some smeared brown and dark red. She ran to the door. She couldn't take her eyes off of his back. They disappeared into Friday's room, and the door closed. The sadness pressed down on Sunday again. Helpless, she began a recount as the leather met her brother's skin. [*crack*] *Twenty-six...*[*crack*] *twenty-seven...*[*crack*] *twenty-eight...*Sunday counted, [*crack*] *twenty-nine...*[*crack*] *thirty...*[*crack*] *thirty-one...*not bothering to hold back the tears anymore [*crack*] *thirty-two...*[*crack*] *thirty-three ...*as each lash of the leather [*crack*] *thirty-four...*[*crack*] *thirty-five...*[*crack*] *thirty-six...*met her brother's back [*crack*] *thirty-seven...*[*crack*] *thirty-eight...*[*crack*] *thirty-nine...*He still didn't cry [*crack*] *forty...*[*crack*] *forty-one...*[*crack*] *forty-two...*[*crack*] *forty-three...*They still said nothing [*crack*] *forty-four...*[*crack*] *forty-five...*[*crack*] *forty-six...*She kept counting in her head [*crack*] *forty-seven...*[*crack*] *forty-eight...*[*crack*] *forty-nine...* until she finally whispered in the darkness [*crack*] "Fifty." The lashing was done.

She heard her father open Friday's door, and walk down the hall and into the living room. The springs in his recliner protested under his weight, and the television clicked on.

She stripped out of her cold wet clothes and folded them. She hid them in the bottom of her closet, and reminded herself to put them in the washer before anyone could point them out in the morning. She slid the closet door closed, careful not to make a sound, and crept to the dresser for a nightgown. She padded to the bed, and slipped between the sheets.

She stared into the blackness. *Why? Why did he take it for me?*

Only one answer came to her, repeating over and over in her mind. *He is my brother. He is my hero...*

Without warning, June burst through the front door and slammed it behind her. She screamed, "Did they come home? Goddamnit, I couldn't concentrate my whole shift! They did this on purpose, Chester! They do this shit to make my life miserable! Miserable! Selfish little bastards. I'm gonna beat the hell outta those two! I'm gonna make them wish they hadn't come home! I'll be so glad when they're gone!"

She stomped down the hallway and Chester shouted, "June!"

He lowered his voice again. "Now gimme just a goddamn minute to tell you what's gone on here."

Sunday could only gather fragments. "That little cocksucker, he thought he could stand up to me...Wednesday, she was good enough to...They took off after that...There wadn't nothin' out there, though...That storm'd drive 'em back, if nothin' else... Friday said he'd take 'em for 'er–"

June screamed, "What?"

She stormed through the kitchen, banging things around. Before Sunday could count the seconds, she was next to girls' bed, with a fistful of Sunday's hair in her clutches. She dragged her flailing daughter from the bed onto the floor. Monday shot up, rubbing her eyes, groggy and swaying. June dragged her across the room and down the hall, and through the dining room. Sunday twisted sideways and locked eyes on her face, beet-red and crazed. June was out of control, screaming toward the living room as they passed, "This little bitch is not gettin' away with it!"

She dragged Sunday through the kitchen, and through the garage door and down the step onto the concrete. Chester was on her heels, frantic, explaining the situation. "If she gets whipped now, it wouldn't be fair to Friday! Don't ya see? He already took all the punishment. He paid for her."

June was hell-bent on equalizing that out once more. "I don't care! She'll take two rounds!"

She screamed toward the garage door where Monday, Tuesday, and Wednesday now cowered behind Chester, petrified she'd turn on them, too. "Goddamnit, somebody bring me the belt!"

Chester grabbed June by the shoulders and shook hard enough for Sunday's hair to slip from her grasp. Sunday scurried out from under them and turned over onto her back to assess what was happening. He pinned June to the washing machine, and shouted over his shoulder, "Sunday, getcher ass to bed!"

Sunday was up and through the door before he could yell over the other shoulder, "All'a'ya, getcher asses to bed!"

Everybody ran.

Chester and June spent most of the night in the garage with the door closed. Sunday believed it was a miracle that no one else was hurt–or worse. Just Friday. Sunday and Friday hadn't escaped that night. But they'd sure as hell had given it a shot.

He's my brother. He's my hero.

THE TRUTH ABOUT SUNDAY MINOR

Life According to Webster

....

N OT FIFTEEN MINUTES after Sunday walked out of
that last group therapy session she was summoned to
Dr. Faus' office for a chat.

As she approached his office, she heard her therapist
pleading quietly with Dr. Faus, "...can't even be sure she's
taking the meds, not really, with everything that's happened."
He assured her, "You're doing fiiine. We'll get all this figured
out." She pled on, "I don't know if I can take this anymore,
and we're walking a thin line with this mess up North, I just—"
She stopped short the moment Sunday stepped through the
doorway.

" We'll discuss this further a little later this afternoon," Dr.
Faus said, and turned his focus to Sunday, "Come on in, Ms.
Minor, and have a seat here."

As she sat down, Dr. Faus continued, "It seems group therapy
isn't progressing for you as we'd hoped. Other participants are
feeling uncomfortable because you are not participating...To
be frank, they are sensing you might not feel...well, they think
you think you're better than them. I think maybe best plan is
for you to refrain from attending for awhile."

*What the hell did that woman say? I didn't do anything
wrong.* Although Sunday didn't care to participate, she couldn't
help but feeling at least a little closer to "normal" listening to
kids her own age share their grievances, no matter how petty.
She'd lost her siblings, the few friends she'd made at school.
She'd been too smart to be a part of continuing education at
Rose Village, and she wasn't allowed on field trips because she
didn't have money. And now she was odd man out once again,
kicked out this time, even more isolated than before.

"You'll be allowed to stay in your room during group sessions. Or you can watch TV in the common area. Whatever you think will be most constructive during that time period. Your one-on-one sessions will increase to four times per week."

She went back to her room while the others finished their group therapy. She flipped through a book from Bo's stack, a copy of something called *A Spell for Chameleon*, but couldn't focus on the words. She wandered to the common area and turned on the TV. She flipped through all five channels. Nothing but news. She didn't bother changing from the last channel and picked up a magazine, instead. She paid no attention to the screen as she flipped through the pages until she caught a few key words.

She sat up and listened to the segment. Those words. They were the same words from another news story, a story she'd watched years ago, the story that changed Sunday's life.

As the news droned on in the background, she reviewed the definition of "consent." She never consented to what her father had done to her. She was simply trained all her life to obey. Her daddy was an authority; he was the adult. Children did not refuse instructions from adults. So she always did as she was told. She would make her bed, she would fold laundry, she vacuumed, she washed dishes, she did her homework, she held the extension cord sometimes for the electric mower, she would "rub his head" whenever he would tell her to, she weeded the garden, painted the garage, mopped the floor, scrubbed the toilets, ironed the clothes when she was told–*all* of it. They were all simply chores, and she did them when she was told to do them. Consent had never played a part in any of her childhood.

For years Sunday attempted to find ways to avoid being alone with Chester, up to and including pretending to be asleep. Nothing, not even a sleeping sister next to her in the very same bed, deterred him from sneaking in at night.

On those nights, he would crawl on his hands and knees into the bedroom–*on his hands and knees*. She would pull the covers tighter over her body, when she felt his hand snaking under the covers to touch her where she didn't want to be touched, acting as if she were still in a her deep slumber. When that didn't work she would shift so that it would be awkward and uncomfortable for him to keep touching her hoping he would give up and crawl away.

It never worked. He would invade until *he* decided when to stop.

There seemed to have been an unspoken agreement that none of the girls talked of his late night visits. Sunday was fairly sure Tuesday was never subjected to them, that she had been spared because she was the baby, the perfect angel. She wasn't a part of any of the scrutiny or the punishment, so she probably escaped Chester's dirty advances, too. *Maybe that's why Momma hovered over her so much. She knew what was happening. Maybe she thought saving Tuesday was good enough.*

Sunday believed Friday never experienced their father's advances because he wasn't a "split-tail," as Chester would refer to the girls on the rare occasion he was in a jovial mood. *He was such an asshole to his own son about everything anyway, it wouldn't make sense that he would humiliate Friday every chance he got for being the way he was, interested in hair and sewing and fashion, and all the other things girls are usually interested in, and then turn around and put him through what we had to deal with.*

Sunday remembered Chester sometimes choosing Friday to stay behind and "rub his head" because of his "sinus headache." For the girls, the excuse was otherwise code for whatever favor Chester decided he wanted after everyone else left. *Still, it doesn't make sense to be so macho, so mean to Friday, and turn around and demand anything like what he makes us do...right?*

She was positive only Wednesday, herself, and Monday were assigned to that chore.

When Chester requested that Sunday be the one to stay behind while the others went out, he would almost immediately command her to follow him into the bedroom. He would ask her to sit in the center of the bed, and lie down beside her. He expected her begin by massage his temples. Sometimes he would fondle her. Sunday was careful not to sit cross-legged, hoping to discourage him. Of course, he was not. Instead, he would tell her exactly how to position herself so he could reach in and take whatever he wanted. Other times, he gradually guided her hands from his temples to wherever he wanted to do whatever he pleased. Sunday hated it, but to disobey was not an option.

Once, however, she did find a way to stop it–at least temporarily. At her limits and desperate to distract him, and every other excuse to leave recycled and worn, when Chester reached for her, a new question popped right out of her mouth: "What time is Momma gettin' home from work?"

Immediately Chester's erection shriveled.

It worked!

After that, she tried to start a conversation with him about her mother every time. She would ask why her momma seemed to hate her so much; why she was mad all the time; what she was planning for his next day off. An effective tactic, a couple of weeks passed before he got wise to her ploy.

"Be quiet now" is what he told her the last time she tried the distraction. He grabbed her hand and pulled it to his penis. "Just be quiet and stroke up and down."

The jig was up.

Sunday recalled the nighttime visits happening a few times a month, and she was held back at the house with Chester at least once a week. She lost count of the number of times; she was constantly being called to satisfy his whims, being touched, groped, and invaded. She could only assume they were the ones required to succumb his urges on the nights he hadn't overtaken her and on the days it was one of them that was called to stay behind instead. The girls didn't talk about what they endured, but she was fairly sure about her assumption.

It seemed so strange now looking back on it from inside that institution, viewing her life like a movie reel on the back wall of her mind. All these pieces fell into place before her eyes. Especially the evening she discovered there were names for what was happening to her and those names were words with true and printed definitions. That moment had truly been the beginning of the end.

. . .

She was twelve at the time, and by that time she liked to tell herself she "had a penchant for vocabulary." In actuality, her sixth-grade English teacher was the one who'd told her so, but "penchant" became her word after that.

Sunday lay on her stomach with her head propped up on her wrists while Friday lay on his back, leaning his head against the couch in front of the TV as the credits for *Night Gallery* scrolled up the screen. June and Wednesday were working the late shift, so as the weekend headline news opener thundered through the speakers, Chester lumbered on to his room. He hated the news. He called Monday in after him to "rub his head." Neither Friday nor Sunday cared about the news either, but *The Twilight Zone* was next, and they never missed an episode.

They stared at the screen as a reporter related the story of a young woman. "…She says she walked in and caught her husband 'fondling' their daughter…"

They cut to the woman on screen, her features blacked out to hide her identity, "He was only playing with her, but I know he shouldn't be playing with her like that. She's just a little girl."

The reporter picked up the story again. "Words from the girl's mother. Her husband is the father of the child…Judgment is pending a court-ordered medical exam. At that time, a determination will be made on whether her husband will be charged with molestation or incest…"

Friday stood up.

Sunday glanced over her shoulder. "Hey! What're you doin'?"

"I'm tired. I'm goin' to bed."

"Aren't you gonna stay up for *Twilight Zone?*"

"No, it's probably a rerun."

Sunday was too distracted to argue.

"Fondle", "molestation", "incest"-all words she never heard before. She worked around the context to try and understand what was happening. What the man had done was obviously against the law, but they didn't say the little girl was in the hospital or that she was hurt or dead. And she was going to have an exam to find out whether these things actually happened to her. They could charge the man with "molestation" or "incest," but not for "fondling." *What does 'fondling' mean? How's that like 'molestation' and 'incest'? I need to look these words up, find out what they mean, and why the mother would be so mad if she walked in and saw it. Why would the mom say, 'She's just a little girl'? Why are these bad words? I mean, FUCK is a bad word. Stabbing and murder, those things are terrible acts. Starved, beaten, all these things I've heard about, but 'molestation', 'incest', 'fondling'...*

She walked into Friday's room, where the Encyclopedia Britannica volumes and the giant Webster's dictionary were kept.

Friday yawned and murmured from his bed in the dark, "What're you doin'?"

"I gotta look up some words."

"For what?"

"Vocabulary."

"You don't have to do homework 'til tomorrow; it's Saturday night."

"I know, but I don't wanna wait if I got time to do my work now."

Sunday pulled the dictionary down off the bookshelf and grabbed a pencil. She darted back out to the living room before Friday could interrogate her any further. She slipped into the kitchen and sat down at the table. The light was still on, so she didn't have to change a thing. *No one should notice me or ask what I'm doing or tell me to stop. If they do, I'll tell 'em I'm just reading.*

She rehearsed her response as she thumbed through the thin sheets of the heavy book. She scanned through the Fs. Her finger skimmed down a page. *Here.*

Fondle: 1. To handle or touch lovingly, affectionately, or tenderly; caress 2. To treat with fond indulgence

Molest: 1. To bother, interfere with or annoy 2. To make indecent sexual advances 3. To assault sexually

Assault? What is assault?

Incest: 1. Sexual intercourse between closely related persons 2. The crime of sexual intercourse, cohabitation, or marriage between persons within the degrees of consanguinity or affinity wherein marriage is legally forbidden

Intercourse? Consang-consang-How do you even pronounce that?

Sunday scribbled the words on a sheet of paper she found folded and crammed into the front cover. *Something is wrong. Something is against the law. The other words...*

She thumbed quickly through the As.

Assault: 1. A sudden, violent attack; onslaught 2. An unlawful physical attack upon another, an attempt or offer to do violence to another, with or without battery, as by holding a stone or club in a threatening manner 3. The stage of close combat in an attack. 4. Rape 5. To make an assault upon; attack; assail

221

Battery. What is the battery used for? Rape. What exactly *is that?*

> Intercourse: 1. Dealings or communication between individuals, groups, countries, etc. 2. Interchange of thoughts, feelings, etc. 3. Sexual relations or a sexual coupling, especially coitus

What is coitus?

> Consanguinity: 1. Relationship by descent from a common ancestor; kinship distinguished from affinity. 2. Close relationship or connection

Sunday didn't want to misinterpret a thing. She turned back to the Bs to check on something.

> Battery: 1. About electricity 2. About a group 3. Military tactic 4. More groups 5. About baseball 6. Navy groups 7. A series of tests 8. the act of beating or battering 9. An unlawful attack upon another person by beating or wounding, or by touching in an offensive manner 10…

None of the rest made sense to her, from what Sunday could tell, so she moved on. With every word read, absorbed, and understood, she forged on to the next, becoming more and more eager to take in the next piece of information, the next clue to her own life.

> Rape: 1. The unlawful compelling of a person through physical force or duress to have sexual intercourse 2. An act of sexual intercourse that is forced upon a person 3. Statutory rape 4. An act of plunder, violent seizure, or… abuse; despoliation; violation 5. The act of seizing and carrying off by force.

What does 'statutory' mean?

Coitus: 1. Sexual intercourse, especially between a man and a woman

Only a few more, and every doubt in Sunday's mind would be flushed from the shadows.

Statutory rape: 1. Sexual intercourse in which at least one person is below the age required to legally consent to the behavior.

Despoliation: 1. The act of plundering 2. The fact or circumstance of being plundered

Plunder. Plunder. Plunder...

Plunder: 1. To rob of goods or valuables by open force, as in war, hostile raids 2. To rob, despoil, or fleece 3. To take wrongfully, as by pillage, robbery, or fraud 4. To take plunder; pillage

And pillage...

Pillage: 1. To strip ruthlessly of money or goods by open violence, as in war; plunder 2. To take as booty
And for final confirmation...

Force: 1. Physical power or strength 2. Strength or power exerted 3. Strength; energy; power; intensity 4. Power to influence, affect, or control 5...18. To compel, constrain, or oblige (oneself or someone) to do something 19....28. to press, urge, or exert (an animal, person, etc) to violent effort 29...30. To rape.

Sunday raised her head from the dictionary, dazed by her revelations, a single word branding itself into the wall of her mind: *Rape.*

I've been raped.

I've been raped.

Oh, my god, I've been raped in so many ways.

I can't even say which definition applies to me most.

I've been raped.

Sunday frantically retraced her steps. *I've been raped.* She read and re-read the words again. *Oh, my god, I've been raped in so many ways.* All these things that had been happening to her, to her sisters, to her brother, all these things possessed names. *I can't say which fits best. I...I...*

They weren't simply "being bad kids" or only "getting a whippin'" or just being "punished."

I've been raped.

Sunday fell back in her chair dumbfounded. Her head swam. *Momma and Daddy, they're the ones who are wrong. They're supposed to be right, and they've been doing this stuff all along... They're supposed to be right, but they've been doing wrong.*

She worked and reworked the pieces so she could be doubly, triply sure that these definitions truly matched up to her history. Self-doubt fueled her frenzy. *All those times they said we deserved to be punished. I'm overreacting. Am I? Am I forcing these words to make them fit? Am I blowing this out of proportion? Is this really happening? Is this the truth?*

There was no room for misunderstandings. She had to be sure.

All that had been happening was against the law. This wasn't a case of two parents taking care of children the best they could. They were committing crimes against their children. They had taken advantage of their innocence.

How much longer is this gonna go on? How does it stop? That little girl on the news–her momma made it stop. How come ours didn't?

Force. That's part of why it's against the law. Maybe I don't understand. Sunday could recall nothing that she and her sisters and brother were not *forced* to do.

She churned through the logic. *There was never a choice. Without choice, it is forced.*

She closed the dictionary. She stared at the list of words she'd scribbled on the sheet of paper. Two hours were gone in the blink of an eye. Someone had turned off the television and the lights in the living room. The house was silent.

She stood and carried the book down the hall, a hall that was somehow different now, and slipped into Friday's room, careful not to disturb him. She slid the dictionary back into its place on the shelf. She tiptoed across the hall into her own room. She eased in under the comforter where Monday burrowed in to sleep.

It is all so different now. Everything has changed.

Sunday lay in bed for hours staring up into the darkness, her mind racing. *These are my parents. Assaulted, battered, raped, and plundered by the two people who shelter, clothe, and feed me. No. The truth is they are criminals.*

Chester and June were constantly praised for the results of their abuse: "Oh, your children are so well behaved." "How in the world do you manage the five of them so gracefully?" "They're so polite…so respectful."

Who's gonna believe me? A nice home…Clean, well-behaved children who make good grades…Both parents hard working and well liked for the most part…No one knows why we're the weird ones. They all just leave us alone.

Bigger questions surfaced, but those too were different now. *Do Momma and Daddy even love us?*

Sunday and her sisters and brother spent all their years begging, pleading, asking their parents to love them.

Is this love? Can't be. How am I gonna tell Friday that Momma doesn't love him? How am I gonna tell Wednesday that Daddy doesn't love her? We're only here to do whatever they want, for their satisfaction. That's all.

They were questions that were still too new to her.

No, that won't work. I can't talk to anyone about this. Friday was there, but he left. He doesn't want to know. The rest won't understand, and they wouldn't believe me anyway. We have been prisoners. We have been in bondage. We have been slaves...

This is the infection in this house.

This is my life according to Webster. It is the truth.

It is an infection. It's not going to get better.

Still no concrete plan existed for what to do with this information, these words and their definitions, her revelations. She rolled herself up and surrendered to an uneasy sleep.

For weeks on end, the news story relentlessly played in her mind. She imagined that lucky little girl in her mother's embrace. *Her momma loved her little girl, and she stopped her daddy. Her momma was the one who stopped it.*

Sunday knew their momma would never do the same for them. She would never want anyone to find out. Ever. These secrets would bring shame to the Minor name. And she was sure no one would believe her if she were the one to tell anyway. *That little girl's momma was old enough to tell. If I told, Momma and Daddy would say nothing happened. They'd say I was crazy. They would send me to reform school, to the nuthouse. They'd whip me over and over until it was time to send me there.*

Her thoughts swirled around memories of the day that stranger, the First Lady, appeared in the good living room, on the good couch, so long ago. Wednesday let her in. And it was then that Sunday made the connection. She finally understood what Wednesday said they couldn't talk about. She also understood why they couldn't talk about it. *No one would ever believe us.*

Even if they did, there was nothing they could do–not in time anyway. The First Lady told Wednesday things didn't work that way. They couldn't just swoop in and save them all. Sunday wavered back and forth on whether to share her research with her sister, always arriving at the same conclusion. *I can't talk to her. That's the thing. That's exactly it. These words and definitions and all the things that have happened to us–they're all exactly what we couldn't talk about that day, and we can't talk about it now. If we talk about it, we'll really be in trouble. Momma and Daddy would finally realize that* we *know what they're doing. And we know they're wrong.*

For a brief moment, she thought maybe the only way out of this was to end her own life, and quickly dismissed by a primal urge to survive.

She kept quiet.

But the secret swelled up inside her chest and in her mind, filling her with anxiety, with a sense of helpless injustice. It also seeped into her well of fear. Her fear of not being perfect was abruptly replaced with a fear of what would happen if her parents caught any glimmer of the truth in her eye. Her mere awareness that everything they were doing was wrong would threaten everything they'd built, and she was petrified they would do whatever it took to eliminate the threat. *No. I can't say they would want to kill me because they'd be in trouble for that, but they would have to take steps to make me…incredible. Not the first definition. Not astonishing or extraordinary. Incredible…as in unbelievable.*

. . .

After that night with her dictionary, Sunday remembered each time the buckle swung through the air, she closed her eyes to mask the truth screaming in her mind. *This is against the law.*

Each time the punishment was finished, she searched their faces for any clue they knew what she knew. *They could lock me up. Or I'll accidentally fall down some stairs. Or accidentally hit my head and become retarded. It'd be easy to quiet me forever. I'll be a vegetable.*

There had been no doubt in her mind they would do whatever was necessary to keep this from coming out.

Over the months that followed, Sunday found herself keeping score. *She's not supposed to do that. He's not allowed to do that.* And each time her own inner voice mocked her in return. *Well... what are you gonna do about it?*

Four More

FOUR MORE YEARS would pass before she finally answered that question.

Sunday flashed through her memories enduring life as a Minor, pausing on the most visible cracks in their very foundation.

June had walked in on them once. Their backs were to her. Wednesday was standing with her pants down next to Chester while he sat in his living room chair. *Momma knew what was going on.* Her momma's horrible gasp is what caused her to pretend to need something from in the kitchen. She passed by the scene in time to capture Wednesday flushed with shame, hurrying to pull her pants up, and Chester weakly offering an excuse. "What the hell's the big deal? I got a sinus headache. She's just rubbin' my head." *Momma didn't do anything to stop him. In fact, she took it out on us.*

The Minor kids changed during those years, too. They grew into themselves, and found their voices, and as best they could, they came into their own.

Wednesday preferred dating black boys, mostly because she was seeking something–anything–as different from the life they led as she could find, Sunday guessed. She thought there was probably something about the way it pissed their daddy off, too. Maybe she kept him away from her that way, like Sunday did talking about their momma. *I dunno.*

Monday got into more and more fights at school. To avoid their parents' wrath, she begged the principal to call Sunday instead of them.

All of them got jobs–Friday got two and joined every club at school that would have him to keep himself away from the house as much as possible.

June continued to spiral downward over those years with the kids being around less and less and outside of the house more and more. She couldn't keep an eye on them, couldn't control them, or punish them–not like she used to. She lost herself in rage almost every time she was alone with them and bore down on them harder and harder.

Sunday guessed Wednesday turning up pregnant just after she turned fourteen was probably the widest crack. Chester and June sent her away with some cover story about being sick. Sunday only found out the truth when the girls at school started calling the Minor girls sluts. The last time, both she *and* Monday took the wenches down in the schoolyard. Mid-scuffle, one of the beat-up girls scurried to rifle through her book bag before waiving the proof like a white flag: a handwritten letter from Wednesday herself with a return address of St. Gerard Majella, the school where they sent pregnant girls before they started showing. *They all lied to us. We looked like fools for defending ourselves.*

Sunday had stomped through the house and, like a grenade, dropped the letter on top of the *Prevention* magazine her momma was reading at the dining table. The Minor house blew up. The fight ended with June falling, writhing on the floor, her fallback theatrics when things got to be too much, she was backed into a corner, and there was nothing left for her to say.

Shortly after that, they moved from their dead end on Rock Knoll to a trailer house out in the sticks. June pled with Chester, saying the move was the only way to save their good name. What finally convinced him was the promise of a *four*-car detached shop for his collection of cars.

• • •

After her evening of poring over the dictionary and the thought of suicide had initially crossed her mind, Sunday returned to the idea of a more "permanent" solution four more times.

The first time came a few months later. She'd been alone in her room trying to concentrate on the word problems in front of her. She couldn't, so distracted was she by the constant drone of that news story. *I can't pretend. I can fly away, but I have to go back at some point. Running away just means someone else is going to get in trouble. There's no other way to stop this. They're not gonna stop, and they're gonna figure out I know what they're doing is wrong. And then they're gonna end me.*

Twelve-year-old Sunday flipped to the next clean lined sheet in her spiral notebook. She didn't want to implicate Friday and Monday, but she needed them to know the truth. She carefully printed:

To Whom It May Concern:

I don't want to be here anymore. I'm sorry I can't take it. You've got to find a way to get out, too.

Your sister,
Sunday

They'll know I'm talking to them…How am I gonna do this anyway? Sunday didn't know much about death or how it could occur. She closed the spiral notebook.

The second time came the following day while she was walking to school. She eyed the passing traffic, and thought about the note again. She considered that being run over by a car might be a good way to go–an accident. Nobody's fault. *Ohhh, that'll hurt really bad, though. And I might not die.*

She walked around with that spiral for a long time. She never thought about actually killing herself again while she carried it, but there was a sense of safety in keeping the note, sort of comforting–if things really got totally unbearable, she already had it written. One less thing to worry about. Although on other pages, she began doodling 2-D headstones marked "R.I.P." like the ones in the black-and-white horror movies on T.V., she never went back to that letter. It was enough to know the words were written there.

She was required to hand in the notebook at the end of each week for a homework grade, but if her teacher ever saw those words, she never said anything to Sunday. At the end of the school year, the spiral was thrown out.

The notion of suicide resurfaced again two years later. The Minors had moved to Bourne, leaving everyone they knew behind. The distance among the Minor kids had already grown wide. And Wednesday had a child to care for now.

Sunday was tired. Tired of school and work and not being happy anywhere, having no one to talk to. Isolation had gotten the better of her. *When we were little, we had each other.*

The real catalyst, though, was when Wednesday tried to run Sunday over with her car. Wednesday got that silver land yacht because she had a child, she needed the room, and she had to be available whenever the demands of motherhood called. Wednesday also had new modern clothes she paid for with part of the money she got to keep to care for the baby, not the hand-me-downs Sunday had to choose from. Sunday would sneak them after she'd left in the mornings

Sunday was walking to the bus stop in her sister's brand new skirt and a pair of platforms. The long flowing maxi was crocheted with a bit of silvery thread, and it made Sunday feel pretty. They'd already fought a number of times about her borrowing Wednesday's clothes. Their eyes met on that street, and Wednesday swerved across the lane and up onto the sidewalk. Sunday leapt out of the way and rolled off the platform and onto her ankle dropping her instantly to the ground just as the front left tire wheeled over her foot. She let out a howl, and her sister drove away. She got up and hobbled on. For the better part of the day, the ache in her heart eclipsed the throbbing in her foot, but when she sat down in the office at The Bon Temp to finish her homework before the start of her shift, she couldn't ignore it any longer. *I don't get to do anything I want to – only what I have to. Adult things. I'm not an adult. I don't wanna be an adult. They work all day; they do chores; they sleep; and then they do it all over again…God! Wednesday tried to kill me. I can't be here anymore.*

Barely able to see through the blur of tears that would no longer be held back, she turned to a new page in a new spiral notebook and feverishly scribbled what she thought should be her last words:

To Whom It May Concern:

I just don't want to do it anymore. Get up at 6 o'clock in the morning. Go to school. She tries to run over me. I take the bus to school. Go to work, and do my homework at work before I have to work. Get off at 2 o'clock in the morning. Do it all over again. I don't want to live like this. If this is the way life is supposed to be, I don't want it.

Sincerely,
Sunday Minor

She spent the next 24 hours thinking about how to end it. *I could swallow a bunch of Aspirin.* Of course, Sunday hadn't been exposed to any kind of pills other than the little white tablets in her medicine cabinet at home–*Jennifer took a bunch of pills in* Valley of the Dolls *and it worked. I would just go to sleep, and never wake up.* She figured all pills ought to have the same effect if you took enough of them.

During the next 24 hours she must've opened that medicine cabinet fifty-two times, closing it again when the voice in her head shamed her for thinking about taking the easy way out. *What good would it do? You gonna leave Friday and Monday here to survive on*

233

THE TRUTH ABOUT SUNDAY MINOR

their own? You're never gonna do it. You're a coward for wanting to die. And a coward for never being able to go through with it.

The next morning, Sunday awoke, went straight to the page in her notebook, and ripped out the letter. She wadded it up, stuffed it in the garbage under last night's scraps, and bagged up the trash so no one would find it.

That was the last time that suicide seemed the best option before she truly made her break.

. . .

And four more weeks of enduring life at Rose Village would pass before she was called to Dr. Faus's office again.

"Sunday, please, come sit." He seemed distracted. "I have some news to share with you. We believe you have been–" The phone rang. He glanced down nervously at the blinking line before continuing again. "You have been cured. You are exhibiting no signs of causing harm to yourself any longer, and are eligible for release." The phone stopped ringing, and Dr. Faus sighed. "There are conditions, however. We've determined your regimen of Thorazine is the key factor to the great strides you've made toward improving your mental health in such a short time."

What? Great strides? I'm cured? How?

Even though she was ready to leave months earlier–she certainly recognized she didn't belong there–she didn't feel any different, just numb and tired from the Thorazine. She wasn't normal yet. *This? This is what normal is? Being doped up for the rest of my life?*

If Dr. Faus gleaned any sense of confusion from Sunday's expression, he ignored that, too. "Now, upon the condition that you agree to continue this pharmaceutical therapy, we will arrange for your release in the morning. Is this agreeable to you?"

Sunday said nothing.

He seemed pleased. "We'll need you to come by here again

in the morning to sign off on paperwork. We'll call your foster parents afterward, and you'll be on your way."

As she made her way back to the common area, images of her first day in the holding tank–the handsome older man, glazed over the same way her momma was after she swallowed those mothballs, the obese naked woman lumbering toward her, the maniacal Asian man hiding behind that column–flashed through her mind. *Momma's the one who should have been sent here. It's her that needs these drugs, not me.*

Mothballs

N OT A SINGLE word. That's how much June said to Sunday the entire time they were there in her mother's hospital room.

Nobody knew exactly how many mothballs June had swallowed the night before–or why. June and Wednesday were arguing when Sunday left for school the previous morning, but anything could set her mother off, and at that point, Sunday simply made sure she wasn't involved.

Only forty-five minutes into Sunday's shift that evening, Wednesday called up to the restaurant, The Bon Temp, where all the Minor kids and their momma worked at least part of the time. They opened at 5 o'clock and closed at ten, but shifts started an hour before, and nobody left until the last dish was dry, which was usually around two in the morning. It was way too early to get a call from anyone from home.

Sunday was the garnish girl, and that night she'd already started soaking the lettuce and was slicing apples for her cart when the manager approached her in the kitchen. "Sunday, Wednesday's on the phone. She wants to talk to you."

"Okay. I'm sorry."

"That's all right. You can take the call in my office."

Sunday was embarrassed by the interruption. Wednesday didn't call her at work. None of them made phone calls during their shifts–work was work. She stepped into the office and pushed the door half-closed before picking up the receiver. "Hello?"

"Momma wants you to come home."

"Wednesday, I have to work. I'm gonna get fired."

"No, you have to come home now."

"Well, Daddy's gonna get mad if I get f–"

"No, you getcher ass home. You need to get home."

"All right. Jeez."

Sunday hung up and stepped out of the office. "I'm sorry, I have to go home for a minute. I'll be right back."

Sunday headed out. She never even took her apron off.

The call didn't make sense, but Sunday couldn't say she wasn't coming. June had never called her away from work before. Their jobs, and the money they brought in were about the only things that came before discipline on June's list of priorities in those days. *That, or chocolate cake with a slice of butter on top. So disgusting.* Each of the Minor kids had to make sure to put in their hours so there was enough money in their paychecks to cover one bill per person each month. And though none of them ever saw a dime of it, the rest went straight into their savings accounts. Chester and June said it was for college.

A half-mile walk down the hill, and a left turn into the mobile home park in Bourne (where they'd moved to a year earlier "to get away from it all"), and she was home. She trotted up the front steps. Her sister swung the door open, and stood aside to let Sunday past.

"She's in our room."

From the bedroom doorway she evaluated her mother curled up in Wednesday's bed, fists clenched against her stomach. The woman didn't say anything, but fat tears were streaming down her grimacing face.

"I caught 'er scarfing down mothballs."

The girls couldn't take their eyes off their mother.

"I stuck my finger down 'er throat to make 'er throw up, but I might not've gotten 'em all out."

They talked like she wasn't there, staring up at them, understanding every word.

Sunday didn't take her eyes off the woman. "Did you call an ambulance?"

"No."

She shot back at Wednesday, "Why not?"

"Do you think we should?"

"What else are we gonna do?"

Wednesday made the call, and Chester drove up as the paramedics closed the ambulance doors. He threw the car into reverse and backed out again. The ambulance sirens screamed as both vehicles raced back down the street.

Sunday wasn't sticking around for her daddy to get home from the hospital; for that, she was sure they'd all find some way to blame her. So she walked back to work.

The return trip was about five times longer than the walk there. *Why would Momma want me there in the first place?*

Deep down, the answer churned in the pit of her stomach. Her momma wanted her to see just what she'd done to her, what she'd driven her to do.

Sunday floated through the next few hours, going through the motions while playing out the hundred scenarios that might lie ahead for her when the shift was finally over. The clock struck two, and the lights went out. Sunday stepped out the back door. Friday was there waiting by the dumpster.

Sunday asked, "Why didn't you go home yet?"

News traveled fast among the Minors, and no doubt he was as terrified of facing the trip home as she was. It was only a matter of time before one of them ended up dead.

"I thought I'd wait for you." Then Friday said what she'd been thinking all night. "We can't go home. Ever."

Running away wasn't a novel idea. They'd imagined how a hundred different ways, and had even tried with no luck. They still returned to the plan time and again. Tonight was no different. They stood there behind the restaurant practically frozen in what they were never more sure would be their last few moments on earth.

Wednesday came peeling into the parking lot, and screeched to a halt about two inches in front of her sister and brother. She was pissed.

She swung open the door and jumped out of the car. "What the hell is going on?"

She sounded exactly like June. She stomped to the front of the car. "I'm stuck at the house waitin' on Daddy while you two are sittin' here shootin' the shit in the dark?"

Friday put his hand on her shoulder and cocked his head to the side, like he did when he was trying to calm one of them down. "Hey, hey, now. We're just tryin' to figure out what we're gonna do."

"What do you mean?"

"Listen, we can't go home. You shouldn't either."

"Where do you think we're gonna go? There's nobody. There's nothing."

"I don't know, but we're not going home."

"Oh, yes, you are!"

Wednesday grabbed her sister by the arm with a mind to drag her back to the car. "You. You aren't going anywhere but home. You started this shit. You're gonna be there to get what's coming."

She yanked her arm from Wednesday's clutch, and as her sister lunged forward again, Friday stepped between them, shoving Sunday out of reach. He grabbed Wednesday's hand and squeezed.

Wednesday whispered, "What's Daddy gonna do when he gets home?"

She shuddered and admitted their daddy called and told her to pick them up. That was the real reason she was there. They talked in hushed voices a while longer. They couldn't figure out why their momma would swallow mothballs in the first place, and who was to blame. Because whoever that was would get it–bad. Wednesday was the "perfect" one and old enough to be on her way out of the house anyway, so this was in no way her fault. Friday was Momma's favorite, so obviously it couldn't be something he did. Monday wasn't even around for the blowup that morning, and Tuesday, well, she never was a part of anything. Sunday didn't say it, but they all nodded in silent agreement.

It's my fault somehow.

They also talked about where they could go. Uncle Vernon no longer visited, so they couldn't just drop in on *him*. Plus, the Uncle Vernon idea hadn't panned out the first time. They had no one to turn to, and nowhere to go. None of them wanted to go back. They agreed they would go together. They loaded into the car and crawled home.

They sat waiting in the living room with the lights off. The moonlight through the shears cast thick shadows that seemed to grow larger around them until they almost swallowed them whole. Waiting there in the darkness, Sunday replayed every moment of that day in her mind. What could she possibly have done to cause her mother to swallow an entire packet of mothballs? The anxiety pressed her deeper and deeper into the couch until finally, the first rumble of Chester's engine slow and low, dissolved it.

Feelings of relief that the waiting was over and fear of what was to come tumbled in the atmosphere around her.

Sunday and the others ignored the impulse to greet him at the door. Embarrassing the family with an altercation in front of the neighbors was out of the question. No one moved a muscle.

What Chester did next was worse than any of the five million things Sunday thought up between walking back to work that evening and the instant he set foot in the trailer.

He opened the front door with his head down and shoulders slumped. He walked past his children to the dining table and leaned all his weight on his stiff, straight arms, head hung, shaking slowly side-to-side.

"She had her stomach pumped. She'll get out tomorrow."

He turned. He eyed Wednesday. He stared at Friday a moment. Then he locked eyes with Sunday. Then...

Nothing.

Resignation.

He's not angry. He's not hurt.

He's just given up.

241

His quietude only increased Sunday's shear panic. She'd never seen this kind of muted unease from him before. Not even when Friday had beaten him at his own game that afternoon before they'd run away for the first time. He'd retreated that day, but he did not resign. This was different.

He eased into the couch next to Wednesday. Sunday's thoughts were reeling. *Is she gonna die? Suicide is against the law. Or worse, is she gonna live?*

She pictured Pandora's Box cracking open, the Minors' secrets billowing out like dark clouds.

Now the secret is out. People will know. The house we live in is wrong. Everything is wrong. So wrong that Momma tried to kill herself.

Sunday couldn't stomach the silence anymore. She stood up. "I'm leaving."

Wednesday shot up. "No, you can't leave. You're only fifteen. I'm leaving. I'm joining the Navy."

Chester spoke. "Your momma's in the hospital. Everybody needs to go to bed. We'll talk about this later."

Friday and Sunday stood on command, and walked to their separate rooms.

Sunday slipped between her sheets, her mind still swimming. *He drove behind the ambulance with Momma. He was by himself when he got home. What happened there? Why is he acting this way? If Momma becomes an invalid, life's gonna be bad. Horrible. I'm not stayin' here to see what that means. If she's a cripple, somebody's gonna be blamed, and that somebody's gonna be me. Where's it gonna come from first? If Daddy has to take care of her, there's never gonna be a time he's not mad. If one of us has to take care of her, we'll never get anything right. If she's crippled we won't even have a chance to prove we're good kids. She'll be a constant reminder of what we did to her, what we drove her to do. We caused it. I caused it. Or else, there'll be nothing to protect us. At least now, Momma has some things she doesn't want him to know about…like the belt buckle…And Daddy. He has things he doesn't want her to know about, too. If she's crippled, there's no reason to hide any of it anymore. She wouldn't be able to do anything about it anyway. There'll be nothing standing in the way of him coming at us, wanting sex or some form of it.*

Wednesday stayed there in the living room with Chester. Sunday listened to them murmuring until she fell into a tumultuous sleep.

The following morning, Sunday awoke with a throbbing headache. She'd tossed and turned all night. She was feeling a little sick to her stomach, in fact. She ignored both and got out of bed. They went through the motions that day: brush teeth, comb hair, get dressed, make breakfast, eat breakfast, clear table, wash dishes, clean counters, sweep and mop. They passed through their routine in silence, save a "breakfast in two minutes" or a "bring me the plates."

They stood in regular formation in front of Chester, who was still sitting at the table staring off into space as the hour approached ten.

"I gotta pick up your momma before noon. Sunday's gonna go with me. Be back in a little while."

Why me?

Chester stood, grabbed his keys, which were still sitting on the table where he left them the night before, and opened the door. Sunday followed him out into a beautiful day. The sun warmed her skin. She took a deep breath before her mind could remind her body, *There's nothing to be happy about today.*

June was in the Methodist Hospital. The medical center was a ways out from Bourne, and the weight of anxiety from the silence between she and her father was compounded by what needed to be said next. *No more waiting.* As soon as they turned onto an open hill country road, she said it: "I want out."

"Wha'd'you mean you want out?"

"I want out of the family."

Chester chewed his upper lip with his bottom teeth, then he nodded. "What'll you do?"

Sunday was shocked he didn't try to talk her out of leaving. He'd held his resignation through the night. *Maybe he thinks this is his chance. Maybe he thinks if he just lets me leave, things could blow over...*

"Well? Where will you go?"

"I'm pretty sure I can stay with my friend Sarah," Sunday lied. She wasn't sure of anything yet.

"What are your plans then with school and whatnot?"

"I'm gonna stay in school, and finish, and I'm gonna keep my job at the restaurant."

Chester made no other comment, and that was okay with Sunday.

Chester parked the car across from the hospital entrance, and the two walked in. He checked with a woman at the front desk, and she told them where to go. They followed her down to the elevator, and she hit the button for floor number five before waving as the door closed. Sunday followed her father out of the elevator and down a short hall, and made a right. They passed four or five rooms and turned, and they found themselves standing in the doorway of her momma's room.

The space was semi-private, set up for two people, but there were no personal things on the bedside table, and the other bed was still made up. There were no flowers. There were no cards. There were no suitcases. There were no bags, except for the two little plastic baggies sitting on the floor at the foot of her bed, each holding a plastic cup and a plastic pitcher; Sunday supposed the gifts were June's consolation prize.

June sat on the far edge of the second bed, staring out the wall-length picture window that overlooked a row of perfectly landscaped treetops set against a clear blue sky.

"Hello, Momma."

Silence.

"How do you feel?"

No response.

June sat there, glazed over, not a flutter of an eyelash, staring out the window. Sunday didn't bother trying to communicate anything else the rest of the time they were there.

"I'm going to see the nurse about signing some papers," said Chester. "Then I'll bring the car around."

Sunday didn't take her eyes off her momma as she nodded okay.

Sunday never went all the way into the room. She straddled the threshold, her ears tuned to the nurses' station and her eyes trained on June.

She glanced over to see her daddy leaning on the counter, his back turned to her and his head resting on a curled up fist, staring down at the sterilized Formica surface.

Sunday scanned the hospital room for any sign of change.

Satisfied her momma wasn't preparing to go ape shit on her, she glanced back to the nurses' station a second time. She studied the nurse Chester was speaking with, a middle-aged woman with more salt than pepper hair. Not more than a few laugh lines. *She's pretty. She's wearing those weird moon shoes nurses do.*

Sunday shifted her attention back to the room. June still hadn't moved a muscle, so Sunday focused on the nurses' station again. The nurse shifted her gaze up from her clipboard to Chester's face every minute or so. She spoke to him in a tone a grownup uses with a toddler, like she knew he didn't entirely understand what she was saying.

Chester seemed to bob his head at the wrong times, like he wasn't listening, as if he just wanted her to hurry up and be finished.

Sunday's gaze fell back to her mother before turning to the station again.

Chester lifted his head and straightened up. He was speaking too low for Sunday to understand his words. Her stomach wrenched. *What's happening? What're they whisperin' about? Are they talking about me? Is he telling her what I've done to drive my mother to this?* She frantically inventoried the week's events over and over again in her head, trying to match one of them to the final scene, until the last flash of the ambulance lights at the end of her block. Nothing fit.

She cast an eye over her mother's body, assessing the damage–*What do mothballs do to you inside? Is she gonna be like this for the rest of her life? What have I done?*–and predicting the future–*She's gonna blow...She's gonna blow up on one of us... all of us.*

Sunday had never seen either of her parents like this before. She couldn't tell which direction trouble was going to come from first.

Chester nodded once more, and inhaled until his chest barreled wide. Sunday's whole body clenched bracing herself for an explosion. *This is it.*

Then...same as the night before...nothing.

He walked past the nurse and down the hall toward the elevator. He never even so much as glanced back at his daughter, still balancing on the threshold of her mother's room, lodged between what had happened and what was to come.

The nurse rolled a wheelchair out from the room next to them and into June's, confirming Sunday's worst fear. *Oh, my god, she's crippled. She can't even walk.*

The nurse bent and struggled to press down the metal foot pedals. She stamped them into place with her foot and rolled the chair to the edge of the bed.

"June, honey, we're gonna need you to stand up, please."

June stood.

Thank god. She's not crippled. She can at least walk.

"Come on over and have a seat in this chair. We're gonna help you down to the car. Time to go home now and get some more rest."

246

June shuffled over, stopped in front of the chair, and blankly stared down at the maroon leather seat.

"Go ahead, dear, and take a seat."

She turned and sat. She moved like a robot, carrying out only the orders she was given. The nurse bent down and placed each of June's feet up on a pedal. Chester stepped back into the room, and searched the room for anything they needed to bring with them. He picked up the wrapped cup and pitcher, and the four of them headed back down to the car.

They must be waiting until we're alone.

June's voice rang in her head…*"You know, your daddy never wanted you. He asked me to get an abortion. Here, have a tuna sandwich." That's why I'm here. They're gonna kill me. This is it. I'm the one that's not going home. It would be too easy for them to end it all right now. They'll report me as a runaway. And with all the others still there, no one would even notice I'm gone.*

The nurse wheeled June out of the Emergency Room doors and around the back of the car to the passenger side. Sunday follow them, then slipped into the back seat behind her mother. They rode all the way home without saying a word.

As soon as they pulled into the driveway, June floated out of the car, somehow no longer needing instruction. She glided through the front door. Her children and husband stared in silence as she floated straight to her room and close the door behind her.

The Minors walked on eggshells the rest of the afternoon, talking in whispers about anything but her. When dinner and chores were done, Sunday was left in her room to her own thoughts.

Why me? Wednesday calling me home, Momma calling me when Wednesday was already there, the school always calling me in to ask why Monday gets into fights, Friday choosing me to run away with, Daddy choosing me to get Momma from the hospital. What could I possibly do at eight, at eleven, at sixteen to help?

And why haven't they ended it yet? They've got to be able to tell I know the truth about everything by now, right? Why hasn't he said anything? Why hasn't she *said anything? When is she gonna blow?*

Little did Sunday know, she would never see her mother walk out of that bedroom again.

Cakewalk

THE LAST DAY Sunday ever woke up under the Minor roof began normally enough–except for the silence. Not a peep was heard from June the whole night and on into the morning. The hush was deafening, more terrifying than any crying, screaming, or fighting ever were. June still had not emerged from self-exile. Sunday was glad to be on her way out the door.

At the bus stop, Friday quipped, "Well, I'm gonna be Momma for Halloween."

Monday snickered. "How? You gonna wear one of her dresses?"

"No. I'm gonna be a zombie."

The three burst into laughter. Sunday needed that.

Still, the question buoyed just below the surface no matter how she tried to drown it with distractions. *When is she gonna blow?*

In front of the school, Sunday leaned into her sister with a final request. "All right, listen. Don't fight with anybody today, okay?"

"Well, if they don't make me mad," Monday said, butting her sister's forehead playfully, "I don't have to fight anybody."

They chuckled.

"Yeah, but don't get mad like Momma, okay?"

"I'm not like Momma."

The three headed their separate ways.

The whole day Sunday was unable to focus. Teachers' voices sounded like far-off echoes. The few friends she knew, if they were around, didn't seek her out that day.

Between bells, she drifted down the halls and into the next classes. No one spoke to her; no teacher called her name.

Rather, Sunday was fixed there on that clean white door to her mother's room, closed, locked, no sound coming out for what seemed like eons already. *She's in there…saving up for me—all her rage bubbling, growing, and expanding like the gasses of red giants.*

"…Red Giants…" Sunday heard the words repeated at the front of her science class.

Every counter will have some mark I missed; every meal I cook will not be good enough; every clock will point out I'm late. As long as Daddy's around, you will hold your temper tight. You will stay the poor, helpless victim. You will need everything. You will lay the back of your hand against your forehead. You will stay broken and overwhelmed. But I see you. I know you'll stop expanding. The only thing you can do to me that hasn't already been done is kill me. And when Daddy's gone. Boom. You will explode. Just like a red giant.

The final bell rang.

Sunday paced to the bus stop trying to imagine what a red giant exploding really looks like, what it feels like–*Shit! My math book!*

She raced back to her locker, powered through the combination, slipped the book under her arm, slammed the locker shut, and ran.

The bus stop was empty. Only those who were waiting for their parents were left. She threw her hands up. *Oh, god. I've done it.*

She spiraled downward into her feet, where her fate rooted around her ankles and between her toes. *This will be the thing. The end of me. I missed the bus. I can't do this.*

She was petrified. Her eyes darted from face to face probing for an out. *Sarah and Wendy!* Snap. The same answer to a question posed for the first time four years ago hit her with a force she couldn't ignore anymore. *I'm not going back.*

Sarah and Wendy weaved toward her. Sarah grabbed her shoulder. "Sunday, what's wrong with you?"

Sunday whispered, "I missed the bus."

"You missed the bus?"

"I missed the bus." Sunday didn't realize she was shaking her head until she was forced to nod. "I have to go to work. And I missed the bus."

"It's okay, you can ride with me. C'mon, let's call my mom."

Yes. Okay. This will work. I can do this. Sunday kept nodding. Sarah led her by the arm while she searched the ground for a plan.

In the office, Sarah waited for the call to connect then said, "Hi, mom, it's me. Sunday needs a ride…No, she's late for work… The Bon Temp. Can you drop her off?"–Sarah cupped her hand over the receiver–"Do you need to go home and change?"

"No. I don't live there anymore."

Sarah eyed her suspiciously while she spoke into the phone. "No. All she needs is to be dropped at the restaurant."

Back at the curb, Sarah cocked her head inquisitively, then decided not to speak. Sunday was relieved she didn't.

The blue pick-up pulled up to the curb, and Sarah's mom, Grace, hollered, "Hey, girls, hop in!"

As she pulled into the street, Grace asked again with a wide grin, "Don't you need to go home and change?"

"No, I don't live there anymore."

"What?"

Sunday repeated what she'd said, only this time a little louder, knowing full well the volume of her voice wasn't the problem. "I'm not gonna live with my family anymore."

"What do you mean you're not gonna live with your family anymore?"

"They'll kill me."

"What? Oh…" Grace's pitch rose with every word. "Well, uh, I-dunno-what-to-do-what-can-I-do…I can't take you to my house because you'd be a runaway, and, well, I'd have to report you."

"That's okay. I'm not going home."

Grace glanced from the road to Sunday and back again. "Honey, please, can't we at least go by there to see what's going on?"

"No. We can't go by there."

Grace searched for a way around this roadblock. "Well, I have to call Mickey to sort this out. I just don't know what I need to do."

That was fine by Sunday. She trusted Grace and Mickey St. Christopher well enough to find out what to do next. That sounded like some kind of plan at least. She could wait her turn, review her options, and make her move. She was sure of three things: *These grownups haven't hurt me. I can trust them to give me my choices. I can choose whichever move I want because any option will be better than going home. And that's it. I will never go back.*

At the last icehouse outside of Bourne, Grace stood in front of the payphone, shaking her head, talking fast between silences left for the advice Mickey offered up on the other end.

Sunday's eyes wandered to a fruit stand across the way. She watched a girl, too young for school, smiling up at her sweet mother. They were sitting next to each other behind carefully laid baskets of fat brown pecans and big orange woven bags filled with grapefruit. They were talking probably about what a wonderful weekend they had. They reminded Sunday of Sarah and Grace. They looked at each other the same way. She saw that look the first time Grace offered her a ride home. And she perceived the same connection again on her sixteenth birthday only a couple weeks back.

Sarah had invited her and Wendy to sleep over. Sunday lied to her momma and daddy when she asked to go. She told them that she and the girls were lab partners in a science project. They would be working all night on the assignment because it was due in two days. Sunday was afraid they'd see right through her lie, although if they did, they never let on.

They didn't mention her birthday, anyway. In fact, outside of the year her mother gifted her new turtlenecks and tights after her father had beaten the life out of her because of the one-inch pen mark on his bedspread and the periodic reminder she should have been aborted, her parents scarcely ever mentioned Sunday's birthday.

After a dip in the St. Christophers' heated pool, Grace came calling for them to come in to help with dinner. As the girls each stood at their stations Grace came to them one at a time beaming over their shoulders and offering up compliments, "Sunday, those cucumbers are sliced perfectly! I was sure this was the job for you."

That same exchange between the girl and her mother at the fruit stand happened when Grace turned to Sarah. Sunday didn't recall what sweet thing Grace said to her daughter. She was fixed on the unspoken words that passed between them instead, her heart aching for the same connection.

Sunday thought about what living there with Grace and Mickey might be like, what it would feel like if they were her real parents.

Grace hung up the payphone and walked back with a touch of relief evident on her face. She swung open the truck, pulled herself up, and slammed the door.

"Okay. You have two choices."

"Yes, ma'am."

"Either I can take you home and you can call the police if you get into trouble, and you need help…or I can take you to the sheriff's department and you can turn yourself in as a runaway."

"It's gonna have to be the sheriff's department."

Graced sighed. "Okay…but you understand…this has got to be your decision. And you can't just walk away from this, Sunday.

You've gotta state your case. You gotta tell 'em why you're not going home. It wouldn't work for you to be named a runaway. You can't just disappear."

"I can do that."

Sunday was caught off guard when Grace turned a block early onto Wendy's street. She pulled into her friend's driveway and threw the gearshift into park.

"Sunday, let's go on in here. I asked Mickey to meet us so we can figure this out together. You need to call your parents and tell them what's going on."

Sunday examined the pieces in front of her, contemplating her next move. *Should I talk to Friday first? No, I can't drag him into this. He'll only try and talk me out of leaving anyway. No matter what she does to him, he loves her. Daddy's the one he hates so much. Is he gonna hate me for this? He can't help but stick up for Momma. He's gonna tell me we can handle it. Tell me, "That's just Momma." Tell me, "We're only gonna be here for a little while longer." I don't want anyone to talk me out of this. I don't want to get anyone in trouble. I don't want anyone to get involved. Not anyone from the inside. Not this time.*

She nodded. *Okay, this will work. If we're here, and Momma and Daddy show up, we're only a block away. I'll need to get from here to there in…in…how long will it take me? …I'll make a run for it. All I gotta do is get to the sheriff's before they get to me. I can do this. I'm only a block away. I can do this.*

"I can do that."

Mickey met them at the door. He took hold of Grace's shoulders, kissed her on the cheek, and they nodded. He nodded to Sunday, lifting her heart a fraction of an inch. A sliver of encouragement, at least. As they walked into the living room, Mickey repeated Grace's instruction calmly, "You're gonna need to call your parents and tell them what's going on."

Sunday nodded, and he handed her the receiver.

"Maybe we won't need to go the sheriff at all."

The image of an exploding red giant flashed in Sunday's mind. *You have no idea.*

Sunday dialed the number. Relief buzzed in her temples when her daddy picked up. *It'll be easier to talk to him.*

"Hello?" Chester huffed on the other end.

"Daddy, it's me. I'm not coming home."

He paused.

"Wha'dyou mean?"

She knew he knew what she meant.

"I mean I can't live there anymore."

"You can't *live* here anymore, huh?"

"No, I told you on the way to the hosp–"

June exploded out of her comatose state in the background, "What the hell is going on? Sunday better get her ass back to this house now! Where the hell is she? Who does she think she–"

Chester's voice became muffled as he cupped his hand over the mouthpiece. "Let'er go, June. Just let her go."

Her screaming grew louder, until the two struggled for the receiver, Chester pleading in the background, "Let'er go…"

She screamed into the phone, "What the hell do you think you're doin'? You better getcher ass to the house immediately or I'm gonna have you placed in reform school."

Sunday was the robot now, "I can accept that."

This enraged her more. She stuttered, "You-you're outta control; Goddamnit, Sunday! I'm..I'm gonna…Goddamnit, it's gonna be the hardest reform school available! Nothing! Just bread…and water…and cleaning…and, and, and punishment!"

Cakewalk.

Sunday was surprised at her own calm and even voice. "It doesn't matter. I'm not living with you anymore."

Obscenities spewed from the receiver. Sunday dropped it to her side. Everyone in the room was fixed on the phone in her hand. She knew they caught the screaming, too. She didn't care anymore. She hung up.

In front of the sheriff's department, Sunday and Grace sat in the truck for a long while, Sunday unconsciously wringing her hands over and over.

"You take your time, honey. No need to rush. I'll be right here."

I can do this. I'm never gonna be able to do this. I can do this. If I get out of this truck, I can't change my mind. I can do this. I can't undo this. Other people will know for sure. That house is poisoned. Even if I want to change my mind…I can say I was kidding. No. No, that would be like admitting that I was the crazy one. That I told people lies about my family. I'm not lying. I can do this-

"If you want me to go in with you, I will."

I have to do this.

"No. I'll go in by myself."

"Okay…well, I'll be right out here waiting for you."

They've never laid eyes on her truck; they won't know it's her.

"Okay."

Sunday slammed the truck door and didn't look back. Time slowed almost to a stop. As she heaved one lead foot in front of the other, her eyes followed the sidewalk straight up to the dark wooden jailhouse door, up the great limestone bricks, to the peak of the thin tin roof, *It's been here for a hundred years,* and into the sky. *I could fly away.*

She opened the door.

A S SUNDAY STEPPED into the jailhouse, the deputy sheriff stepped out from behind the front counter with a grin.

"Well, young lady, what can I do for you?"

"I'm a runaway."

"A runaway?" He pulled a notepad from his front shirt pocket.

"Yessir."

"Okay. Well, give me your name and phone number, and we'll go from there."

Sunday rattled off the information. The deputy sheriff's grin faded as she continued more urgently, "I'm not going home. If you make me go home, you'll have to pick me up again and again, for as many times as you want. I'm not gonna live there anymore."

He laid the pen and notepad on the counter behind him, nodding slowly. "Hmmm. Well, we're gonna have to talk about this." He puffed his chest, and hiked his pants by the belt loops. "Do your folks know where you are?"

"Yessir."

"Do they know *exactly* where you are?"

"Yessir. They know I'm on my way to turn myself in."

"Turn yourself in?"

"Yessir."

"Well, what is it you've done that you have to turn yourself in for?"

"I'm a runaway, sir."

"I see...Well, right now, we have to determine whether or not being a runaway is against the law. If you're running away, you may not have broken the law. We gotta find out why you're leaving."

"Okay...My brother and younger sister. They're getting off work. Nobody's gonna be able to pick them up. We need to get them before they go home."

"Who's your brother?"

"Friday Minor. He's working at the Smokehouse tonight."

The sheriff smiled again. "Oh yeah. I know Friday."

Everybody did. Away from the family and away from school, Friday was respected, appreciated, and admired. At the Smokehouse Café, he bussed the tables of wealthy city officials, local police officers, and mom-and-pop shop owners from around town. He moved up to waiter pretty quickly, and within a few weeks after that the owner gave him his own set of keys. He was tipped far better than even waiting tables at The Bon Temp because of how he treated people. He anticipated what a customer needed before they knew themselves, clearing the table as soon as the last fork was laid down, pulling the Tabasco from his apron as soon as a patron opened his mouth. No one ever received any more or less respect and service by Sunday's brother just because of who they were. Police officers never worried they wouldn't have time to sit down to lunch when they sat in his section. And the mayor could enjoy a meal with plenty of time leftover to rub elbows with the locals before his lunch hour was up. Friday always wanted to make sure everyone he came face to face with was comfortable and happy. Of course this guy knew who Friday was.

"He gets off at 8 o'clock."

"Okay. I can send Officer White over to pick him up."

It was time. She wanted Friday there.

As he leaned over the reception desk to pick up the CB radio receiver, he asked her, "Who's your sister?"

"Monday Minor."

"Where's she work?"

"With me down at the Bon Temp. She gets off at ten tonight."

"All right, we'll get 'er picked up. You wanna wait to talk with us until your brother gets here?"

Sunday nodded.

He called Officer White and gave a series of numbers out over the receiver. "White here. What can I do ya for?"

"I need you to pick up a Friday Minor down at the Smokehouse."

"Ten-four. Do I need to arrest him?"

"Nope. Just a person of in'erest."

"Well, I know that young man. He's friendly with my daughter."

"He's done nothin' wrong. We only wanna talk to 'im."

"We?"

The sheriff rolled his eyes and raised his voice. "Just pick 'im up, will ya?"

"Copy that. I'm on Main Street. Gimme about five minutes."

"Okay, see you in a few."

The sheriff leaned back over the counter, and clicked the CB back into place.

He turned to Sunday. "You wanna wait in here for your brother, or you wanna wait outside?"

"I'll wait outside."

Sunday trotted back down the jailhouse steps toward Grace's truck. She rolled down the window as Sunday walked up.

"I'm still here! I'll be here 'til you tell me I can go."

Sunday nodded, and cupped her fingers over the window jamb. "I don't think I want you here when my parents get here. I don't want them to see you."

"How about if I go back to Wendy's house and wait to hear from you?"

"Okay. That'll be good."

Grace pulled out of the space in front of the jailhouse, and Sunday turned back to the jailhouse steps. She saw the sheriff watching her in the window. White's patrol car pulled up, and she whipped around and locked eyes with Friday. He jumped out before the car was in park.

Sunday raced toward him, and their embrace amplified the ache in her heart. She couldn't hold back anymore, and tears came streaming down her face.

"I'm sorry, Friday. I'm so sorry…No one else…I–"

He hugged tighter. "Everything's gonna be okay now. It's gonna be okay."

They sat down on the front stoop next to each other.

Friday whispered, "Everything's gonna be all right. It's gonna be okay now."

Officer White walked past the pair and through the door, as the deputy sheriff stepped out.

"Why don'tch'all come on in here with me?"

He ushered them into a back room and pointed to a couple of seats at a long folding table. There were three cameras positioned around the room. As they followed the order, the sheriff walked to the camera closest to him, shifted the angle, pointing the lens toward Sunday and Friday, and pressed a button. Once he checked that the red light was on, he stepped behind the table and sat down across from them.

"Now. Let's get down to business. Why are you running away?"

"Because my mother's crazy…"

He left room for an explanation.

"I don't wanna live there anymore because there's no tellin' what's gonna make her blow up day after day."

The sheriff formulated the next question carefully. "Well, do you think she's sick?"

"I dunno."

"Well…we understand she was in the hospital this weekend."

How?

She tried to mask her surprise with a shrug. "Yeah, I think she accidentally swallowed some mothballs."

He leaned over the table with his hands clasped in front of him, and lowered his voice. "People don't swallow mothballs by accident, sweetheart."

He leaned back again. "Friday...how do you feel about what's goin' on here?"

Friday shrugged. "If she wants to go, she needs to go."

"Okay...Well, wha'd'ya think about what she's saying about your mother?"

"She's my mother."

The sheriff's jaw flexed, and he nodded. "Is your sister right?"

Friday looked the sheriff directly in the eye. "Yeah."

"Well, let's talk about how y'all get punished..."

Sunday answered, "When we're bad we get whipped."

"How old are you?"

"I'm sixteen."

"You still get whipped?"

"Yeah."

He turned to Friday. "And how old are you?"

"Seventeen."

"Aren't y'all a little old for whippin's?"

Sunday explained, "If we live with them, we go by their rules. Or we get punished."

"I see." The deputy sheriff raised his eyebrows. "And you don't want to go by their rules anymore."

"No, sir, I don't."

"And what do they use when they're whippin' you?"

"Momma usually uses a belt. And Daddy just uses his hands."

"Show me, how does your daddy use his hands?"

Sunday put her hand up and balled her fist. "Like this."

She raised it to show him. "And then he hits you."

"How many times?"

"Only two or three times usually. He doesn't usually hit you a whole lot. He just hits you real hard."

"So now, how many times does your momma hit you with the belt?"

"Only 'til she gets tired."

The sheriff's head jerked back. "What do you mean "til she gets tired'?"

"'Til she gets outta breath…or she falls down."

"Falls down? What do y'all do when she falls down?"

Friday jumped in. "We try'n make sure there's not a chair in the way or something."

The sheriff pushed further. "How long does that last?"

"Oh, just a couple minutes," Friday said.

"How often does this happen?"

"Once or twice a week."

"How is she when she gets up?"

"She's usually sad and quiet and stays in her room for awhile–"

Sunday finished his thought, "–but sometimes if she's not too tired, she'll whip you again."

"Friday, is that true?"

Friday stared down at his hands, wringing them over and over. "Yeah."

"Why did you say a minute ago that it's over after just a couple minutes?"

"She's my mother, sir."

There was a long pause. Sunday glanced over at the red light on the camera.

The sheriff finally asked, "Do you think your parents love you?"

Sunday lied. "I think they do."

"Is that the only way…the only contact they have with y'all?"

"No. They talk to us…They talk to each other and stuff."

"No, what I'm askin' is…the whippin's, is that the only way they touch you?"

The sound of her own voice suddenly grew muffled. Stories fell from her mouth, but she couldn't make out the words. Her vision toggled between memory inside and reality outside.

First, the whipping…the kicking…

Then the sheriff's frown sinking deep.

Then waking on the floor after her momma choked her.

Then the sheriff raising a sympathetic brow.

Then the splinter of wooden spoon raised high above her momma's head.

Then her brother next to her in the camera room, silent and wringing his hands.

Then the blisters on his hands from being punished for setting fires.

The tsunami of truth crashed through her soul, filling the room. There was no way to stop it now. It was happening too fast. The words flowed up and out of her like that gospel hymn from so long ago.

Sunday's world faded to black.

She slipped back into that pew. A montage of request after request from her father to stay back, stay behind, come in here, rub my head. The lights dimmed and the familiar shadow of her father slithered across the floor of her room dark room while the rest of the world slept.

The deputy sheriff shot a finger up and boomed, shocking her back into her chair, "Hold on."

He picked up the phone and dialed.

Friday squeezed Sunday's shoulder. "It's gonna be okay."

Sunday didn't take her eyes off the sheriff.

"Peyton! Getcher ass over here. We've got incest."

What? What have I done? Momma! She was the reason I walked in here! Not Daddy! What did I say?

Her eyes were burning and swollen. Her cheeks were wet and her mouth was sore from her permanent frown. Her chin wouldn't stop trembling. She was terrified. Friday's eyes were as big as hers. *That…that's not what I meant to say! What did I say?*

Sunday's brother squeezed her shoulder again. "It's gonna be okay."

She didn't believe him.

The sheriff hung up and peered down at the children across the table. "Y'all...we're gonna take a break here. Give you a minute to getcher selves together. Y'all wanna wait in here or do y'all wanna go outside?"

What just happened? What did I say?

Sunday couldn't remember a word she said. The last hour was a blur. She forgot her swollen eyes. She forgot her wet cheeks. She forgot to catch her breath. She forgot her words.

Friday spoke for the both of them. "We wanna go outside."

He led his sister out of the room and out onto the jailhouse stoop.

They sat together arm in arm with their knees up and their fingers laced, bodies huddled together, exhausted. Just as she leaned her head on her brother's shoulder, a car pulled up in front of them. Sunday knew that rumble anywhere. She raised her head to meet her father's icy stare. He shook his head slowly as if deeply disappointed.

Friday lifted his sister by the elbow. "Here, let's go back inside."

As if the sheriff had been keeping tabs, he appeared in the doorway and escorted them back in. He pointed to a different room than they'd been in before. "White, I want you to take them in here. I'll be doing interviews in the camera room."

Sunday had a view into the doorway of the camera room from where she sat. She fought the urge to fly away.

June's voice boomed through the front office next. "Somebody better tell me what the hell is going on here!"

Friday and Sunday locked eyes. White stared at them.

The sheriff responded outside, "Mrs. Minor, I need you to follow me in here."

She followed the sheriff and another officer into the camera room, and he pushed the door only half-closed. Sunday and her brother craned their necks to see what was going on.

White worked to distract them. "What grade are you in?"

June loomed over the table next door. "I asked you, what the hell is going on?"

"Tenth," Sunday whispered to White.

"Eleventh," Friday said, neither of them taking their eyes off the scene in the next room.

The sheriff leaned forward to match June's stance, and narrowed his eyes to match hers. "Don't you think it's about time we all found out?" He sounded disgusted. "Have a seat."

She did as she was told and slid into the chair in front of her, backpedaling quickly. "Wha-wha'd'you mean by that?"

White raised his voice to the two children. "Do you play any sports?"

They responded in unison, "No."

June regained her footing across the way. "What are you talking about? I have no idea what the hell you're sayin' to me!"

The sheriff challenged, "Well, this has been goin' on for a looong while now, hasn't it, June?"

White raised his voice another notch. "Are you planning to go to college?"

Sunday caught sight of June out of the corner of her eye gasping for air, fanning herself before she collapsed to the floor, writhing out of control. *There! See! That's why I came here. Can't they see? Thank God everybody can see it. She's the crazy one.*

Officer White catapulted toward the door. "Get an ambulance out here!"

Sunday stiffened when White turned back to her and her brother. He opened his mouth to say something, decided against it, and bolted for the camera room.

He grabbed the door handle of the camera room, and stared at June flailing on the floor like a madwoman. He glanced over his shoulder at Sunday and Friday, taking in everything. He closed the camera room door, then came back, and closed their door, too.

In minutes the ambulance sirens filled the air. She heard the scuffle of paramedics rushing in, instructing each other what to do. They whisked her mother away.

Next, the sheriff boomed on the other side of the door, "Mr. Minor, I need you to come in here. We need to talk."

Chester spoke for the first time sounding equally official. "I understand."

"Exactly how the hell long has this been happening, Chester?" The camera room door click closed.

An eternity seemed to pass before the muffled voices quieted. The door clicked open again. The sheriff plodded past their room, calling out, "I'm heading out. Gotta pick up the younger sister."

Finally, White opened their door and leaned in. "You two. Go on and get some fresh air."

On her way out, Sunday scanned the jailhouse for her father. He was nowhere to be seen. All this in-and-out to the front stoop, her mother being carted out, her father being called in, this wasn't how things were supposed to happen.

Outside, the cruiser hadn't yet come to a complete stop when Monday swung open the passenger door and hit the ground running, heading straight for Sunday, screaming, "He was the best father we ever had!"

She leapt forward and grabbed a fistful of her sister's hair. They tumbled to the ground. Monday pinned her sister with one fist and pummeled her with the other, still screaming, "None of us are gonna have any place to go now! What's gonna happen now, huh? We're never gonna have any place to live!"

Sunday defended herself from the blows, pushing and yelling back, "Quit it! Get off 'a me!"

Monday screamed back desperately, "They took care of us! You need to keep your mouth shut! You messed up the whole family! They left us now, and they were the only people who could love us!"

Friday lunged toward Monday and yanked hard, attempting to pull her away, but she was locked in on her target.

Sunday screamed back, "Leave me alone! I'm not going home!"

Monday yanked down on her hair, and beat a fist against her sister's side, yelling, "You have to go home! There's no place else!"

She spit more accusations and pummeled harder with both fists. The panic rose in her voice. "If you don't come home, we're all gonna get in trouble!"

Officer White rushed over and shoved Friday to the side. He grabbed Monday by both shoulders and lifted her at least a foot above the ground. "C'mon, scrappy."

She tried to jerk away from him, but he was too strong. He restrained her and carried her to the side, her feet flailing beneath her. "C'mon, let's go."

"No! She's talkin' about my dad."

The two of them disappeared around the corner. Once she quieted down, Monday marched back around the building, head down, still seething. White trailed behind and motioned Sunday and Friday toward the door.

The group stepped inside the jailhouse in time for Sunday to watch her daddy, hands cuffed behind him, being escorted by the sheriff up the stairs where the jail cells were. He turned his head and burrowed daggers into her soul. Nausea twisted her stomach and threatened to erupt from her throat.

The sheriff clomped back down the stairs.

"Time for us to go. Sunday, go ahead and call your ride."

He pointed to Monday and Friday. "You two are comin' with me."

They caravanned to the Bourne house. The police cruiser pulled into Chester's spot, and Grace and Sunday pulled in behind.

"Honey, run inside and get your things. You're gonna be stayin' with us until the court decides what to do next."

She was first to reach the front door, and Wednesday yanked it wide open. In a split second, she laced her fingers through Sunday's hair and dragged her to the floor. Wednesday cocked her clenched fist high above her head.

The sheriff stepped into the doorway and warned, "I suggest you release her before I have to bring you up on charges of assault to a minor."

Wednesday immediately dropped her fist and let go of Sunday's hair. Sunday launched down the hall to claim her property. She slid open the closet door and yanked a single pair of slacks and a turtleneck from their hangers. She whirled around and stopped. The gold letters of her bible there on the bedside caught her eye. She hesitated. *Why bother?*

She grabbed it anyway and stepped out.

As the truck pulled away, Sunday's mind raced. *Everyone just needs to catch their breath. I didn't mean to tell them about Daddy. I'll fix this. What did they even ask me? How could I tell them? They can stay with Daddy. They can't stay with her. I'll make them understand. I'll make the police understand. Sure, Daddy shouldn't be allowed around children, but we're used to his requests. And we're almost all grown anyway. Momma, she was the crazy one. She was the sick one. She was the one liable to kill us. It was her that made me run. Something went wrong in there. How come the others want to stay? They know what living there with her is like, and they stay with her anyway.*

As the distance grew between Sunday Minor and home, her racing heartbeat began to slow. Her racing thoughts lulled. The truth finally hit Sunday. She'd done it. She would never spend another night at the Minor house.

I made it out.

Square One

OVER A YEAR had passed since Sunday thought she'd made it out. Just like that, the decision was made, and truth be told, she never did spend another night in the Minor household. But she hadn't really made it *out*-out, had she?

She thought she'd found a life, first with the St. Christophers, and then with the Kindlys, but soon enough she'd come to find that no, the truth wasn't finished with her yet. And now too much time had passed since any sense of freedom stirred in her. She was to be released in the morning. She wasn't sure what her next move would be. Although she knew she wasn't exactly "normal" yet, despite what Dr. Faus said, she was ready for anything–ready to get out of there at least. She stepped into the common area at Rose Village for the last time, and chose a seat next to Bo.

"You gonna go bowling with us tomorrow night?"

"No."

"Why not? You don't go, nobody goes."

"I won't be here. They're releasing me."

Bo chuckled. "Everybody knows they don't let people outta here. What gives?"

"That's what Dr. Faus said. They're releasing me."

Bo sat up straight and rubbed the tops of her thighs anxiously. "Bullshit. Nobody gets out. They're transferring you."

"No bullshit. I'm getting out. Dr. Faus said I was better."

"Bullshit. People don't get better here."

Sunday nodded. She agreed with that for sure. She shrugged. "I dunno…All I do know is, I'm leavin' tomorrow."

Bo stood over Sunday. "You're serious. You're leaving."

Sunday nodded.

Bo knocked her head back. "Ha!"

She threw her arms up and shouted, "Sunday's cured! She's goin' home!"

She dropped back down to give Sunday a hug. "Ha, haaa! You're goin' home."

Bo stood again and cheered, "They cured one!"

Blain and Ray jumped out of their chairs with a "Whoo-hoo!" and a "Yeah!" Other patients started clapping. The quiet murmurs in the room turned to chatter, and the chatter turned to cheers. People jumped up on chairs and bounced, pumping their fists, cheering, "They cured one!"

With that, someone turned up the volume on the TV full blast. One nurse began calling out over the loudspeaker from inside their booth, "What's going on in there? Is everything okay? Can *someone please* turn down the television?" while another one picked up the phone and dialed for help.

The room was fast becoming frenzied. The nurse pleaded urgently through the intercoms from behind the glass, "Calm yourselves. Relax yourselves," but no one paid any attention.

Out of nowhere, Blain picked up one of the big orange block chairs and hurled it against the wall, shattering the wooden parts to pieces. The nurse screamed into the phone, "It's happening! They're out of control!"

Ray bolted out of the crowd to the pile of rubble and picked up one of the legs. "Good a slugger as any!" He ran to the nurses' station, and began pounding on the shatterproof glass. His raw animalism set the room ablaze with energy.

Patients' expressions shifted from excited to angry. They bounced around the room and against one another. The little ones became frightened. They scattered out to the edges of the room, huddling in corners. And one at a time, they sought Sunday out. Within minutes a gaggle of ducklings tightly encircled her waist.

She observed the nurses frantically dialing numbers on all phones and barking into their receivers from inside their station-turned-cage.

They're gonna blame this on me. What am I gonna do?

The entire ward was consumed by chaos.

An announcement blew from the highest volume over the intercom, "You are all free to go."

The room fell silent.

What? – Wait – why?

"I repeat. The doors are unlocked. You are all free to go."

Everyone looked around at one another.

What's happening?

Blain broke out, "Yeah! Let's go!" He bolted for the door.

No one wasted another second.

Bo was the first to follow. "I'm outta here!"

All the teens made a break for the door.

Why is this happening?

The nurse continued on the loudspeaker, "The police have been notified."

Oh shit! They're comin' for me. I am not taking the blame for this!

Sunday stared down at her ducklings. *What the hell am I gonna do with you…*

"Follow me."

She led the children through the doors, and across the front lawn. She passed through the iron gates, and like hatchlings behind their momma, they followed her across the road and into the woods. They hid in the bushes avoiding the searchlights, ducking when they were shined their way, and listening to sirens approaching from every direction. Squad cars swarmed the hospital grounds, and policemen poured out of them.

The children were crying, and Sunday tried to console them one at a time. "Shh. It's gonna be okay. Y'all are all gonna go home. I promise."

Shit. I didn't think anything through. Why am I here? Why do I have to make all the decisions? It's okay. Sit tight. We gotta wait out the cops.

She pulled herself together and sat guard until the last police car departed the Rose Village grounds. The excitement finally subsided, and she crept out onto the curb and eyed the icehouse down the road. She turned back to the wide-eyed group and signaled for them to come out.

"Okay. Does everybody have their phone numbers memorized?"

They all nodded, except for Lizzy. She started to cry. "I don't. I don't know my number."

"You're okay. Lydia's gonna take you home with her. Her parents'll figure out how to help you." Lydia was thirteen, and seemed as close to normal as anybody else. She nodded at Lizzy to confirm.

Traveling in the same single file line, they trekked down to the icehouse, and when Sunday stepped inside, she gathered them all protectively. The man behind the counter eyed them cautiously. "Y'all from down the street?"

Sunday nodded.

"Need the phone, don'tcha?"

"Yessir. There's six of us, but only five are making calls."

"I'm not in the business of givin' away free phone calls."

Sunday eyed him suspiciously, and chose her words carefully. "Sir...I don't have any money...We won't be long."

Sunday detected the cogs turning in his head. *God, please don't let him do anything to us.*

Finally, he sighed. "All right. Go on. You can use the phone in the back. But you can't get picked up here."

Once the last of the ducklings placed her call, Sunday made one of her own.

Mr. Kindly sounded groggy. "Hello?"

She was glad to hear a familiar voice. "It's me, Sunday. I've been released."

"At this time of night?"

She wasn't prepared for that. "I'm...I'm not sure what happened...but everybody's out."

272

"What do you mean everybody?"

"I dunno. I was gonna be released tomorrow and everybody got excited...I dunno. The nurses unlocked the doors and let everybody out."

"Where are you?"

"I'll be across the street from the gates."

"Are you in trouble?"

"I don't think–"

"Don't get in anybody's car."

"Well, the police–"

"Nobody's."

"Okay."

She walked back down to the gates, and waited.

She was back to square one.

How did this happen? Is it finished? Did I really make it?

She nodded slowly as the realization materialized in her mind.

I really did. I made it out.

Sunday Minor examined the chess pieces of a new board, and hope crept into a far corner of her mind. She wondered what her next move might be.

Epilogue

LTHOUGH THE INCREDIBLE release of Sunday Minor and the other patients of Rose Village was never clearly explained, one can point to the social and political atmosphere around the time in which the event happened. Investigations into state and federal institutions had long since gotten underway due to the mounting evidence of inadequate care and inappropriate practices. Several years before Sunday was admitted, a number of exposés had uncovered a number of cases in mental facilities, such as children being fed tranquilizers like candy and "chemical handcuffing" of delinquent children whether they needed the drugs or not. Out of those, dozens of lawsuits citing drug treatment misuse in juvenile and mental institutions arose. By the time she'd entered the asylum, a series of U.S. Senate hearings in late 1975 on "The Abuse and Misuse of Drugs in Institutions" had already concluded. In fact, cover-to-cover, the third transcribed volume of the first session of the hearings alone specifically referenced Thorazine a total of 433 times. Perhaps the case can be made that such public scrutiny combined with budget cuts not yet publically addressed at Rose Village was what ultimately informed the nurses' decision to release the locks and open the gates. However, this is only speculation.

Also in the weeks leading up to her assignment as a ward of the state and of Mr. and Mrs. Kindly, through private conversations with Sunday, the St. Christophers came to truly understand the Minor children's grave situation living with their mother, even though their father was gone. The St. Christophers arranged for the children to speak out against their mother one last time to the authorities. Sunday's heart broke to learn none of the others had corroborated her story, all of them clinging to their only version of normal. They all chose to stay…for a while anyway.

Wednesday Minor did enlist in the Navy as she promised the night Chester came home from the hospital after June swallowed the mothballs.

The next year, Friday Minor enlisted in the Navy, too, before going on to become a nurse, doing exactly what he loved–helping people.

Monday Minor stayed with June until four months after she'd given birth to her first child, at which time June kicked her out for reasons unknown.

Tuesday stayed the longest, never having been subjected to the same maliciousness the others endured. She found holding a job for more than a few weeks difficult, and quit when she got bored. It never made sense for her to want to get away.

In the end, Chester Minor was charged with two counts of child molestation, and he pleaded guilty to only one–Monday. He claimed he was never told what he was charged with, but Sunday knew the police couldn't put you in jail without telling you why. For the countless times he had terrorized, demanded, and secretly slinked into their rooms at night to sexually assault his children, for all the years of beating them, sometimes to the brink of death, with balled up fists and jutted jaw, red-faced and enraged, he was convicted on a *single* count of molestation. He was sentenced to two to five years, and then released early. Afterward Chester got a job as a school bus driver, but not long after he started, an anonymous complaint was filed and he was promptly let go.

June Minor divorced her husband shortly after he was convicted. Still, for all her insanity and rage, for all the damage she wrought on a daily basis, mentally *and* physically; for all the abuse, from telling her children she was convinced they set out to make her life miserable and that she and Chester had always considered abortion to choking them and leaving them for dead;

for all the beatings with her hands, with the buckle end of a belt, with paint sticks, with brushes, with spoons–whatever was nearest to her in the height of a rage–over things as ridiculous as tetanus from a rusty nail making her look like a bad mother, or a child's hair gone straight before church when she'd taken the time to set it in curlers, or one of the children dropping and breaking a glass, or a grade slipping a point or two–for everything–apart from the day Chester was arrested, she never saw the inside of a police station, she never saw the inside of a courtroom, and she never saw the inside of a nut house. No, the psychiatric ward had stood in wait, holding a room for Sunday instead. And eventually, when all June's children were finally grown and gone, June simply disappeared.

The weeks following Sunday Minor's release were an improvement, having weaned her six-month Thorazine intake from five times a day down to zero, but it is no surprise that this was only the calm before the storm.

When the haze wore off, Sunday's past absolutely assaulted her. And this time, she refused to go gently back into the grips of her truth. Instead she hurled herself wildly into the darkness, forging her way toward anything that resembled the light.

A whirlwind affair with her foster father, she was sure, had been true love until her trysts shattered the Kindly home. Following the ruin, to replace the family she felt she lost, she sought comradery among a motley crew of bikers–which became a life of non-stop speed, crank, and "being nice" to her boyfriend's associates in order to earn her keep–until her life had been put at stake.

That night, Sunday did the last thing she thought she would ever have to do again. She called her momma. And her momma did come. She did allow her back…but not without an underlying plan of her own. A marriage was arranged with a soldier on his way to Italy, a dowry was given, and a send-off planned–all under Sunday's nose…

It seemed she would never be able to be free to live her own life, free to make her own choices. That was, until the night she locked eyes with the man who vowed to truly love her, who did protect her, and who, in the end, brought her as close to normal as she would ever get, in fact.

Although her life was not without its turbulent times, against all odds Sunday did escape; she did find love; she did build a successful career; she did raise a family of her own, one she loved in a way she'd never known.

But, even then, the truth was most certainly not finished with Sunday Minor.

Made in United States
Orlando, FL
07 May 2024

46617709R00163